BBC

DOCTOR WHO

THE TWELFTH DOCTOR

VOL 6: SONIC BOOM

"Very strong story with an intensely fun new companion and smooth new look!"
NEWSARAMA

"The art and coloring is terrific!"
DOCTOR WHO NEWS

"Gives me the same sort of feeling I get settling in to watch an episode..."
WE THE NERDY

"Absolutely delightful."
THE GEEK GIRL PROJECT

"As always, *Doctor Who: The Twelfth Doctor* delivers the goods!"
THE FANDOM POST

"The latest from Titan Comics is touching, heartfelt, and visually spectacular."
BLOGTOR WHO

"A smart, funny romp through the world of comic books. Absolutely recommended."
SCI FI PULSE

"Exciting, fast-moving, funny and mysterious."
GEEK MOM

"Clever and funny!"
CAPELESS CRUSADER

"Perfect, enjoyable and intriguing!"
MCM BUZZ

"The Twelfth Doctor's comic adventures are something insanely special!"
WARPED FACTOR

"Titan's Twelfth *Doctor Who* comics are everything that's good about comic books."
FANBOY NATION

TITAN COMICS

SENIOR COMICS EDITOR
Andrew James

ASSISTANT EDITORS
Jessica Burton, Amoona Saohin

COLLECTION DESIGNER
Andrew Leung

TITAN COMICS EDITORIAL
Tom Williams, Lauren McPhee

PRODUCTION SUPERVISOR
Maria Pearson

PRODUCTION CONTROLLER
Peter James

SENIOR PRODUCTION CONTROLLER
Jackie Flook

ART DIRECTOR
Oz Browne

SENIOR SALES MANAGER
Steve Tothill

PRESS OFFICER
Will O'Mullane

COMICS BRAND MANAGER
Chris Thompson

ADS & MARKETING ASSISTANT
Tom Miller

DIRECT SALES & MARKETING MANAGER
Ricky Claydon

COMMERCIAL MANAGER
Michelle Fairlamb

HEAD OF RIGHTS
Jenny Boyce

PUBLISHING MANAGE
Darryl Tothill

PUBLISHING DIRECTO
Chris Teather

OPERATIONS DIRECTO
Leigh Baulch

EXECUTIVE DIRECTOR
Vivian Cheung

PUBLISHER
Nick Landau

For rights information contact Jenny Boyce
jenny.boyce@titanemail.com

Special thanks to Steven Moffat, Brian Minchin, Mandy Thwaites, Matt Nicholls, James Dudley, Edward Russell, Derek Ritchie, Scott Handcock, Kirsty Mullan, Kate Bush, Julia Nocciolino and Ed Casey for their invaluable assistance.

BBC WORLDWIDE

DIRECTOR OF EDITORIAL GOVERNANCE
Nicholas Brett

DIRECTOR OF CONSUMER PRODUCTS AND PUBLISHING
Andrew Moultrie

HEAD OF UK PUBLISHING
Chris Kerwin

PUBLISHER
Mandy Thwaites

PUBLISHING CO-ORDINATOR
Eva Abramik

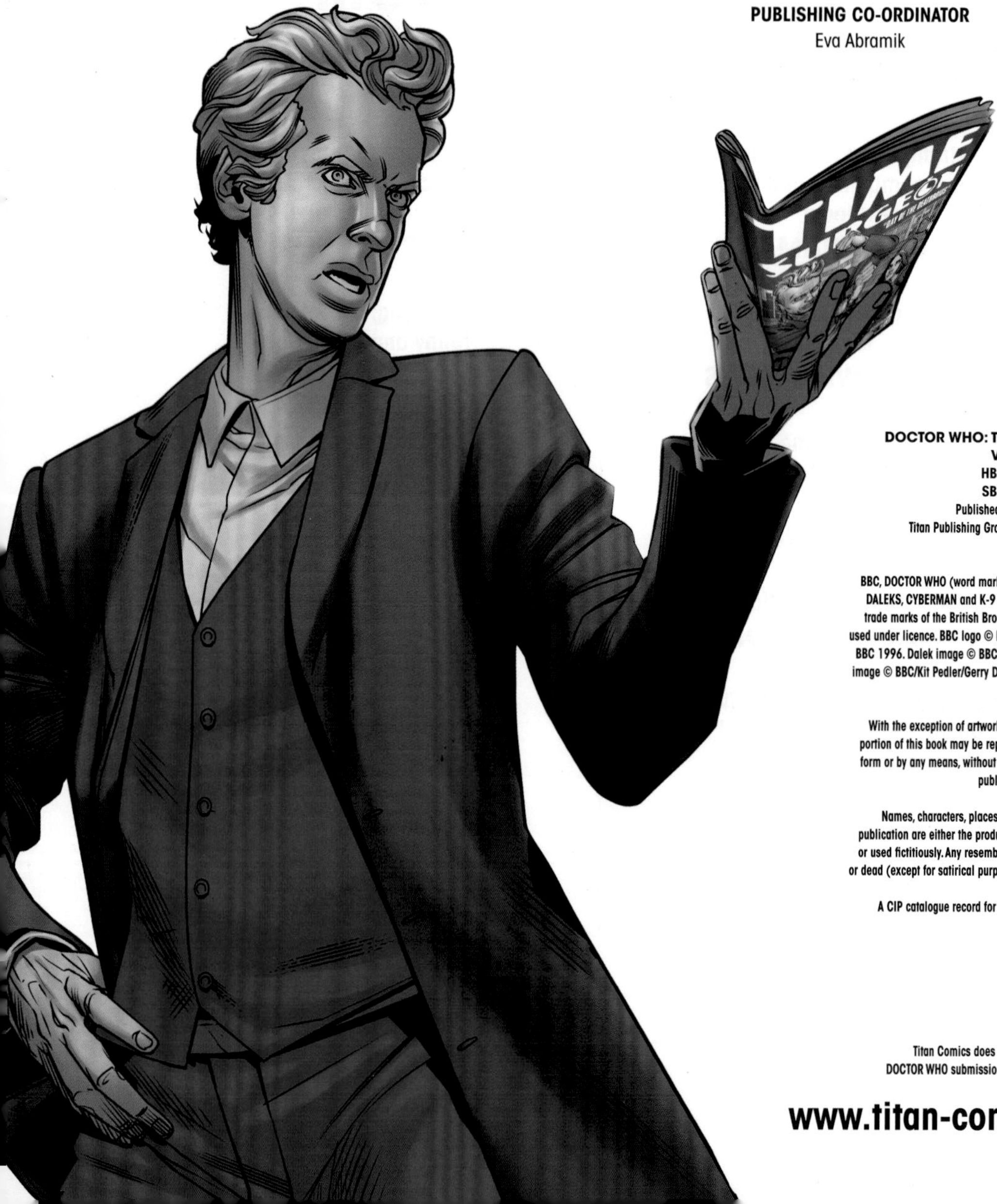
TIME SURGEON

DOCTOR WHO: THE TWELFTH DOCTC
VOL 6: SONIC BOO
HB ISBN: 97817858601
SB ISBN: 97817858601
Published by Titan Comics, a division
Titan Publishing Group, Ltd. 144 Southwark Stre
London, SE1 0

A CIP catalogue record for this title is available from
British Libra
First edition: July 20

10 9 8 7 6 5 4 3

Printed in Chi

www.titan-comics.con

DOCTOR WHO

THE TWELFTH DOCTOR

VOL 6: SONIC BOOM

WRITER:
ROBBIE MORRISON

ARTISTS:
MARIANO LACLAUSTRA
& RACHAEL STOTT
WITH AGUS CALCAGNO
& FER CENTURION

COLORISTS:
CARLOS CABRERA,
HERNÁN CABRERA
& RODRIGO FERNANDES
WITH JUAN MANUEL TUMBURUS

LETTERS: RICHARD STARKINGS
AND COMICRAFT'S
JIMMY BETANCOURT

DOCTOR WHO

THE TWELFTH DOCTOR

THE DOCTOR

Last of the Time Lords of Gallifrey. Never cruel or cowardly, he champions the oppressed across time and space. Even without a regular companion to show off to, the Doctor still manages to find adventure – and danger – wherever he goes!

TRAVELING ALONE

Since the departure of Clara, and after dropping off space bassist Hattie back on the Twist, the Doctor has been adventuring alone. Will he offer a spot on the TARDIS to anyone else? Who could he next meet on his travels?

THE TARDIS

'Time and Relative Dimension in Space'. Bigger on the inside, this unassuming blue box is your ticket to unforgettable adventure. The Doctor likes to think he's in control, but more often than not the TARDIS takes him where and when he needs to be...

PREVIOUSLY...

With one-time traveling companion, Hattie, the Doctor came face to face with a haunted house of endless corridors and rooms – in which a whole family had been lost! Puzzling out the secret of the house – that it was a dying TARDIS – the Doctor helped it to its rest, and saved the family within. Returning Hattie to the Twist, and to her burgeoning musical career, the Doctor continued on his way, alone again... Where will he travel to next?

When you've finished reading the collection, please email your thoughts to doctorwhocomic@titanemail.com

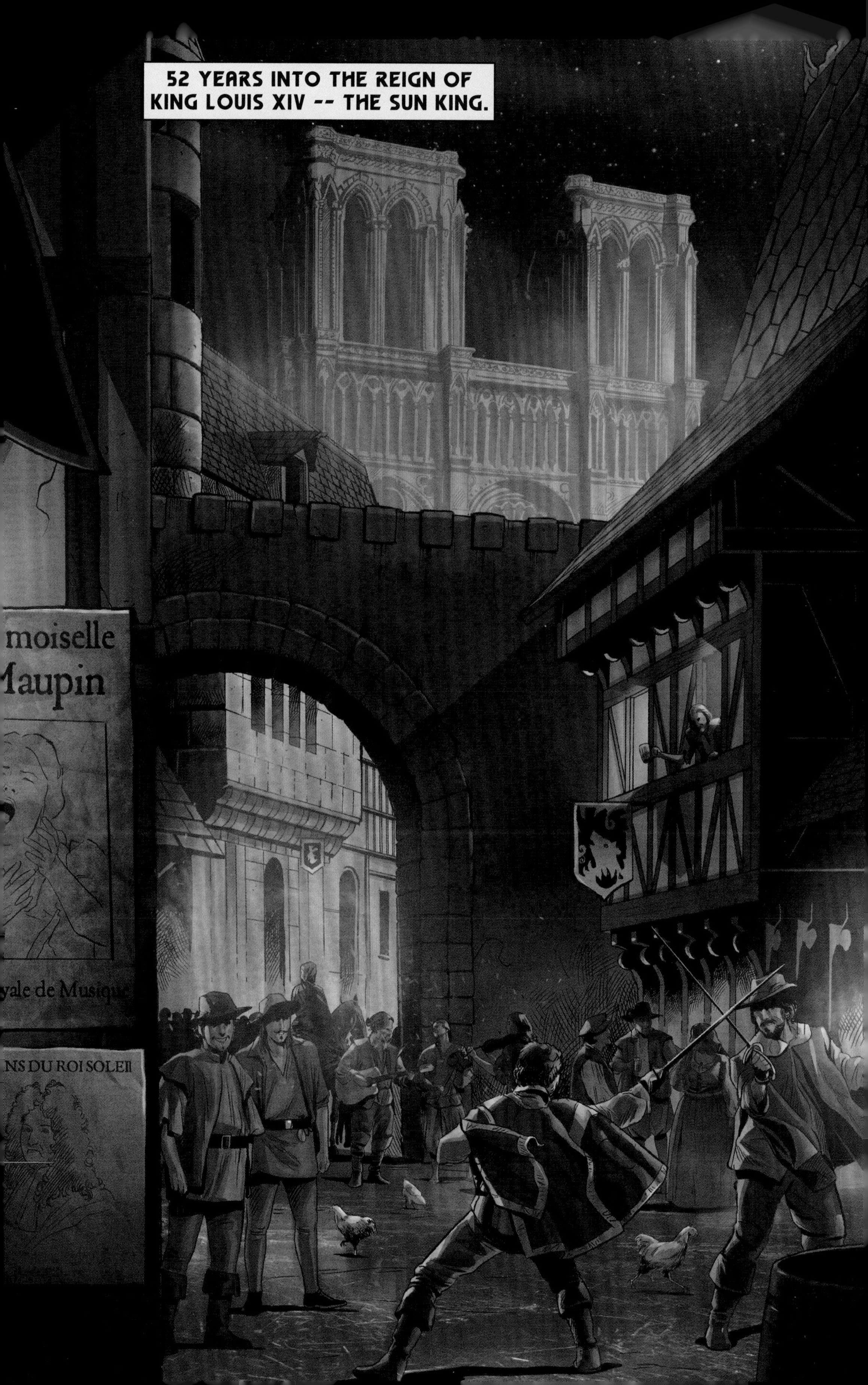
52 YEARS INTO THE REIGN OF
KING LOUIS XIV -- THE SUN KING.
moiselle
Maupin
yale de Musique
NS DU ROI SOLEII

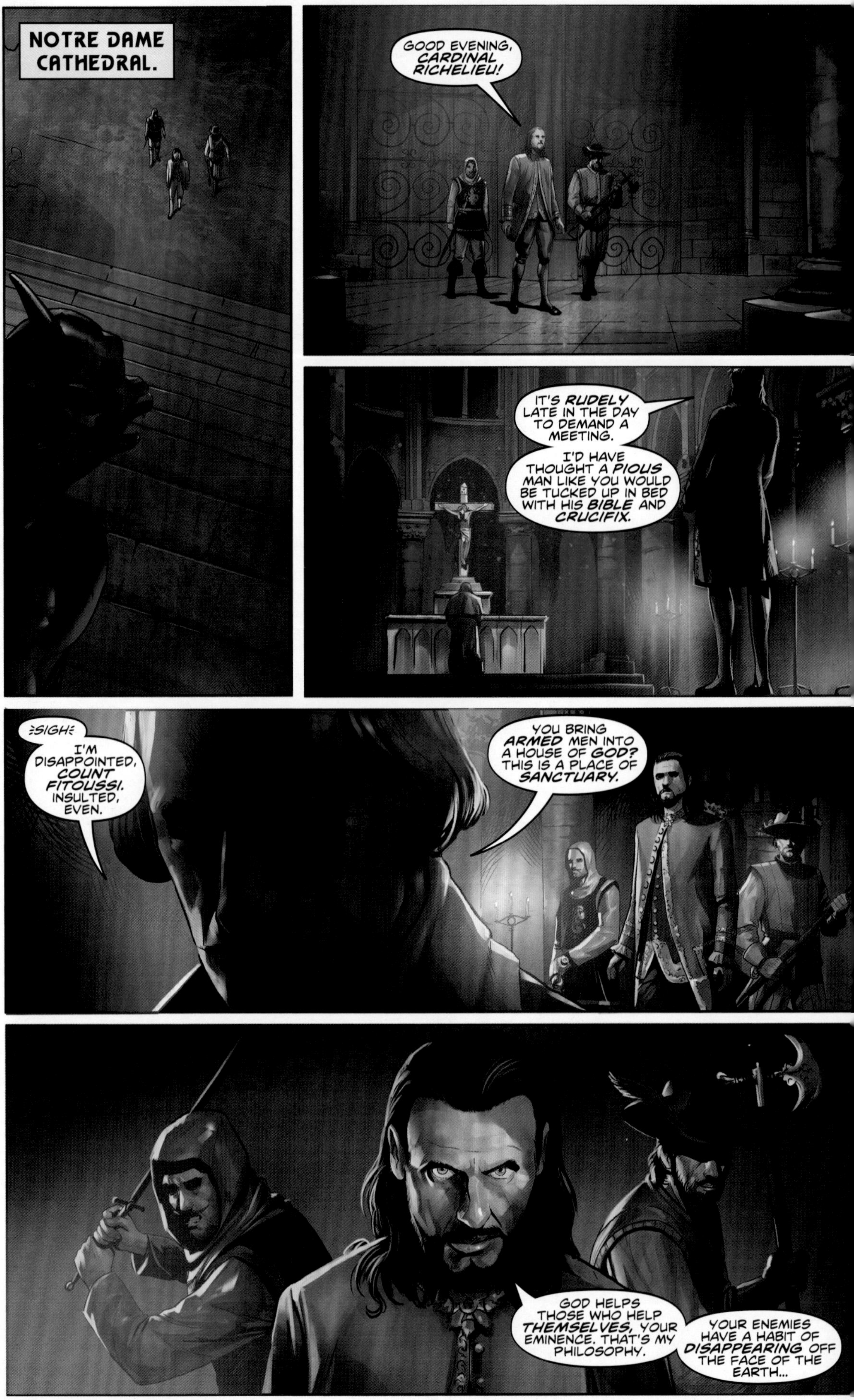
NOTRE DAME CATHEDRAL.
GOOD EVENING, CARDINAL RICHELIEU!
IT'S RUDELY LATE IN THE DAY TO DEMAND A MEETING.
I'D HAVE THOUGHT A PIOUS MAN LIKE YOU WOULD BE TUCKED UP IN BED WITH HIS BIBLE AND CRUCIFIX.
SIGH
I'M DISAPPOINTED, COUNT FITOUSSI. INSULTED, EVEN.
YOU BRING ARMED MEN INTO A HOUSE OF GOD? THIS IS A PLACE OF SANCTUARY.
GOD HELPS THOSE WHO HELP THEMSELVES, YOUR EMINENCE. THAT'S MY PHILOSOPHY.
YOUR ENEMIES HAVE A HABIT OF DISAPPEARING OFF THE FACE OF THE EARTH...

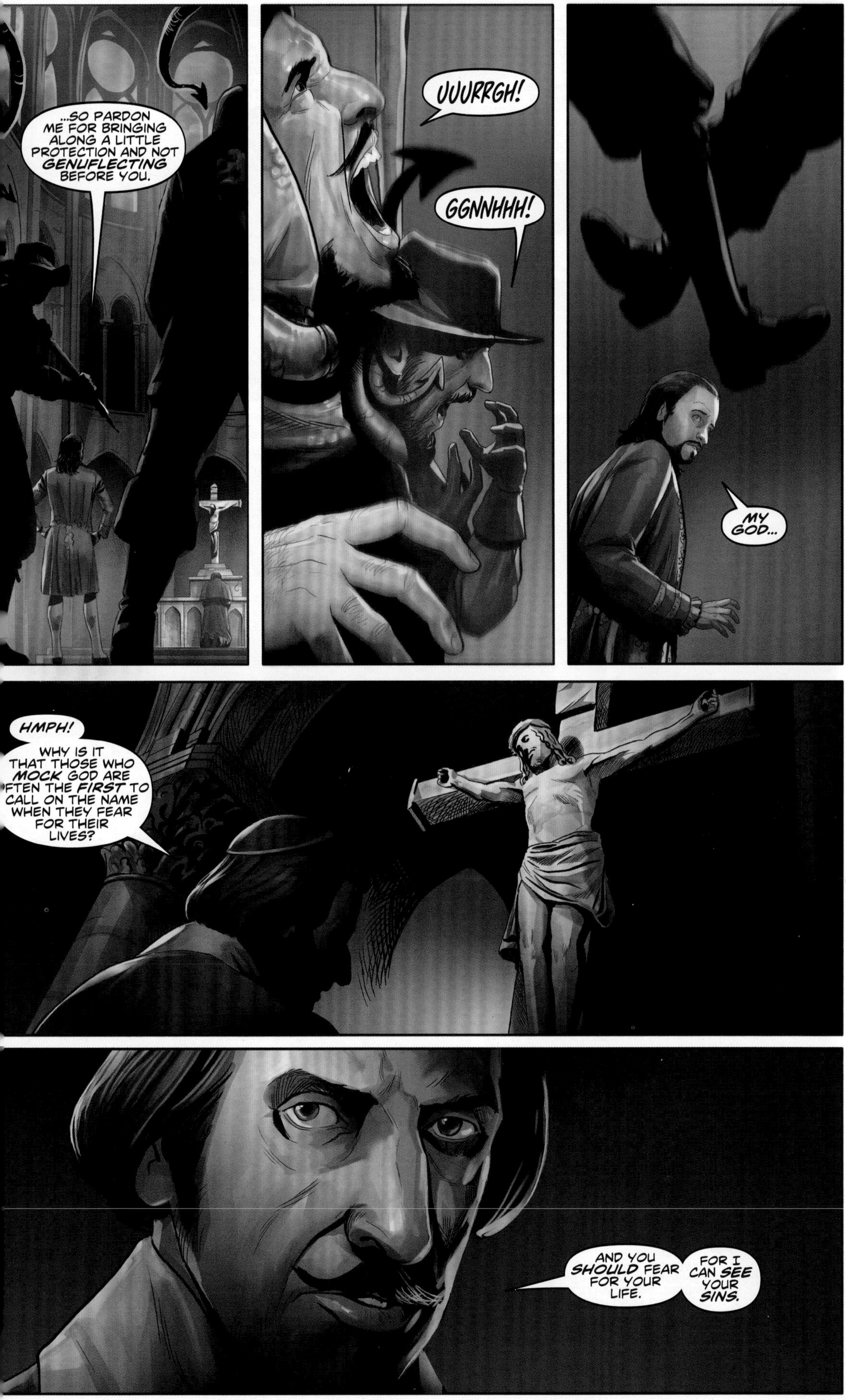
...SO PARDON ME FOR BRINGING ALONG A LITTLE PROTECTION AND NOT GENUFLECTING BEFORE YOU.
UUURRGH!
GGNNHHH!
MY GOD...
HMPH!
WHY IS IT THAT THOSE WHO MOCK GOD ARE OFTEN THE FIRST TO CALL ON THE NAME WHEN THEY FEAR FOR THEIR LIVES?
AND YOU SHOULD FEAR FOR YOUR LIFE.
FOR I CAN SEE YOUR SINS.

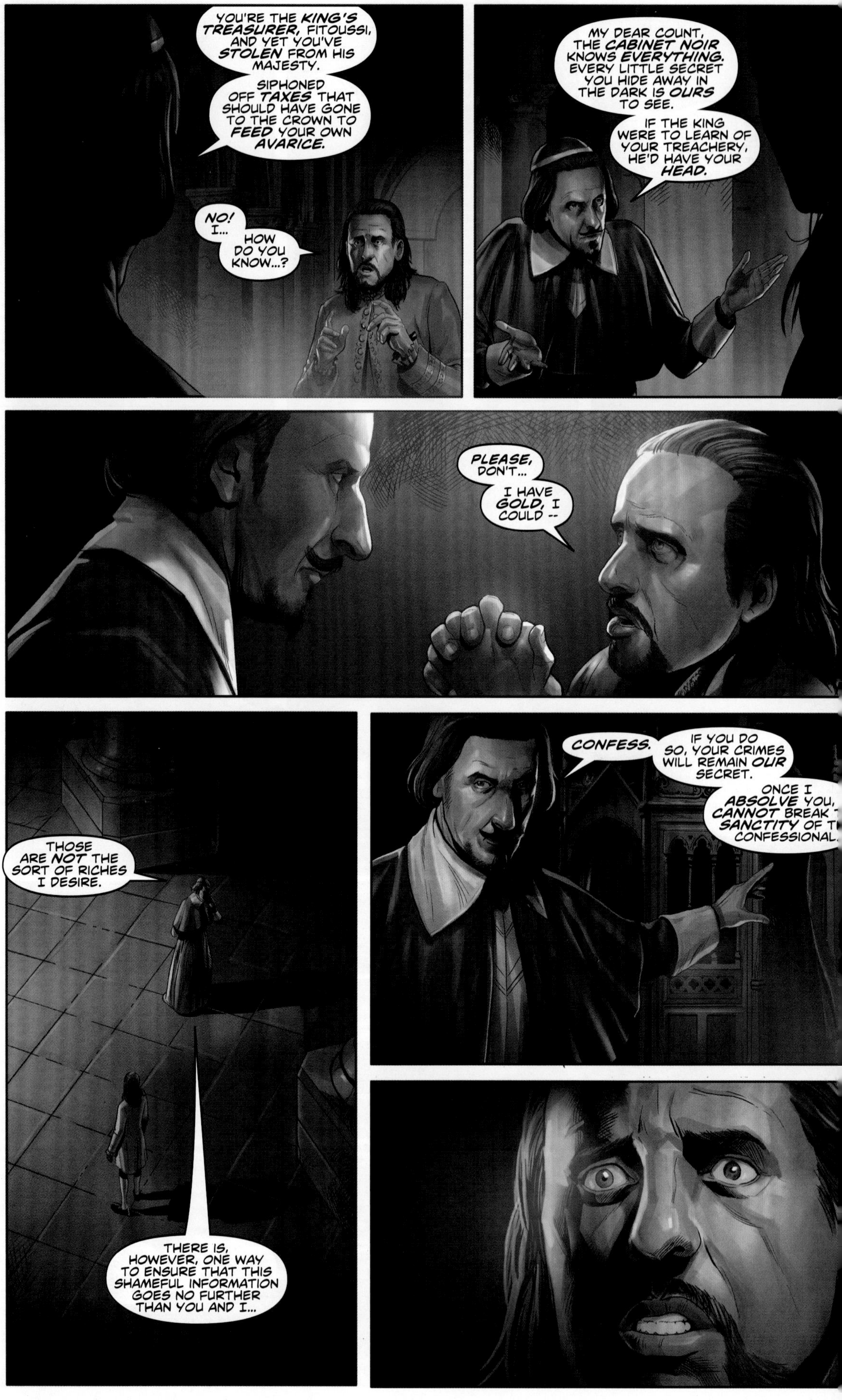
YOU'RE THE KING'S TREASURER, FITOUSSI, AND YET YOU'VE STOLEN FROM HIS MAJESTY.
SIPHONED OFF TAXES THAT SHOULD HAVE GONE TO THE CROWN TO FEED YOUR OWN AVARICE.
NO! I... HOW DO YOU KNOW...?
MY DEAR COUNT, THE CABINET NOIR KNOWS EVERYTHING. EVERY LITTLE SECRET YOU HIDE AWAY IN THE DARK IS OURS TO SEE.
IF THE KING WERE TO LEARN OF YOUR TREACHERY, HE'D HAVE YOUR HEAD.
PLEASE, DON'T...
I HAVE GOLD, I COULD --
THOSE ARE NOT THE SORT OF RICHES I DESIRE.
THERE IS, HOWEVER, ONE WAY TO ENSURE THAT THIS SHAMEFUL INFORMATION GOES NO FURTHER THAN YOU AND I...
CONFESS.
IF YOU DO SO, YOUR CRIMES WILL REMAIN OUR SECRET.
ONCE I ABSOLVE YOU, CANNOT BREAK SANCTITY OF CONFESSIONAL.

KKRRUNCH

KKKRRASH

GULP!

B-BLESS ME, FATHER, FOR I HAVE SINNED! IT...

IT'S BEEN A *LIFETIME* SINCE MY LAST CONFESSION!

I HAVE *SWINDLED* THE KING, *BLACKMAILED* NOBLEMEN TO DO MY BIDDING!

I HAVE *LIED* AND *CHEATED*, BEEN *UNFAITHFUL* ON COUNTLESS OCCASIONS, ORDERED THE *KILLING* OF MY ENEMIES! I HAVE --

SUCH *WICKEDNESS.*

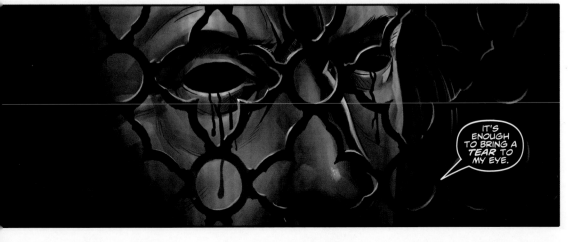

IT'S ENOUGH TO BRING A *TEAR* TO MY EYE.

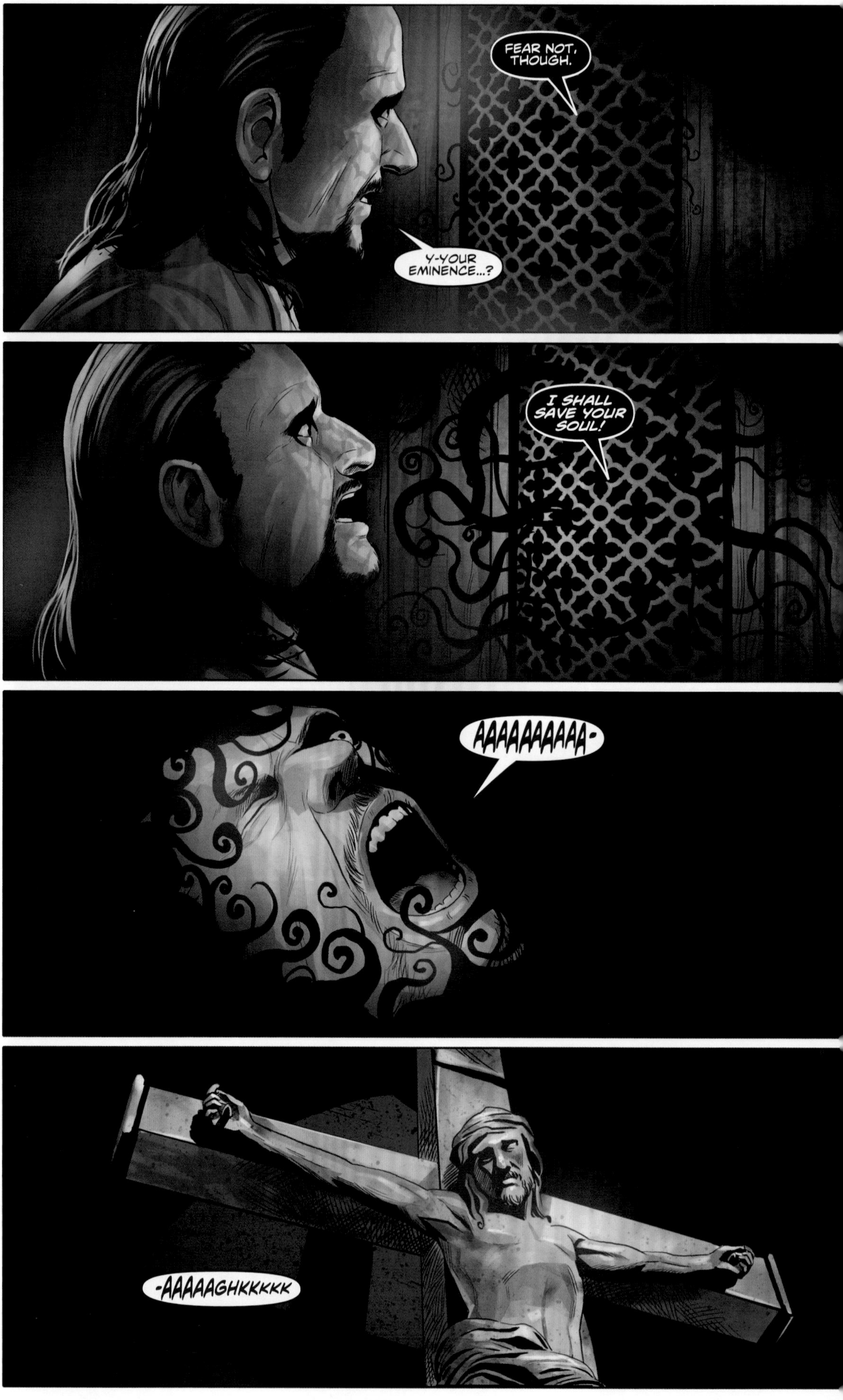
FEAR NOT, THOUGH.
Y-YOUR EMINENCE...?
I SHALL SAVE YOUR SOUL!
AAAAAAAAAA-
-AAAAAGHKKKKK

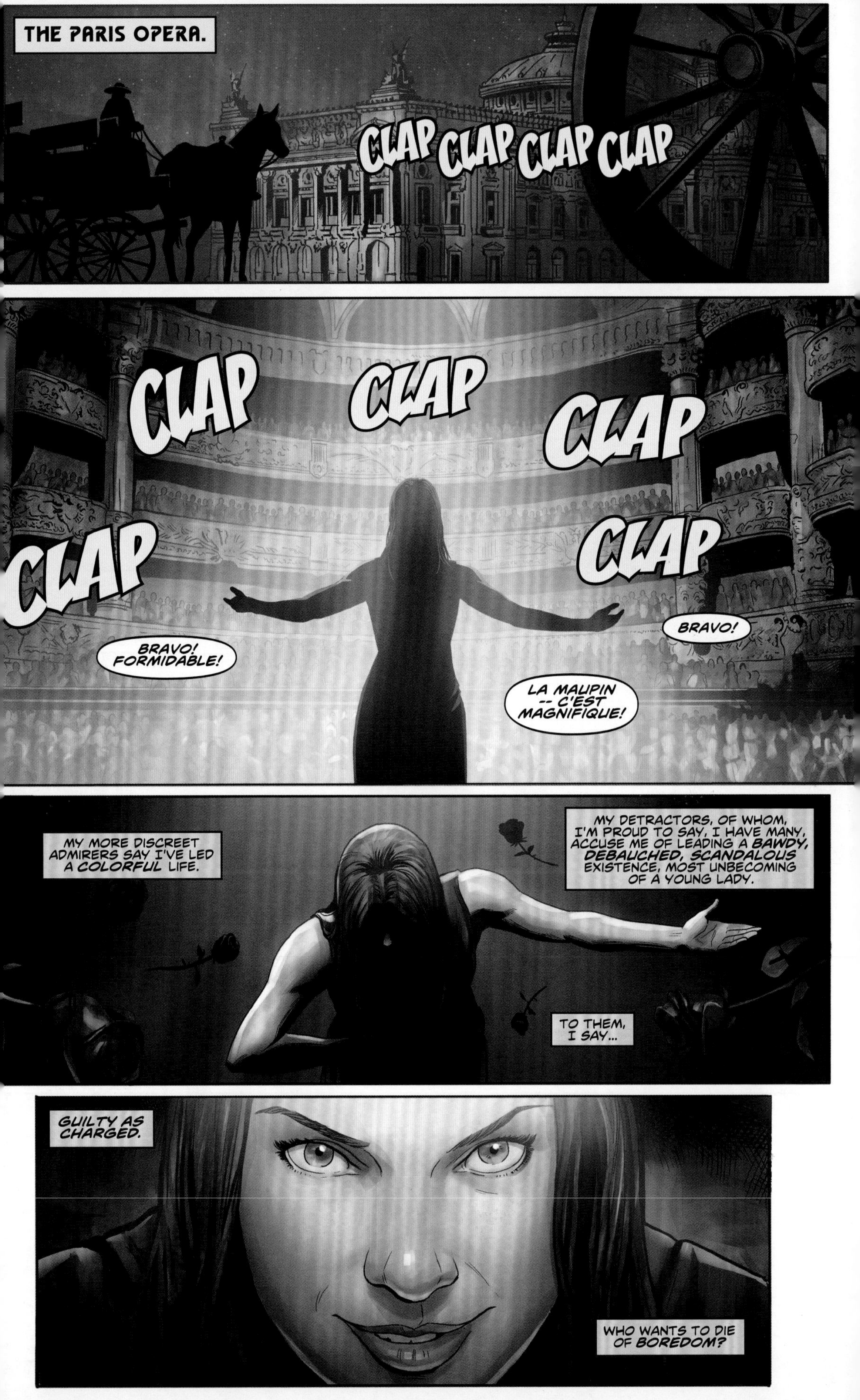
THE PARIS OPERA.
CLAP CLAP CLAP CLAP
CLAP
CLAP
CLAP
CLAP
CLAP
BRAVO! FORMIDABLE!
BRAVO!
LA MAUPIN -- C'EST MAGNIFIQUE!
MY MORE DISCREET ADMIRERS SAY I'VE LED A *COLORFUL* LIFE.
MY DETRACTORS, OF WHOM, I'M PROUD TO SAY, I HAVE MANY, ACCUSE ME OF LEADING A *BAWDY, DEBAUCHED, SCANDALOUS* EXISTENCE, MOST UNBECOMING OF A YOUNG LADY.
TO THEM, I SAY...
GUILTY AS CHARGED.
WHO WANTS TO DIE OF *BOREDOM?*

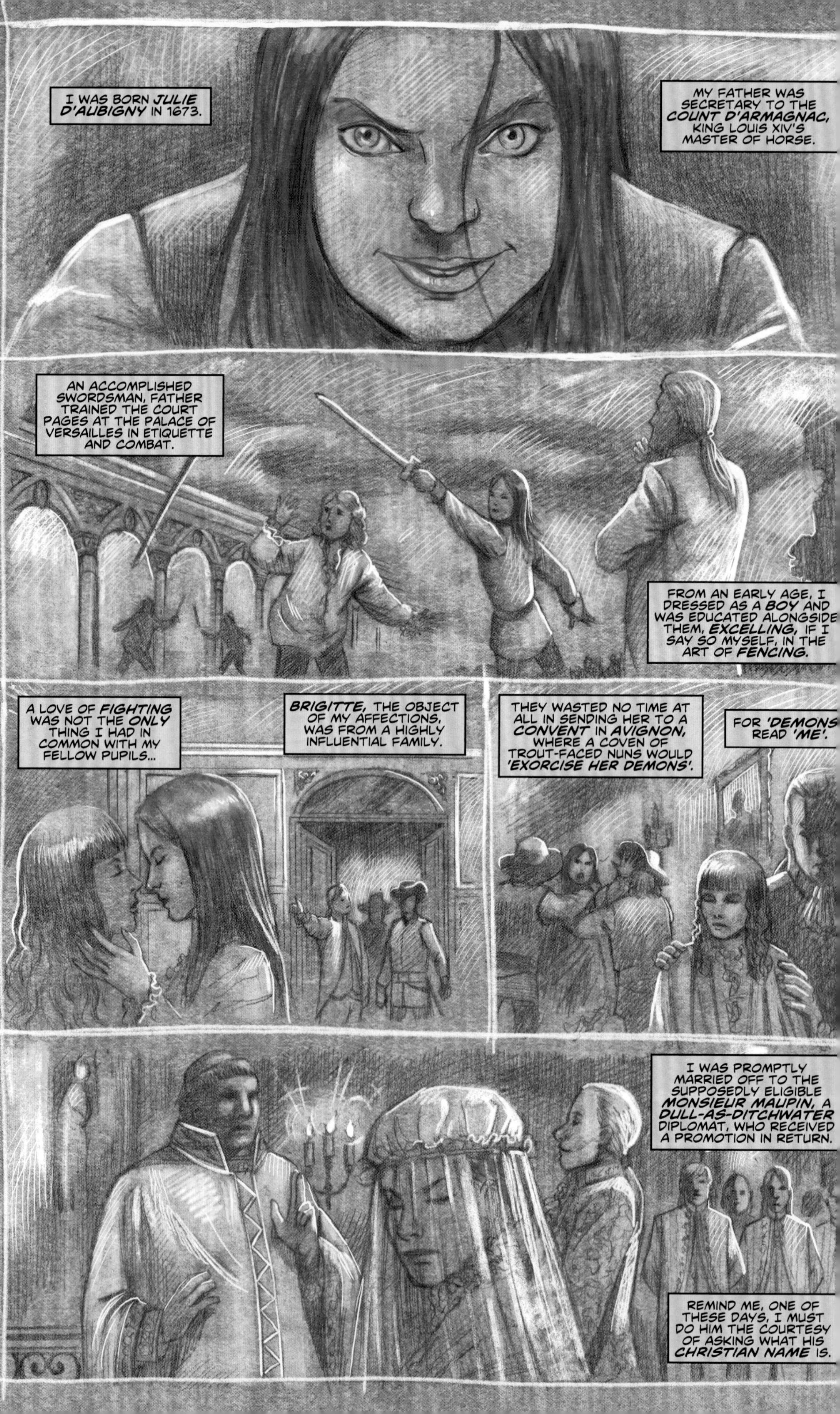
I WAS BORN JULIE D'AUBIGNY IN 1673.
MY FATHER WAS SECRETARY TO THE COUNT D'ARMAGNAC, KING LOUIS XIV'S MASTER OF HORSE.
AN ACCOMPLISHED SWORDSMAN, FATHER TRAINED THE COURT PAGES AT THE PALACE OF VERSAILLES IN ETIQUETTE AND COMBAT.
FROM AN EARLY AGE, I DRESSED AS A BOY AND WAS EDUCATED ALONGSIDE THEM, EXCELLING, IF I SAY SO MYSELF, IN THE ART OF FENCING.
A LOVE OF FIGHTING WAS NOT THE ONLY THING I HAD IN COMMON WITH MY FELLOW PUPILS...
BRIGITTE, THE OBJECT OF MY AFFECTIONS, WAS FROM A HIGHLY INFLUENTIAL FAMILY.
THEY WASTED NO TIME AT ALL IN SENDING HER TO A CONVENT IN AVIGNON, WHERE A COVEN OF TROUT-FACED NUNS WOULD 'EXORCISE HER DEMONS'.
FOR 'DEMONS' READ 'ME'.
I WAS PROMPTLY MARRIED OFF TO THE SUPPOSEDLY ELIGIBLE MONSIEUR MAUPIN, A DULL-AS-DITCHWATER DIPLOMAT, WHO RECEIVED A PROMOTION IN RETURN.
REMIND ME, ONE OF THESE DAYS, I MUST DO HIM THE COURTESY OF ASKING WHAT HIS CHRISTIAN NAME IS.

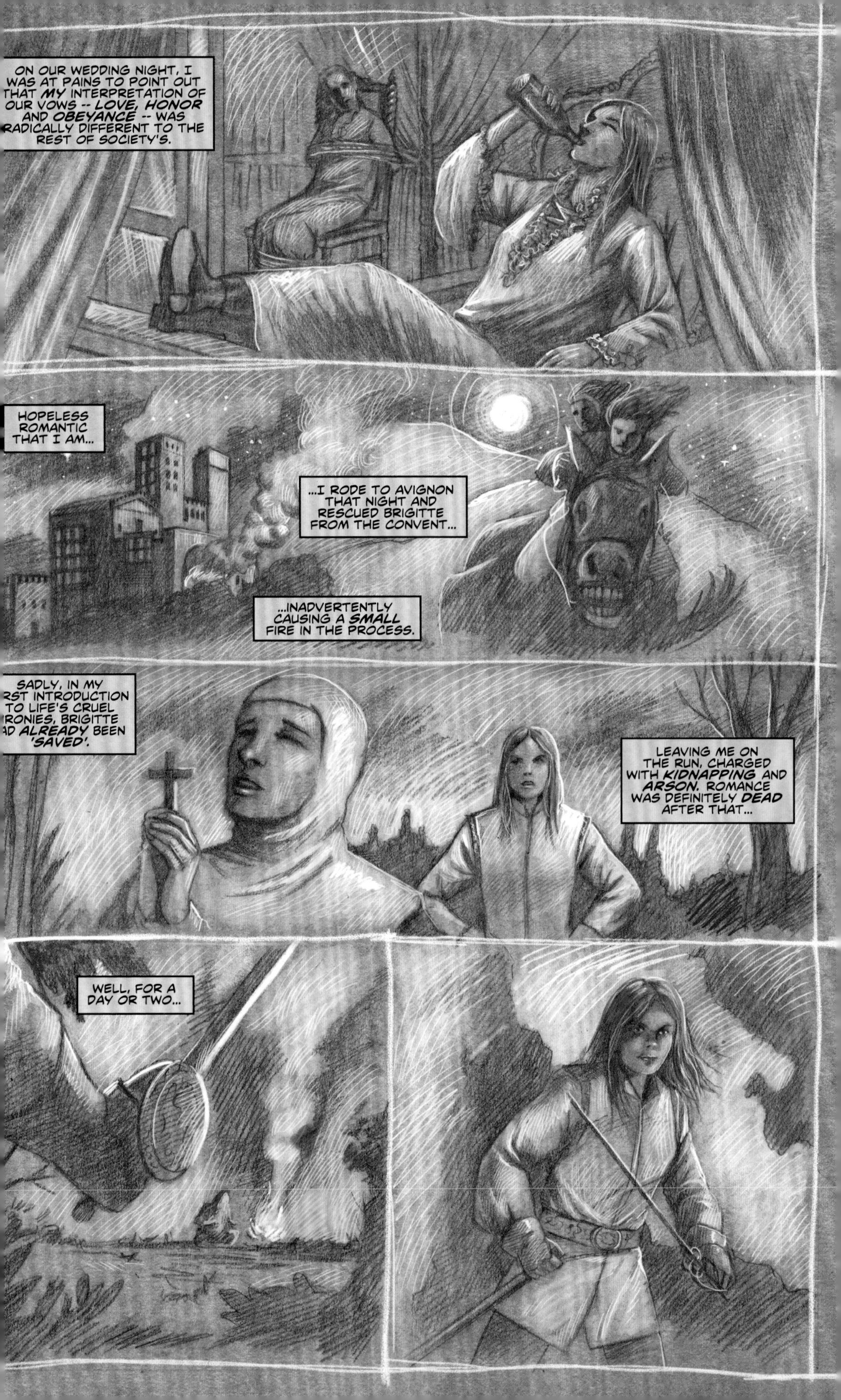
ON OUR WEDDING NIGHT, I WAS AT PAINS TO POINT OUT THAT MY INTERPRETATION OF OUR VOWS -- LOVE, HONOR AND OBEYANCE -- WAS RADICALLY DIFFERENT TO THE REST OF SOCIETY'S.
HOPELESS ROMANTIC THAT I AM...
...I RODE TO AVIGNON THAT NIGHT AND RESCUED BRIGITTE FROM THE CONVENT...
...INADVERTENTLY CAUSING A SMALL FIRE IN THE PROCESS.
SADLY, IN MY RST INTRODUCTION TO LIFE'S CRUEL RONIES, BRIGITTE AD ALREADY BEEN 'SAVED'.
LEAVING ME ON THE RUN, CHARGED WITH KIDNAPPING AND ARSON. ROMANCE WAS DEFINITELY DEAD AFTER THAT...
WELL, FOR A DAY OR TWO...

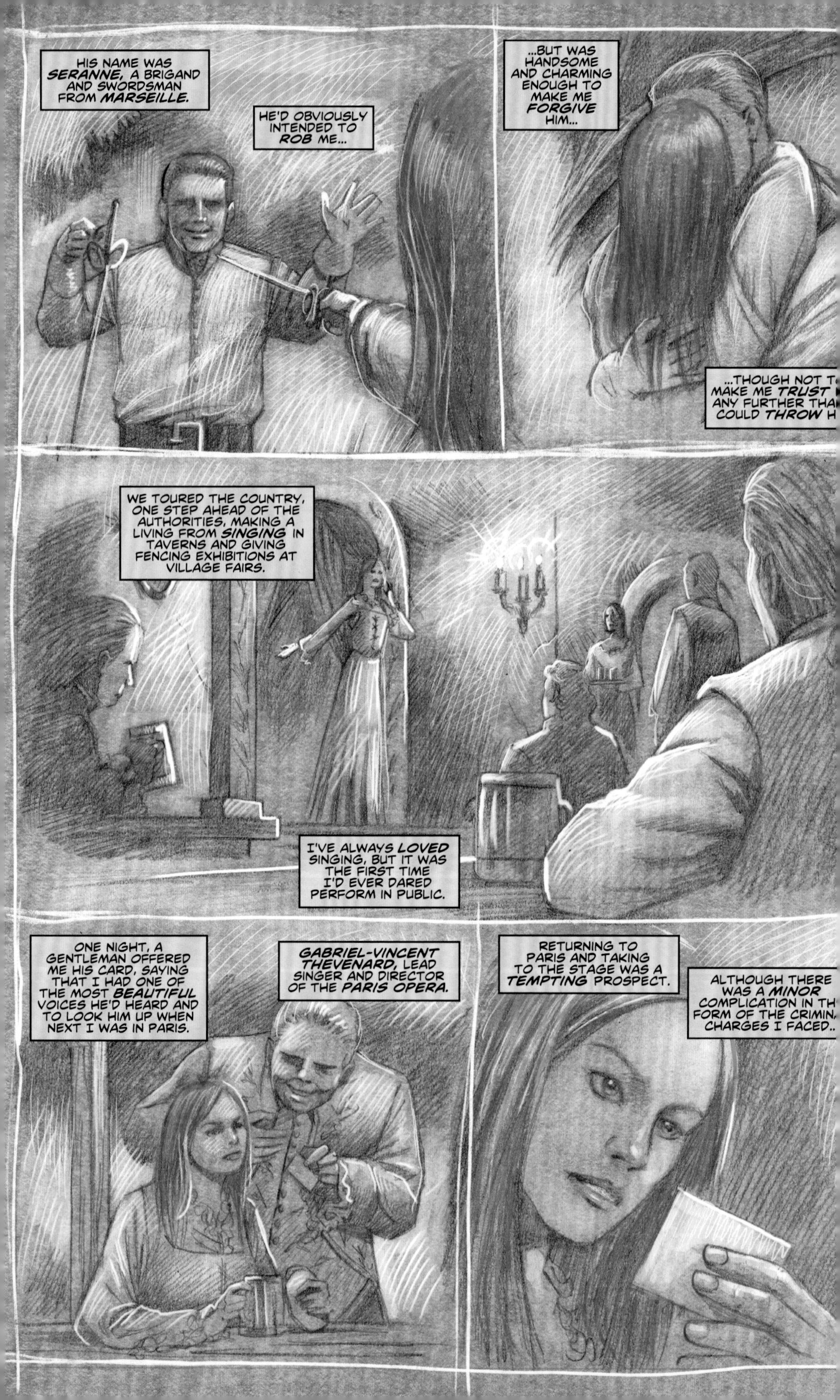

HIS NAME WAS SERANNE, A BRIGAND AND SWORDSMAN FROM MARSEILLE.
HE'D OBVIOUSLY INTENDED TO ROB ME...
...BUT WAS HANDSOME AND CHARMING ENOUGH TO MAKE ME FORGIVE HIM...
...THOUGH NOT T MAKE ME TRUST ANY FURTHER THA COULD THROW H
WE TOURED THE COUNTRY, ONE STEP AHEAD OF THE AUTHORITIES, MAKING A LIVING FROM SINGING IN TAVERNS AND GIVING FENCING EXHIBITIONS AT VILLAGE FAIRS.
I'VE ALWAYS LOVED SINGING, BUT IT WAS THE FIRST TIME I'D EVER DARED PERFORM IN PUBLIC.
ONE NIGHT, A GENTLEMAN OFFERED ME HIS CARD, SAYING THAT I HAD ONE OF THE MOST BEAUTIFUL VOICES HE'D HEARD AND TO LOOK HIM UP WHEN NEXT I WAS IN PARIS.
GABRIEL-VINCENT THEVENARD, LEAD SINGER AND DIRECTOR OF THE PARIS OPERA.
RETURNING TO PARIS AND TAKING TO THE STAGE WAS A TEMPTING PROSPECT.
ALTHOUGH THERE WAS A MINOR COMPLICATION IN TH FORM OF THE CRIMIN CHARGES I FACED...

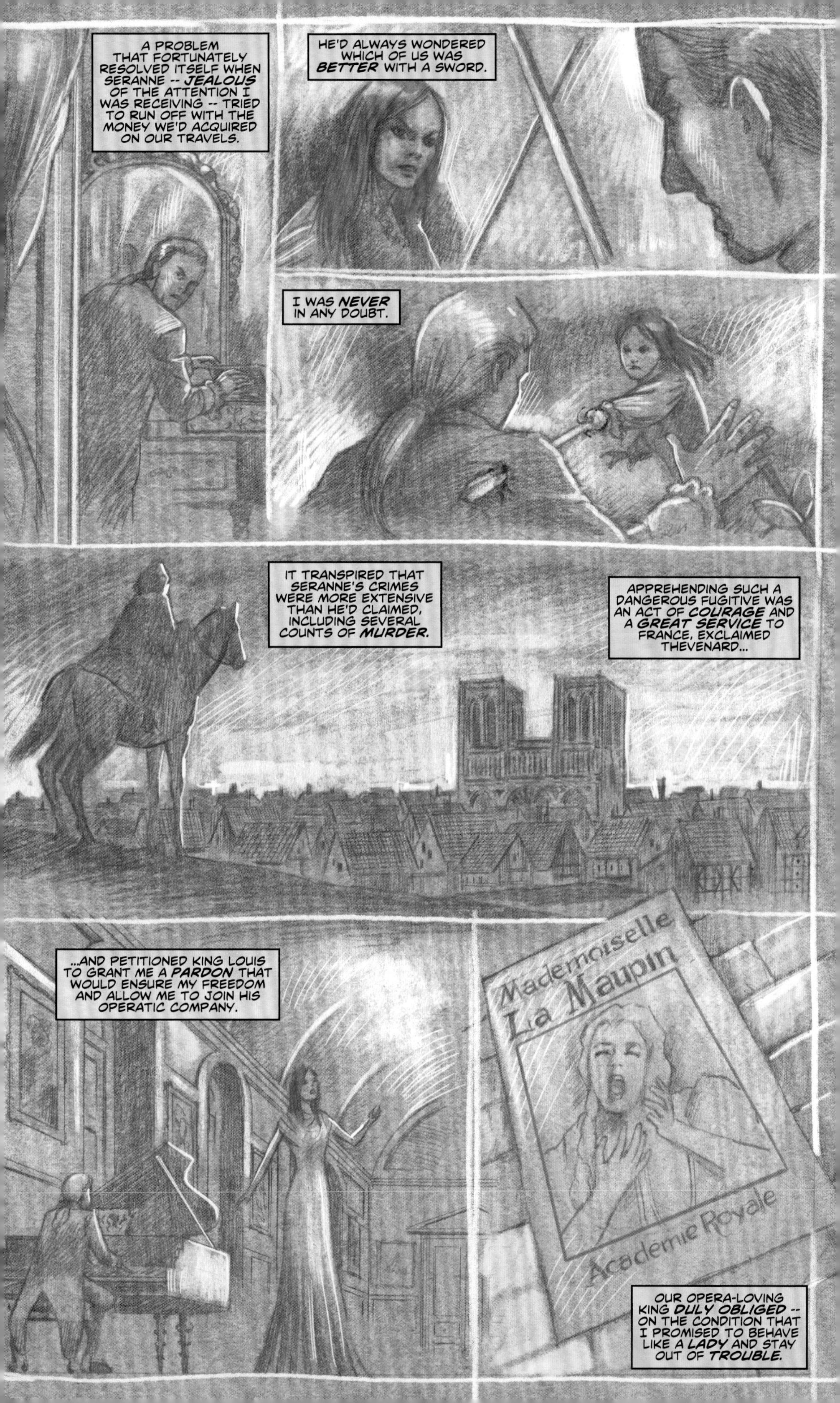
A PROBLEM THAT FORTUNATELY RESOLVED ITSELF WHEN SERANNE -- *JEALOUS* OF THE ATTENTION I WAS RECEIVING -- TRIED TO RUN OFF WITH THE MONEY WE'D ACQUIRED ON OUR TRAVELS.
HE'D ALWAYS WONDERED WHICH OF US WAS *BETTER* WITH A SWORD.
I WAS *NEVER* IN ANY DOUBT.
IT TRANSPIRED THAT SERANNE'S CRIMES WERE MORE EXTENSIVE THAN HE'D CLAIMED, INCLUDING SEVERAL COUNTS OF *MURDER*.
APPREHENDING SUCH A DANGEROUS FUGITIVE WAS AN ACT OF *COURAGE* AND A *GREAT SERVICE* TO FRANCE, EXCLAIMED THEVENARD...
...AND PETITIONED KING LOUIS TO GRANT ME A *PARDON* THAT WOULD ENSURE MY FREEDOM AND ALLOW ME TO JOIN HIS OPERATIC COMPANY.
Mademoiselle
La Maupin
Academie Royale
OUR OPERA-LOVING KING *DULY OBLIGED* -- ON THE CONDITION THAT I PROMISED TO BEHAVE LIKE A *LADY* AND STAY OUT OF *TROUBLE*.

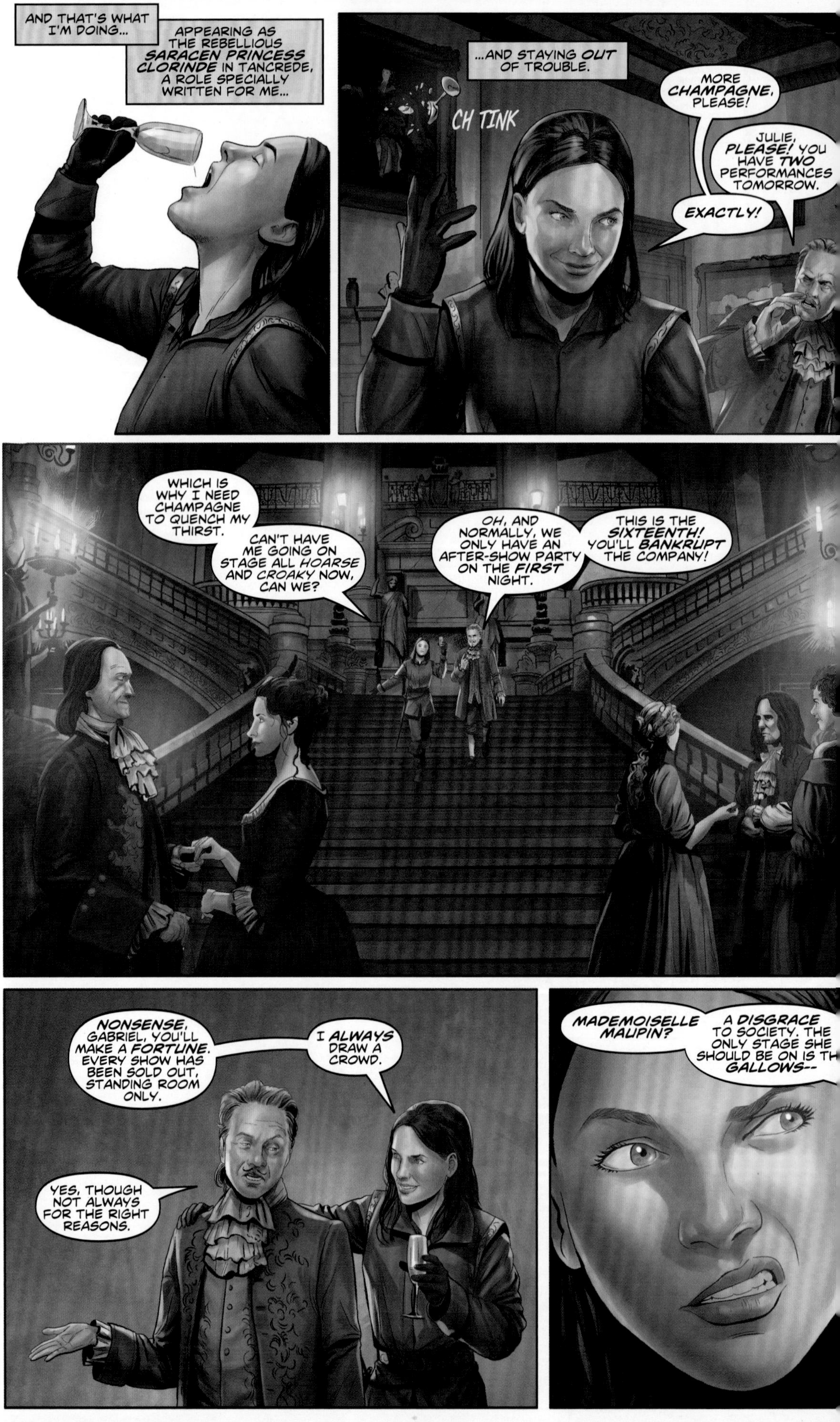
AND THAT'S WHAT I'M DOING...
APPEARING AS THE REBELLIOUS SARACEN PRINCESS CLORINDE IN TANCREDE, A ROLE SPECIALLY WRITTEN FOR ME...
...AND STAYING OUT OF TROUBLE.
CH TINK
MORE CHAMPAGNE, PLEASE!
JULIE, PLEASE! YOU HAVE TWO PERFORMANCES TOMORROW.
EXACTLY!
WHICH IS WHY I NEED CHAMPAGNE TO QUENCH MY THIRST.
CAN'T HAVE ME GOING ON STAGE ALL HOARSE AND CROAKY NOW, CAN WE?
OH, AND NORMALLY, WE ONLY HAVE AN AFTER-SHOW PARTY ON THE FIRST NIGHT.
THIS IS THE SIXTEENTH! YOU'LL BANKRUPT THE COMPANY!
NONSENSE, GABRIEL, YOU'LL MAKE A FORTUNE. EVERY SHOW HAS BEEN SOLD OUT, STANDING ROOM ONLY.
I ALWAYS DRAW A CROWD.
YES, THOUGH NOT ALWAYS FOR THE RIGHT REASONS.
MADEMOISELLE MAUPIN?
A DISGRACE TO SOCIETY. THE ONLY STAGE SHE SHOULD BE ON IS TH GALLOWS--

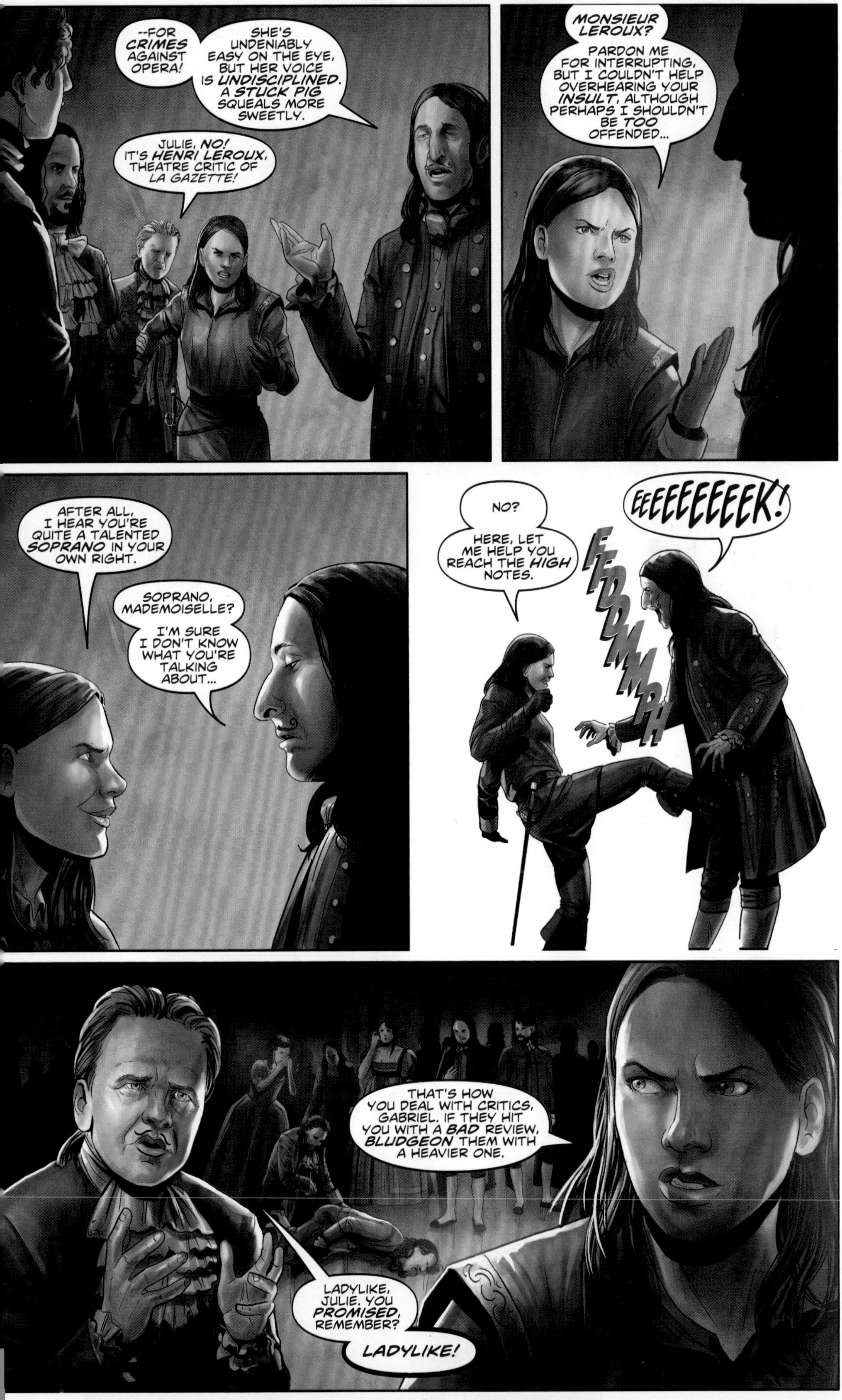

--FOR CRIMES AGAINST OPERA!
SHE'S UNDENIABLY EASY ON THE EYE, BUT HER VOICE IS UNDISCIPLINED. A STUCK PIG SQUEALS MORE SWEETLY.
JULIE, NO! IT'S HENRI LEROUX, THEATRE CRITIC OF LA GAZETTE!
MONSIEUR LEROUX?
PARDON ME FOR INTERRUPTING, BUT I COULDN'T HELP OVERHEARING YOUR INSULT, ALTHOUGH PERHAPS I SHOULDN'T BE TOO OFFENDED...
AFTER ALL, I HEAR YOU'RE QUITE A TALENTED SOPRANO IN YOUR OWN RIGHT.
SOPRANO, MADEMOISELLE?
I'M SURE I DON'T KNOW WHAT YOU'RE TALKING ABOUT...
NO?
HERE, LET ME HELP YOU REACH THE HIGH NOTES.
FFDUMMPH
EEEEEEEEEK!
THAT'S HOW YOU DEAL WITH CRITICS, GABRIEL. IF THEY HIT YOU WITH A BAD REVIEW, BLUDGEON THEM WITH A HEAVIER ONE.
LADYLIKE, JULIE. YOU PROMISED, REMEMBER?
LADYLIKE!

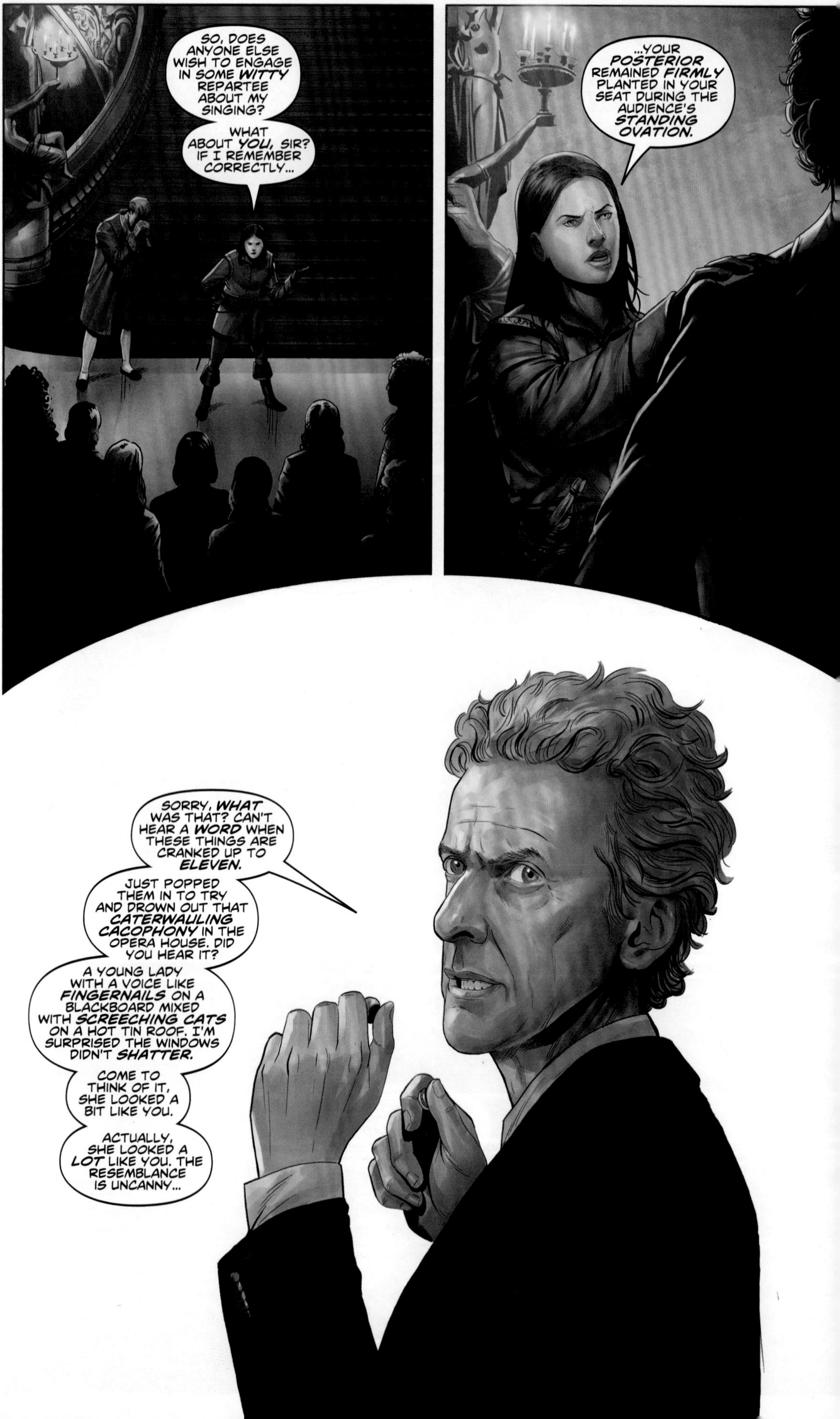
SO, DOES ANYONE ELSE WISH TO ENGAGE IN SOME WITTY REPARTEE ABOUT MY SINGING?
WHAT ABOUT YOU, SIR? IF I REMEMBER CORRECTLY...
...YOUR POSTERIOR REMAINED FIRMLY PLANTED IN YOUR SEAT DURING THE AUDIENCE'S STANDING OVATION.
SORRY, WHAT WAS THAT? CAN'T HEAR A WORD WHEN THESE THINGS ARE CRANKED UP TO ELEVEN.
JUST POPPED THEM IN TO TRY AND DROWN OUT THAT CATERWAULING CACOPHONY IN THE OPERA HOUSE. DID YOU HEAR IT?
A YOUNG LADY WITH A VOICE LIKE FINGERNAILS ON A BLACKBOARD MIXED WITH SCREECHING CATS ON A HOT TIN ROOF. I'M SURPRISED THE WINDOWS DIDN'T SHATTER.
COME TO THINK OF IT, SHE LOOKED A BIT LIKE YOU.
ACTUALLY, SHE LOOKED A LOT LIKE YOU. THE RESEMBLANCE IS UNCANNY...

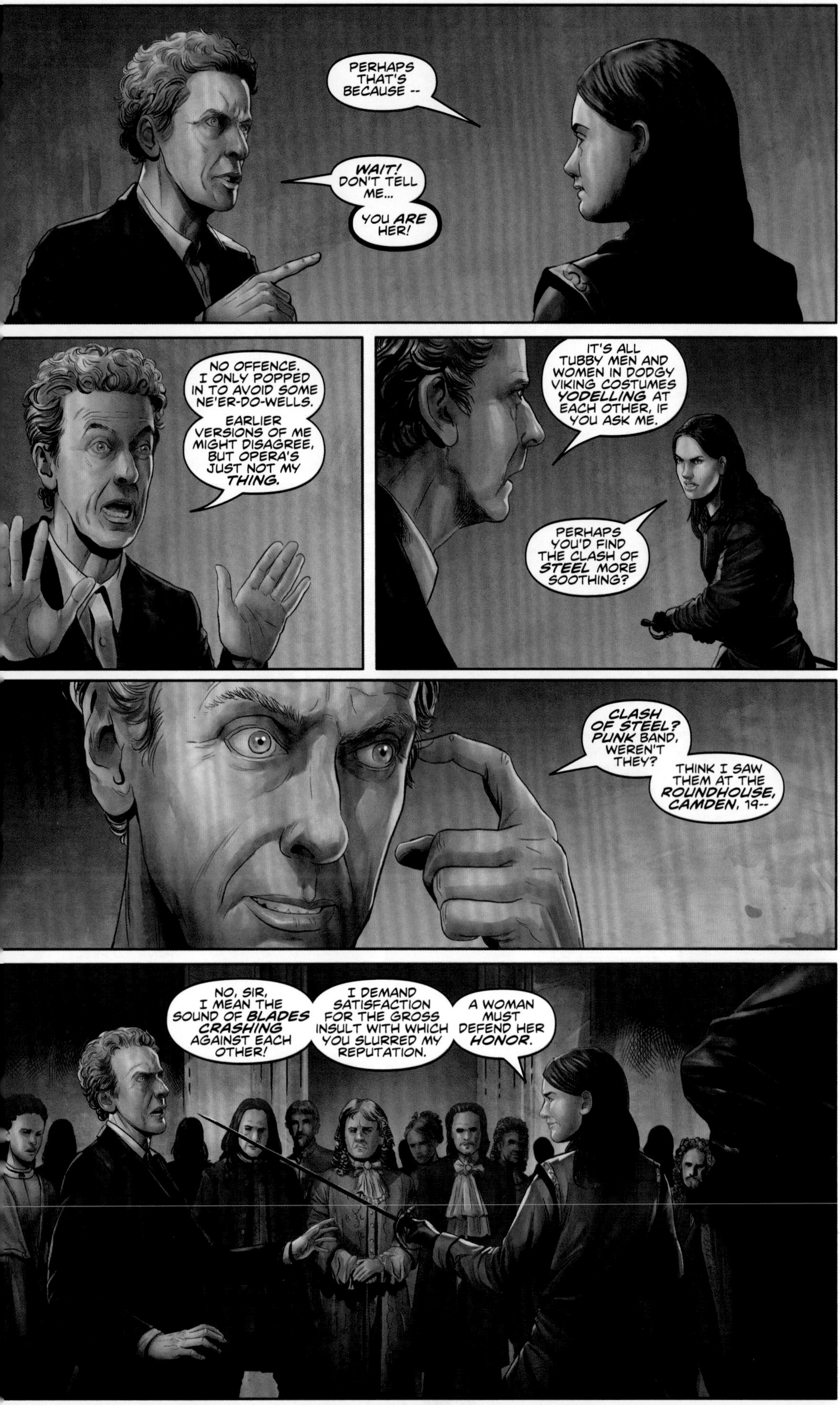
PERHAPS THAT'S BECAUSE --
WAIT! DON'T TELL ME...
YOU ARE HER!
NO OFFENCE. I ONLY POPPED IN TO AVOID SOME NE'ER-DO-WELLS.
EARLIER VERSIONS OF ME MIGHT DISAGREE, BUT OPERA'S JUST NOT MY THING.
IT'S ALL TUBBY MEN AND WOMEN IN DODGY VIKING COSTUMES YODELLING AT EACH OTHER, IF YOU ASK ME.
PERHAPS YOU'D FIND THE CLASH OF STEEL MORE SOOTHING?
CLASH OF STEEL? PUNK BAND, WEREN'T THEY?
THINK I SAW THEM AT THE ROUNDHOUSE, CAMDEN, 19--
NO, SIR, I MEAN THE SOUND OF BLADES CRASHING AGAINST EACH OTHER!
I DEMAND SATISFACTION FOR THE GROSS INSULT WITH WHICH YOU SLURRED MY REPUTATION.
A WOMAN MUST DEFEND HER HONOR.

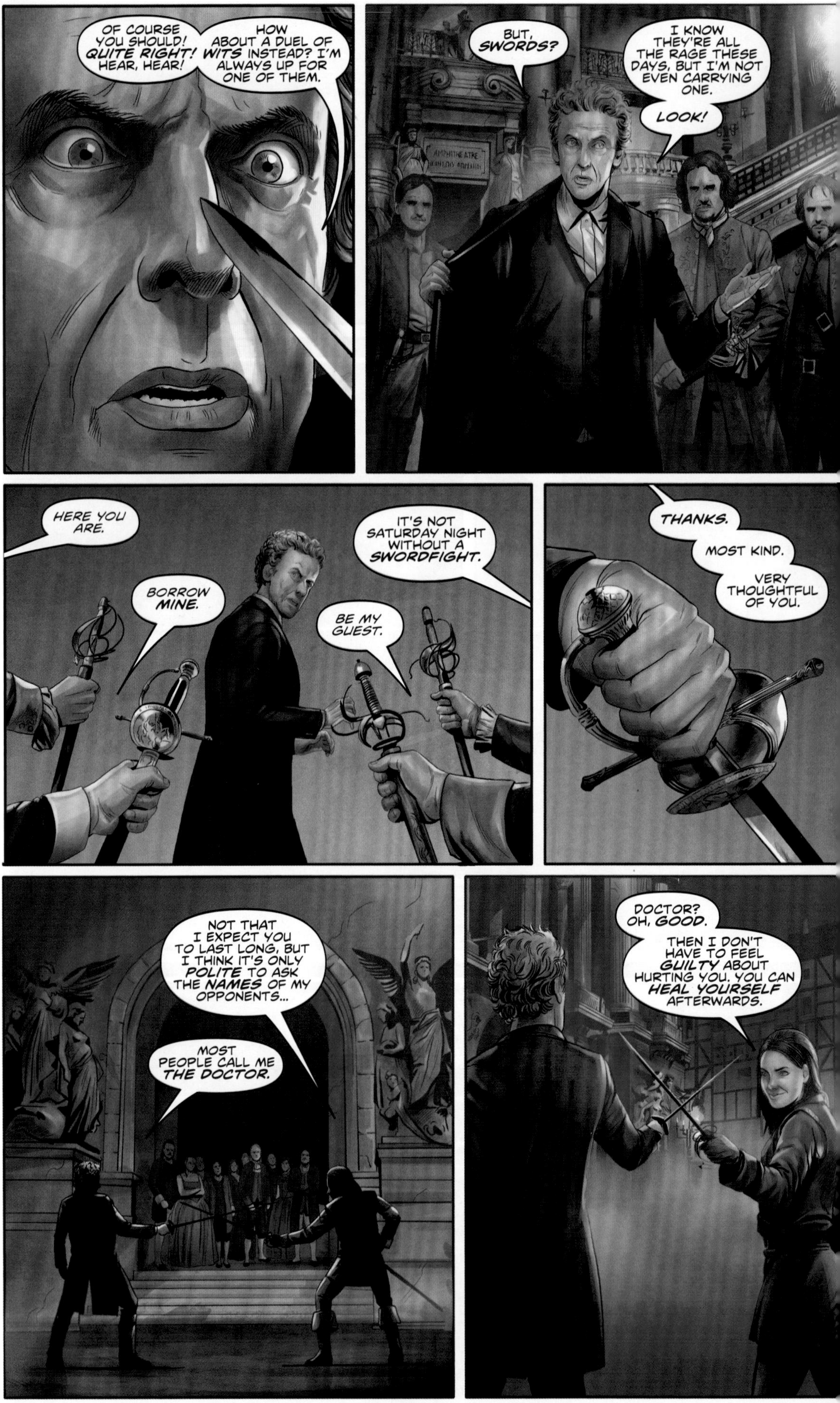
OF COURSE YOU SHOULD! QUITE RIGHT! HEAR, HEAR!
HOW ABOUT A DUEL OF WITS INSTEAD? I'M ALWAYS UP FOR ONE OF THEM.
BUT, SWORDS?
I KNOW THEY'RE ALL THE RAGE THESE DAYS, BUT I'M NOT EVEN CARRYING ONE.
LOOK!
AMPHITHEATRE
HERE YOU ARE.
BORROW MINE.
BE MY GUEST.
IT'S NOT SATURDAY NIGHT WITHOUT A SWORDFIGHT.
THANKS.
MOST KIND.
VERY THOUGHTFUL OF YOU.
NOT THAT I EXPECT YOU TO LAST LONG, BUT I THINK IT'S ONLY POLITE TO ASK THE NAMES OF MY OPPONENTS...
MOST PEOPLE CALL ME THE DOCTOR.
DOCTOR? OH, GOOD.
THEN I DON'T HAVE TO FEEL GUILTY ABOUT HURTING YOU. YOU CAN HEAL YOURSELF AFTERWARDS.

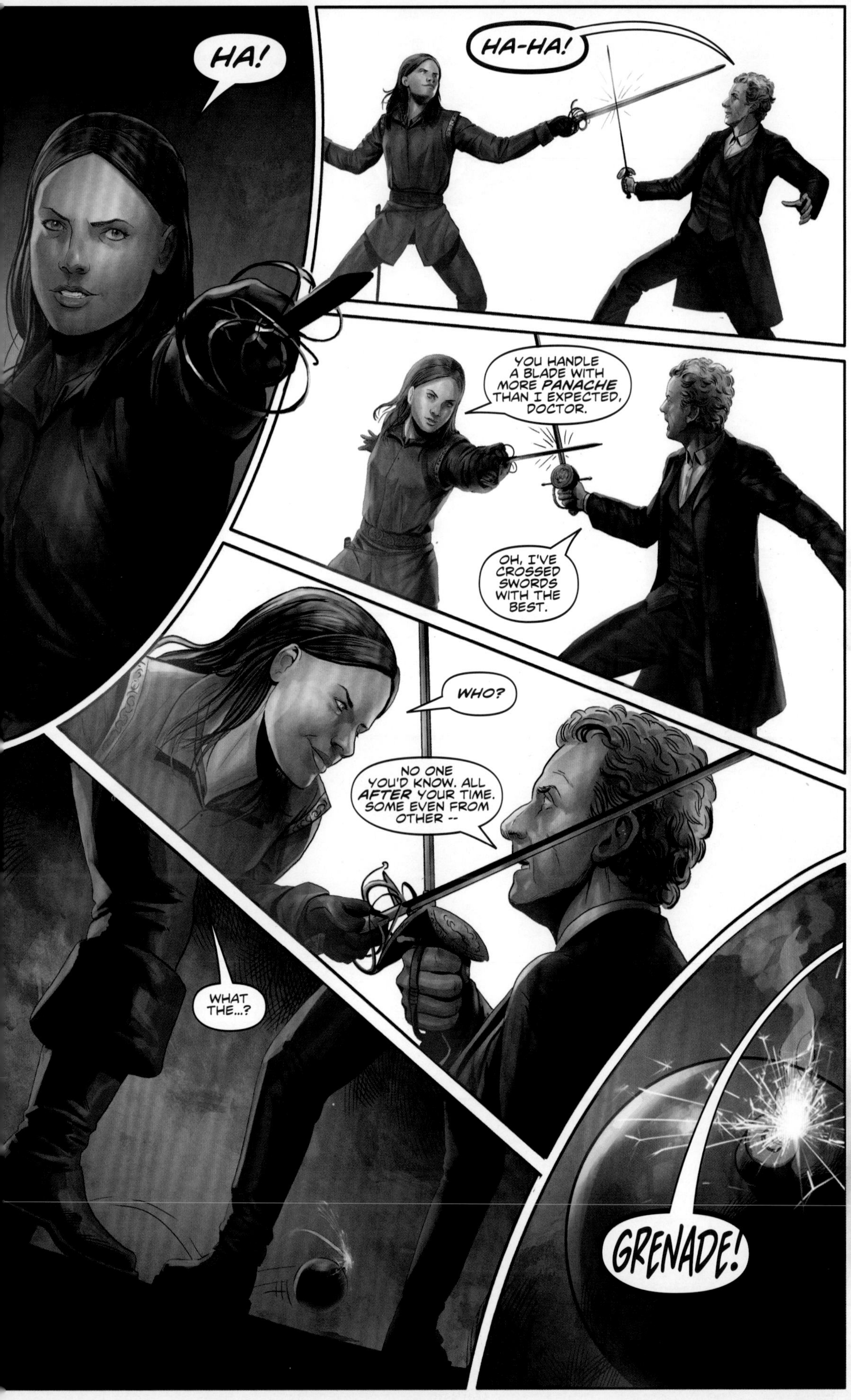
HA!
HA-HA!
YOU HANDLE A BLADE WITH MORE PANACHE THAN I EXPECTED, DOCTOR.
OH, I'VE CROSSED SWORDS WITH THE BEST.
WHO?
NO ONE YOU'D KNOW. ALL AFTER YOUR TIME. SOME EVEN FROM OTHER --
WHAT THE...?
GRENADE!

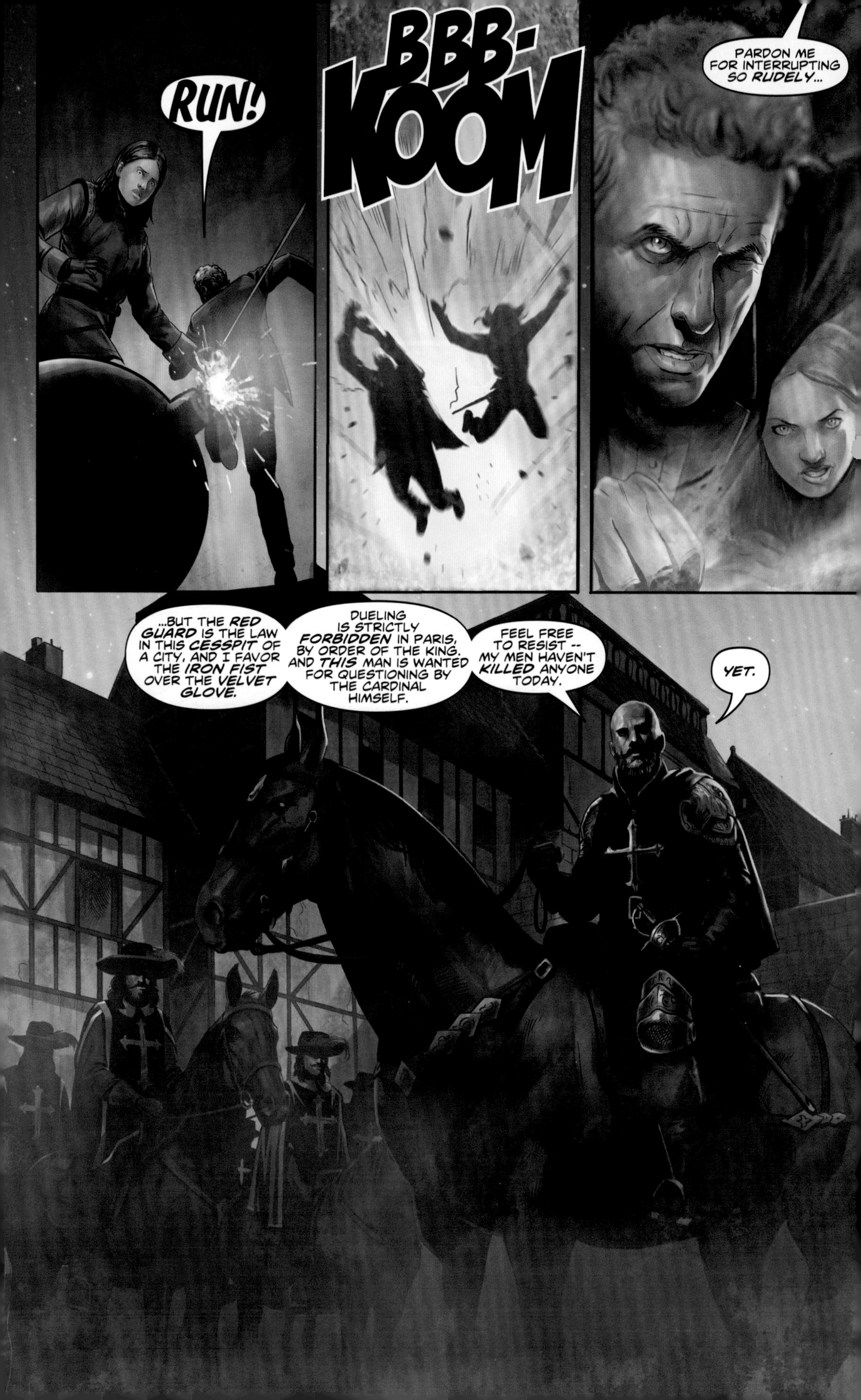
RUN!
BBB-KOOM
PARDON ME FOR INTERRUPTING SO RUDELY...
...BUT THE RED GUARD IS THE LAW IN THIS CESSPIT OF A CITY, AND I FAVOR THE IRON FIST OVER THE VELVET GLOVE.
DUELING IS STRICTLY FORBIDDEN IN PARIS, BY ORDER OF THE KING. AND THIS MAN IS WANTED FOR QUESTIONING BY THE CARDINAL HIMSELF.
FEEL FREE TO RESIST -- MY MEN HAVEN'T KILLED ANYONE TODAY.
YET.

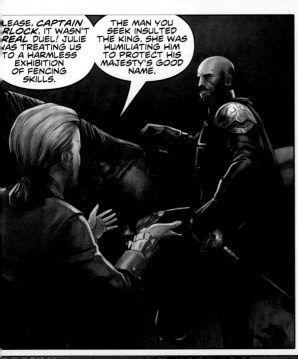

PLEASE, *CAPTAIN RLOCK*, IT WASN'T A *REAL* DUEL! JULIE WAS TREATING US TO A HARMLESS EXHIBITION OF FENCING SKILLS.

THE MAN YOU SEEK INSULTED THE KING. SHE WAS HUMILIATING HIM TO PROTECT HIS MAJESTY'S GOOD NAME.

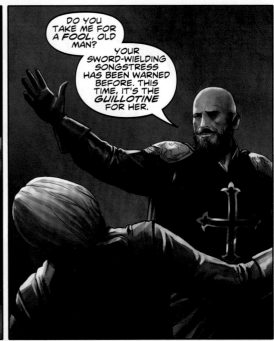

DO YOU TAKE ME FOR A *FOOL*, OLD MAN?

YOUR SWORD-WIELDING SONGSTRESS HAS BEEN WARNED BEFORE. THIS TIME, IT'S THE *GUILLOTINE* FOR HER.

IF YOU WANT MY HEAD, CAPTAIN, YOU'LL HAVE TO TAKE IT YOURSELF.

A *PLEASURE*, MADEMOISELLE.

IT WON'T LOOK SO PRETTY STUCK ON A *SPIKE* ON THE CITY WALLS.

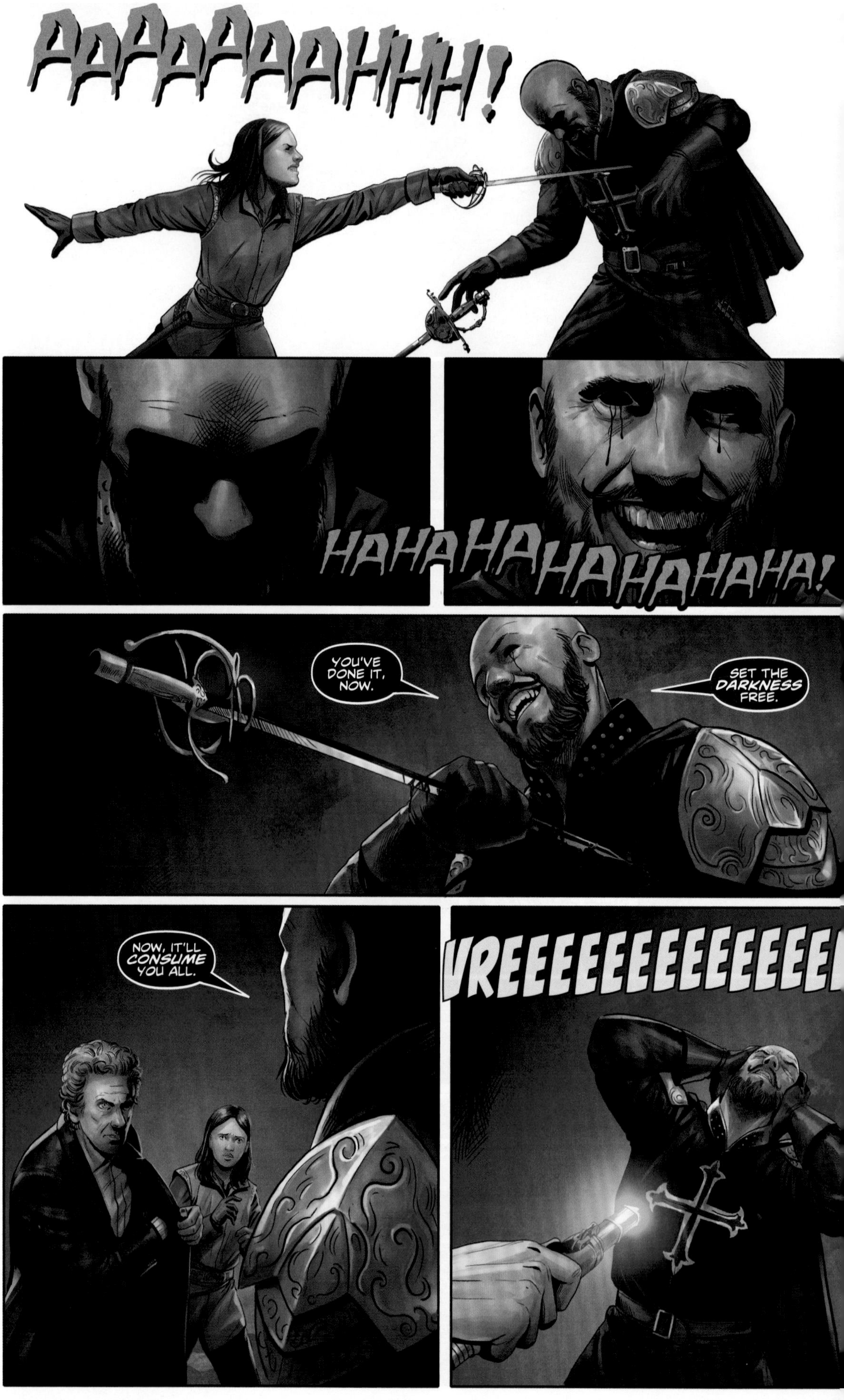
AAAAAAAAHHHH!
HAHAHAHAHAHAHAHA!
YOU'VE DONE IT, NOW.
SET THE *DARKNESS* FREE.
NOW, IT'LL *CONSUME* YOU ALL.
VREEEEEEEEEEEEEE

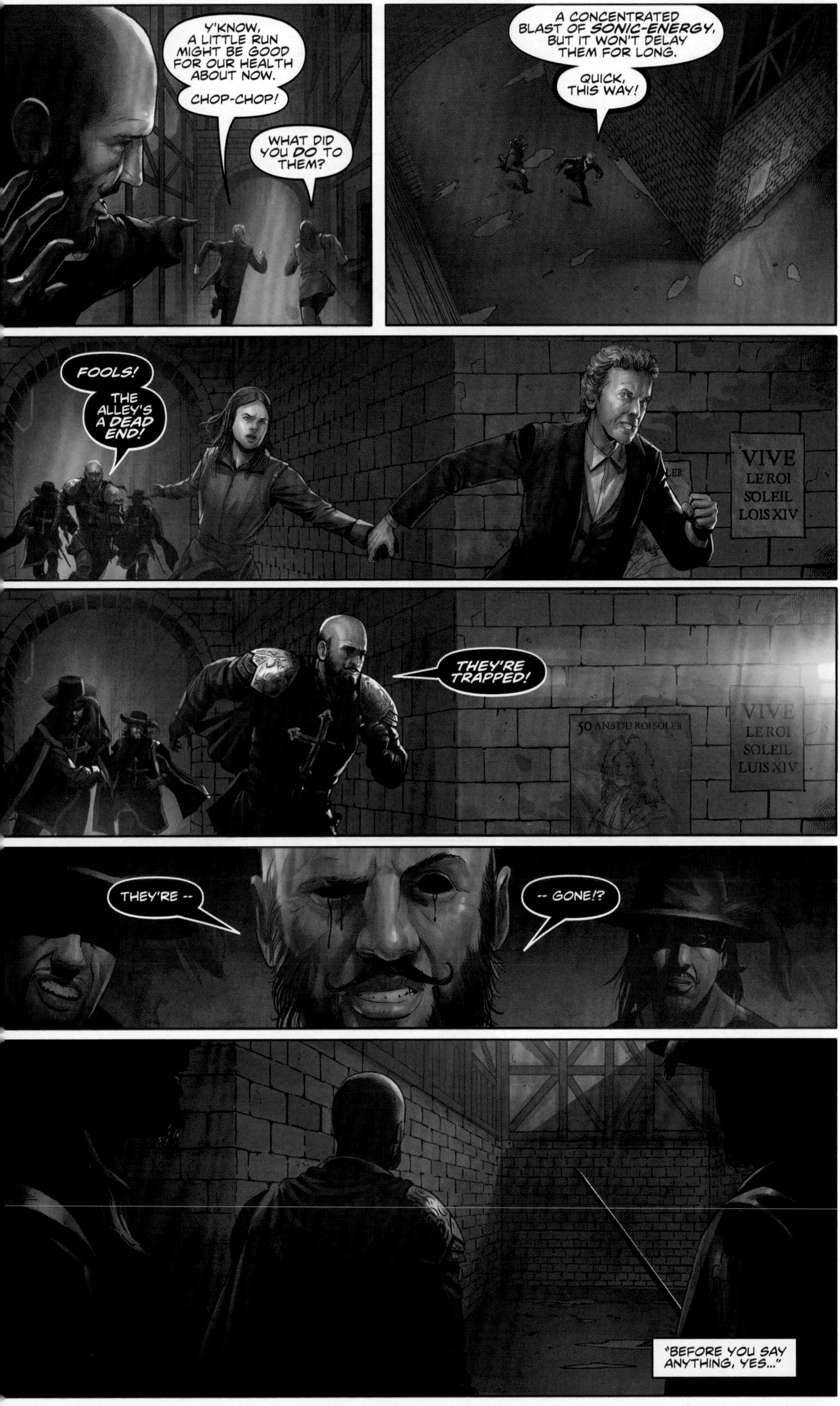
Y'KNOW, A LITTLE RUN MIGHT BE GOOD FOR OUR HEALTH ABOUT NOW.
CHOP-CHOP!
WHAT DID YOU DO TO THEM?
A CONCENTRATED BLAST OF SONIC-ENERGY, BUT IT WON'T DELAY THEM FOR LONG.
QUICK, THIS WAY!
FOOLS!
THE ALLEY'S A DEAD END!
VIVE LE ROI SOLEIL LOIS XIV
THEY'RE TRAPPED!
50 ANS DU ROI SOLEIL
VIVE LE ROI SOLEIL LOIS XIV
THEY'RE --
-- GONE!?
"BEFORE YOU SAY ANYTHING, YES..."

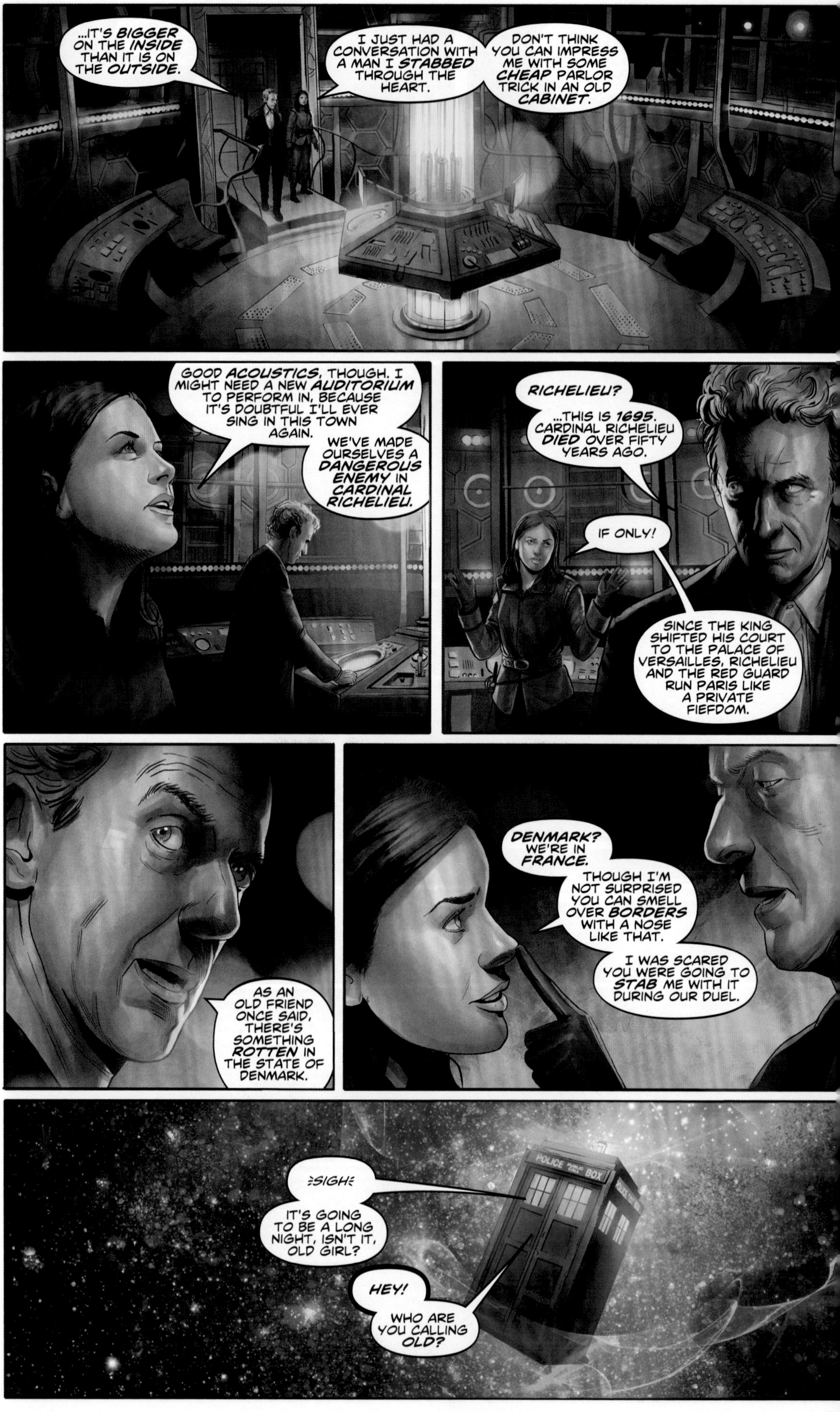

...IT'S BIGGER ON THE INSIDE THAN IT IS ON THE OUTSIDE.
I JUST HAD A CONVERSATION WITH A MAN I STABBED THROUGH THE HEART.
DON'T THINK YOU CAN IMPRESS ME WITH SOME CHEAP PARLOR TRICK IN AN OLD CABINET.
GOOD ACOUSTICS, THOUGH. I MIGHT NEED A NEW AUDITORIUM TO PERFORM IN, BECAUSE IT'S DOUBTFUL I'LL EVER SING IN THIS TOWN AGAIN.
WE'VE MADE OURSELVES A DANGEROUS ENEMY IN CARDINAL RICHELIEU.
RICHELIEU?
...THIS IS 1695. CARDINAL RICHELIEU DIED OVER FIFTY YEARS AGO.
IF ONLY!
SINCE THE KING SHIFTED HIS COURT TO THE PALACE OF VERSAILLES, RICHELIEU AND THE RED GUARD RUN PARIS LIKE A PRIVATE FIEFDOM.
AS AN OLD FRIEND ONCE SAID, THERE'S SOMETHING ROTTEN IN THE STATE OF DENMARK.
DENMARK? WE'RE IN FRANCE.
THOUGH I'M NOT SURPRISED YOU CAN SMELL OVER BORDERS WITH A NOSE LIKE THAT.
I WAS SCARED YOU WERE GOING TO STAB ME WITH IT DURING OUR DUEL.
POLICE BOX
SIGH
IT'S GOING TO BE A LONG NIGHT, ISN'T IT, OLD GIRL?
HEY!
WHO ARE YOU CALLING OLD?

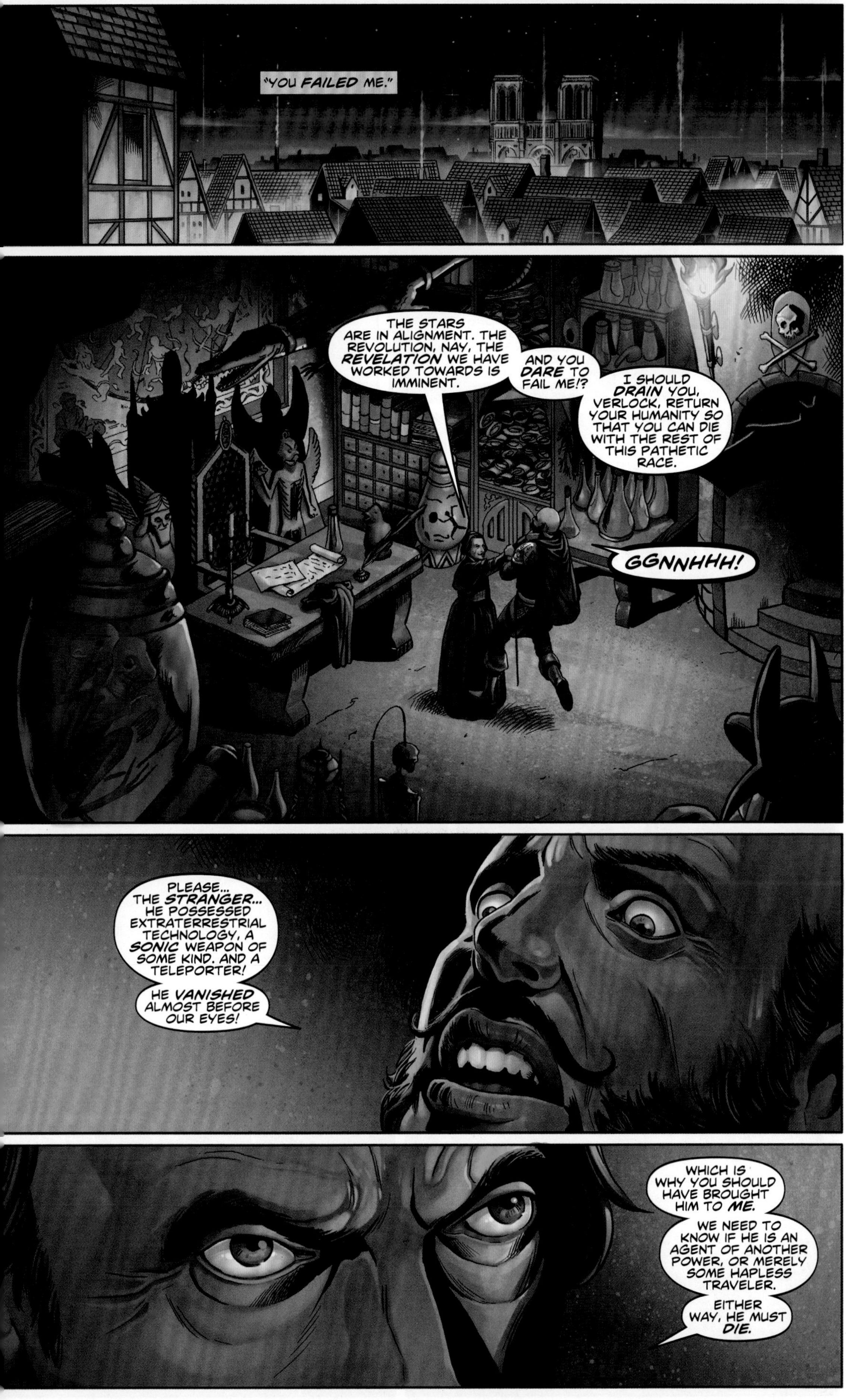
"YOU FAILED ME."
THE STARS ARE IN ALIGNMENT. THE REVOLUTION, NAY, THE REVELATION WE HAVE WORKED TOWARDS IS IMMINENT.
AND YOU DARE TO FAIL ME!?
I SHOULD DRAIN YOU, VERLOCK, RETURN YOUR HUMANITY SO THAT YOU CAN DIE WITH THE REST OF THIS PATHETIC RACE.
GGNNHHH!
PLEASE... THE STRANGER... HE POSSESSED EXTRATERRESTRIAL TECHNOLOGY, A SONIC WEAPON OF SOME KIND. AND A TELEPORTER!
HE VANISHED ALMOST BEFORE OUR EYES!
WHICH IS WHY YOU SHOULD HAVE BROUGHT HIM TO ME.
WE NEED TO KNOW IF HE IS AN AGENT OF ANOTHER POWER, OR MERELY SOME HAPLESS TRAVELER.
EITHER WAY, HE MUST DIE.

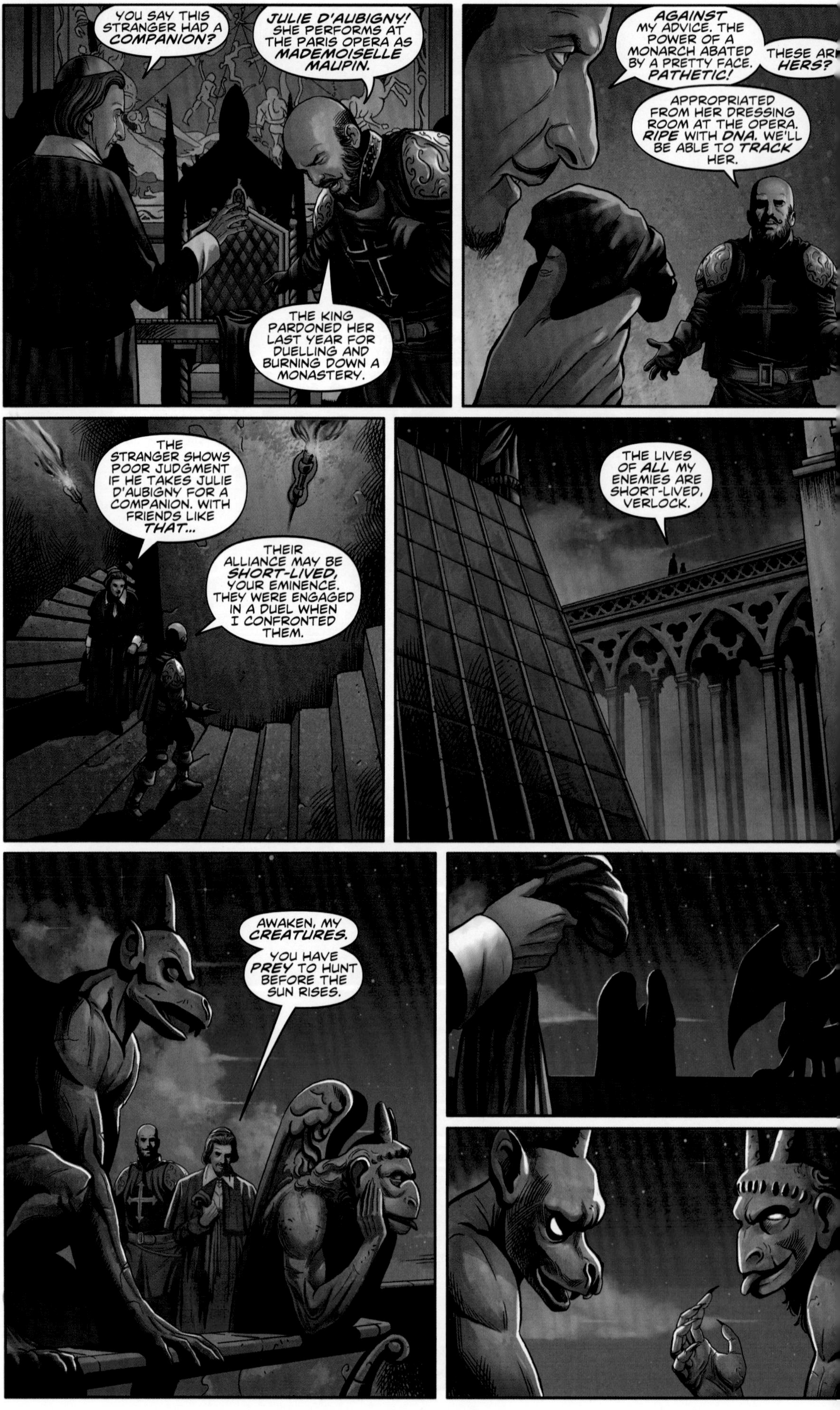
YOU SAY THIS STRANGER HAD A COMPANION?
JULIE D'AUBIGNY! SHE PERFORMS AT THE PARIS OPERA AS MADEMOISELLE MAUPIN.
THE KING PARDONED HER LAST YEAR FOR DUELLING AND BURNING DOWN A MONASTERY.
AGAINST MY ADVICE. THE POWER OF A MONARCH ABATED BY A PRETTY FACE. PATHETIC!
THESE AR HERS?
APPROPRIATED FROM HER DRESSING ROOM AT THE OPERA. RIPE WITH DNA. WE'LL BE ABLE TO TRACK HER.
THE STRANGER SHOWS POOR JUDGMENT IF HE TAKES JULIE D'AUBIGNY FOR A COMPANION. WITH FRIENDS LIKE THAT...
THEIR ALLIANCE MAY BE SHORT-LIVED, YOUR EMINENCE. THEY WERE ENGAGED IN A DUEL WHEN I CONFRONTED THEM.
THE LIVES OF ALL MY ENEMIES ARE SHORT-LIVED, VERLOCK.
AWAKEN, MY CREATURES.
YOU HAVE PREY TO HUNT BEFORE THE SUN RISES.

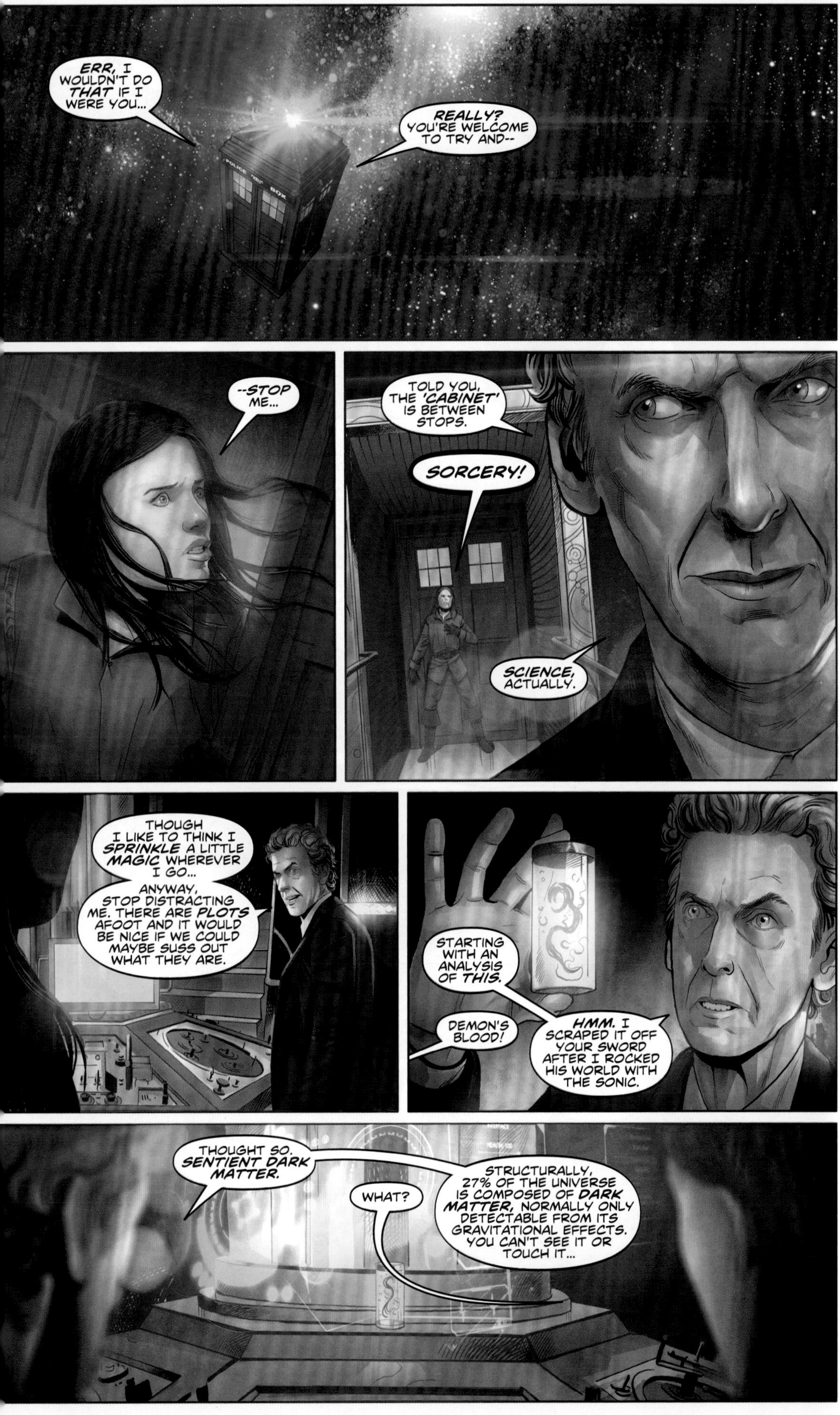
ERR, I WOULDN'T DO THAT IF I WERE YOU...
REALLY? YOU'RE WELCOME TO TRY AND--
--STOP ME...
TOLD YOU, THE 'CABINET' IS BETWEEN STOPS.
SORCERY!
SCIENCE, ACTUALLY.
THOUGH I LIKE TO THINK I SPRINKLE A LITTLE MAGIC WHEREVER I GO...
ANYWAY, STOP DISTRACTING ME. THERE ARE PLOTS AFOOT AND IT WOULD BE NICE IF WE COULD MAYBE SUSS OUT WHAT THEY ARE.
STARTING WITH AN ANALYSIS OF THIS.
DEMON'S BLOOD!
HMM. I SCRAPED IT OFF YOUR SWORD AFTER I ROCKED HIS WORLD WITH THE SONIC.
THOUGHT SO. SENTIENT DARK MATTER.
WHAT?
STRUCTURALLY, 27% OF THE UNIVERSE IS COMPOSED OF DARK MATTER, NORMALLY ONLY DETECTABLE FROM ITS GRAVITATIONAL EFFECTS. YOU CAN'T SEE IT OR TOUCH IT...

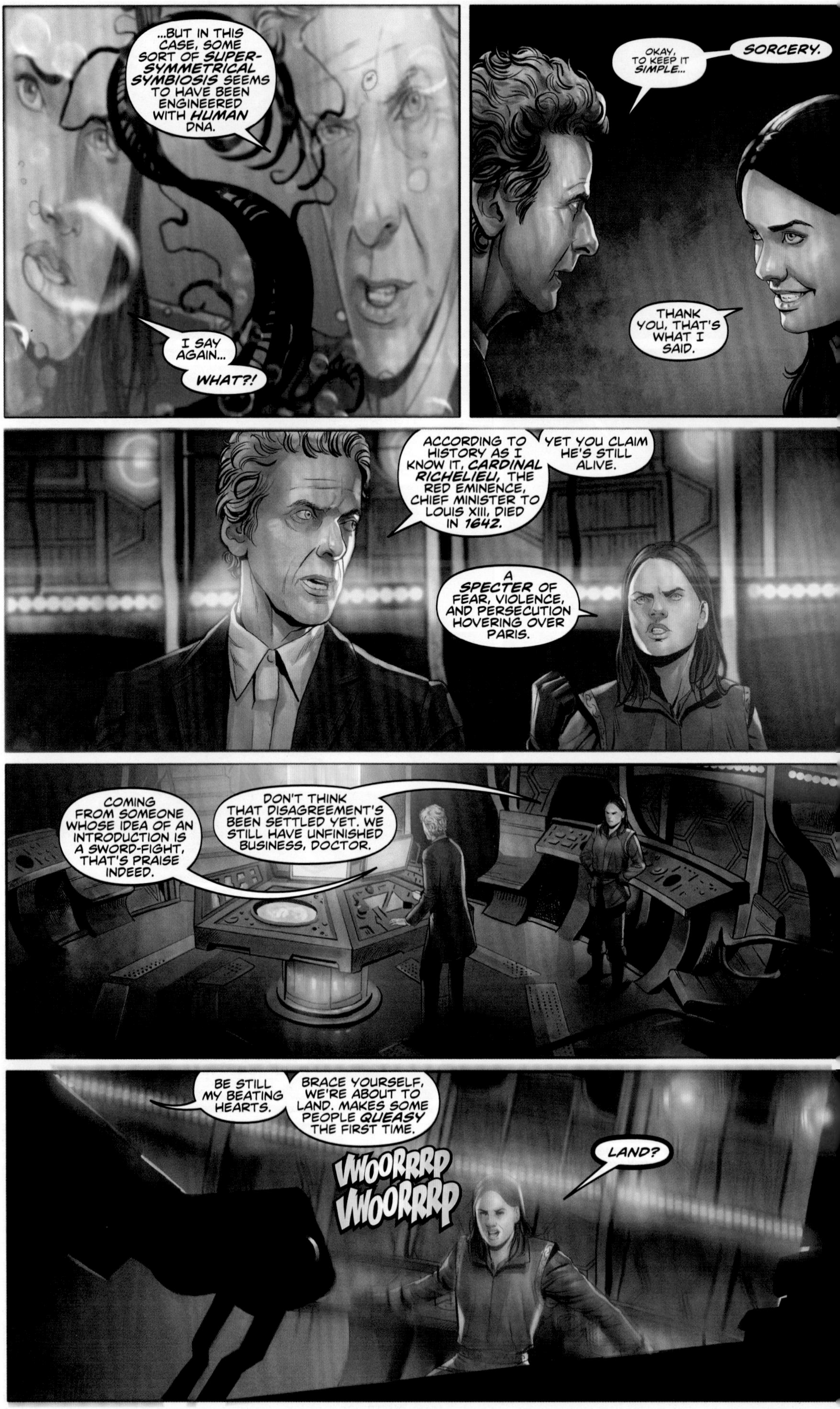
...BUT IN THIS CASE, SOME SORT OF SUPER-SYMMETRICAL SYMBIOSIS SEEMS TO HAVE BEEN ENGINEERED WITH HUMAN DNA.
I SAY AGAIN...
WHAT?!
OKAY, TO KEEP IT SIMPLE...
SORCERY.
THANK YOU, THAT'S WHAT I SAID.
ACCORDING TO HISTORY AS I KNOW IT, CARDINAL RICHELIEU, THE RED EMINENCE, CHIEF MINISTER TO LOUIS XIII, DIED IN 1642.
YET YOU CLAIM HE'S STILL ALIVE.
A SPECTER OF FEAR, VIOLENCE, AND PERSECUTION HOVERING OVER PARIS.
COMING FROM SOMEONE WHOSE IDEA OF AN INTRODUCTION IS A SWORD-FIGHT, THAT'S PRAISE INDEED.
DON'T THINK THAT DISAGREEMENT'S BEEN SETTLED YET. WE STILL HAVE UNFINISHED BUSINESS, DOCTOR.
BE STILL MY BEATING HEARTS.
BRACE YOURSELF, WE'RE ABOUT TO LAND. MAKES SOME PEOPLE QUEASY THE FIRST TIME.
LAND?
VWOORRRP
VWOORRRP

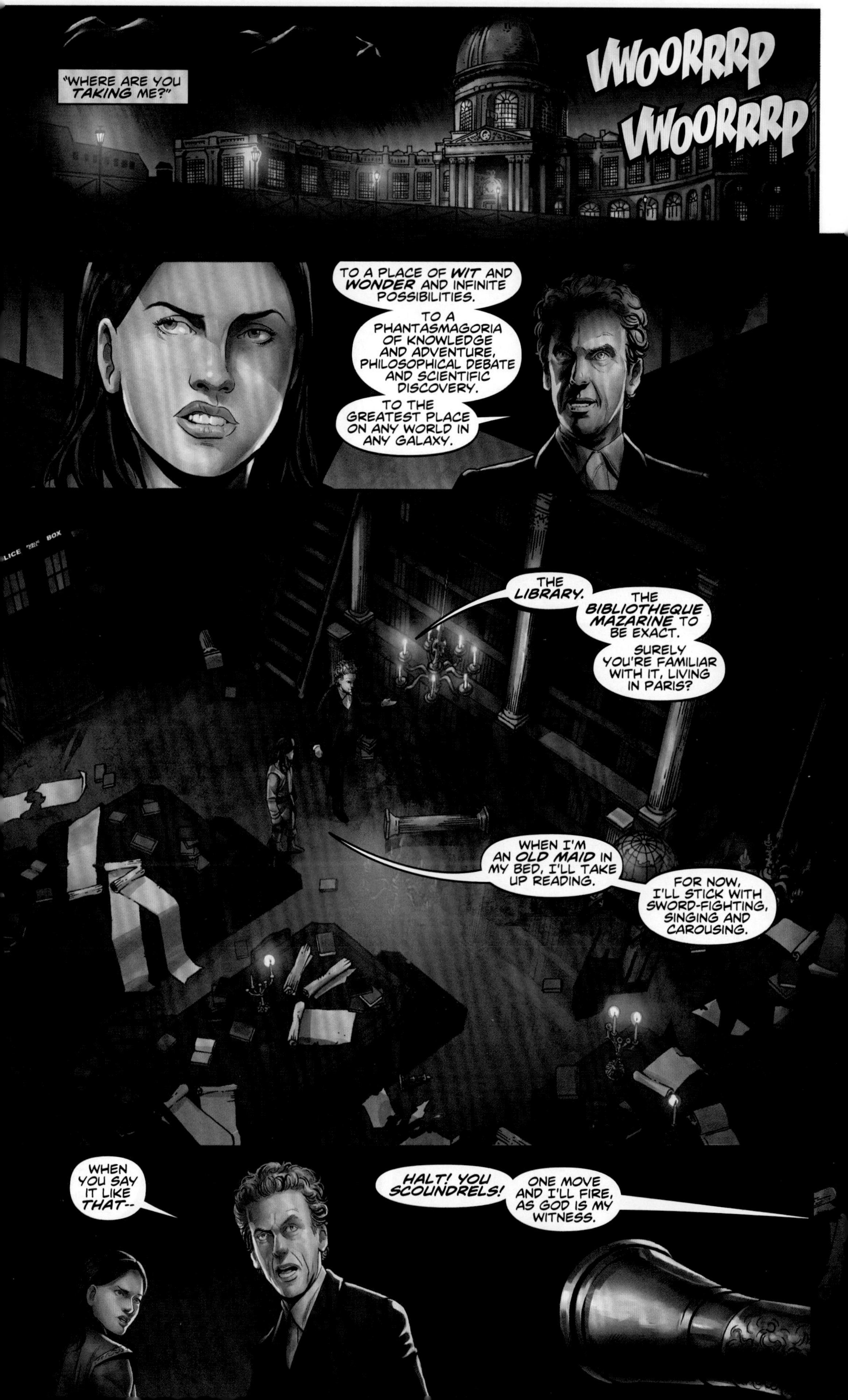

"WHERE ARE YOU TAKING ME?"
VWOORRRP
VWOORRRP
TO A PLACE OF WIT AND WONDER AND INFINITE POSSIBILITIES.
TO A PHANTASMAGORIA OF KNOWLEDGE AND ADVENTURE, PHILOSOPHICAL DEBATE AND SCIENTIFIC DISCOVERY.
TO THE GREATEST PLACE ON ANY WORLD IN ANY GALAXY.
THE LIBRARY.
THE BIBLIOTHEQUE MAZARINE TO BE EXACT.
SURELY YOU'RE FAMILIAR WITH IT, LIVING IN PARIS?
WHEN I'M AN OLD MAID IN MY BED, I'LL TAKE UP READING.
FOR NOW, I'LL STICK WITH SWORD-FIGHTING, SINGING AND CAROUSING.
WHEN YOU SAY IT LIKE THAT--
HALT! YOU SCOUNDRELS!
ONE MOVE AND I'LL FIRE, AS GOD IS MY WITNESS.

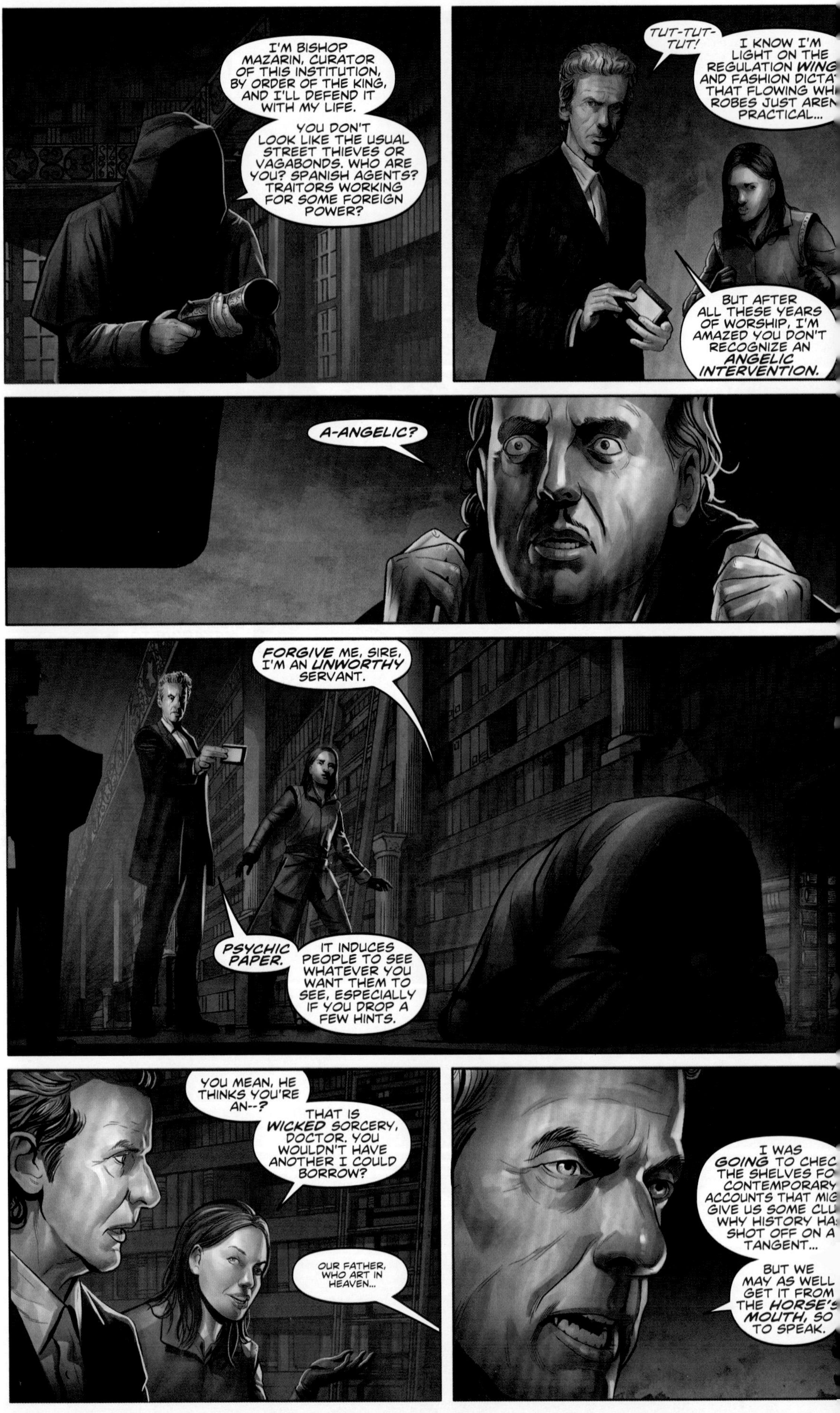
I'M BISHOP MAZARIN, CURATOR OF THIS INSTITUTION, BY ORDER OF THE KING, AND I'LL DEFEND IT WITH MY LIFE.
YOU DON'T LOOK LIKE THE USUAL STREET THIEVES OR VAGABONDS. WHO ARE YOU? SPANISH AGENTS? TRAITORS WORKING FOR SOME FOREIGN POWER?
TUT-TUT-TUT!
I KNOW I'M LIGHT ON THE REGULATION WINGS AND FASHION DICTA THAT FLOWING WH ROBES JUST AREN PRACTICAL...
BUT AFTER ALL THESE YEARS OF WORSHIP, I'M AMAZED YOU DON'T RECOGNIZE AN ANGELIC INTERVENTION.
A-ANGELIC?
FORGIVE ME, SIRE, I'M AN UNWORTHY SERVANT.
PSYCHIC PAPER.
IT INDUCES PEOPLE TO SEE WHATEVER YOU WANT THEM TO SEE, ESPECIALLY IF YOU DROP A FEW HINTS.
YOU MEAN, HE THINKS YOU'RE AN--?
THAT IS WICKED SORCERY, DOCTOR. YOU WOULDN'T HAVE ANOTHER I COULD BORROW?
OUR FATHER, WHO ART IN HEAVEN...
I WAS GOING TO CHEC THE SHELVES FO CONTEMPORARY ACCOUNTS THAT MIG GIVE US SOME CLU WHY HISTORY HA SHOT OFF ON A TANGENT...
BUT WE MAY AS WELL GET IT FROM THE HORSE'S MOUTH, SO TO SPEAK.

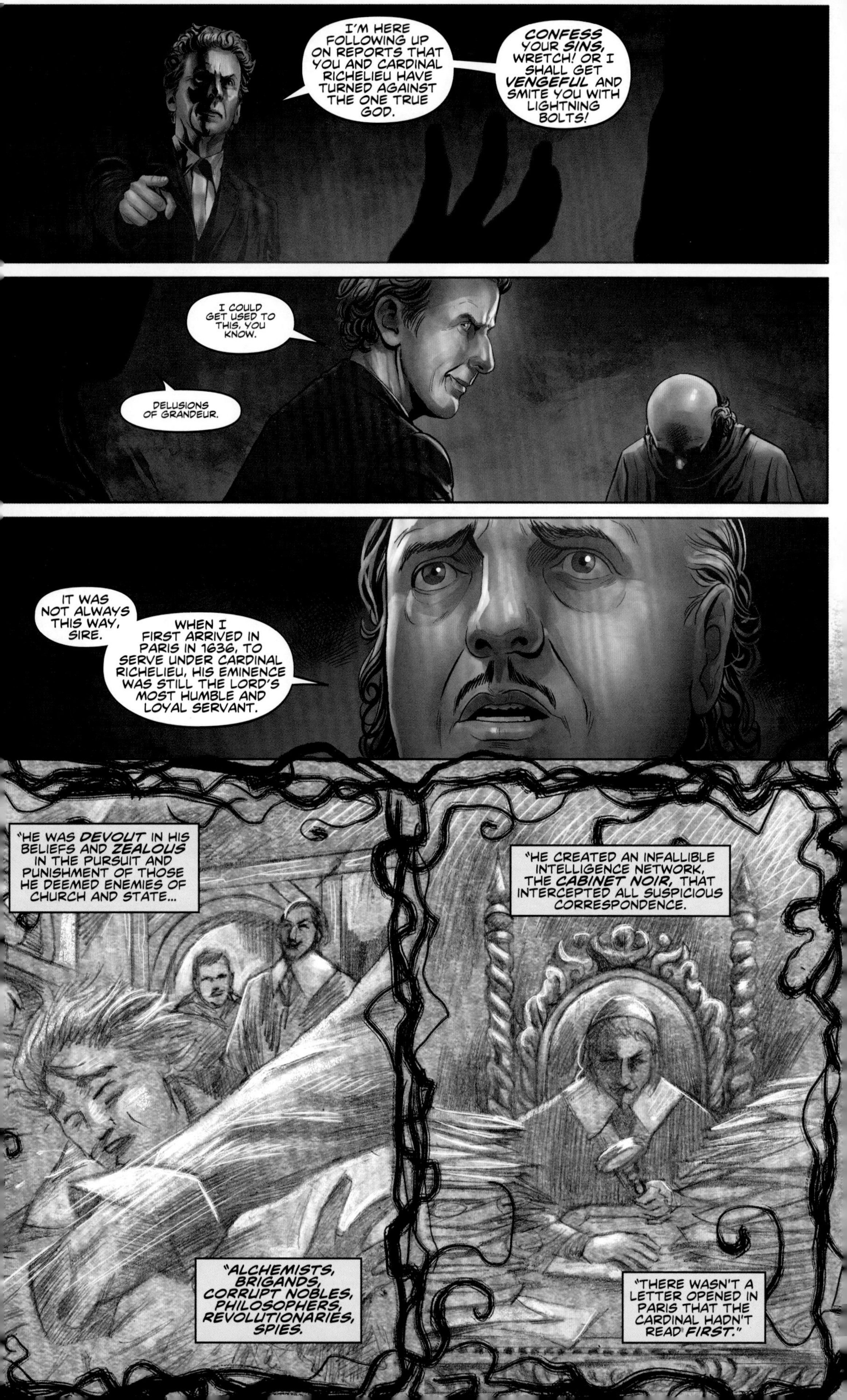

I'M HERE FOLLOWING UP ON REPORTS THAT YOU AND CARDINAL RICHELIEU HAVE TURNED AGAINST THE ONE TRUE GOD.
CONFESS YOUR SINS, WRETCH! OR I SHALL GET VENGEFUL AND SMITE YOU WITH LIGHTNING BOLTS!
I COULD GET USED TO THIS, YOU KNOW.
DELUSIONS OF GRANDEUR.
IT WAS NOT ALWAYS THIS WAY, SIRE.
WHEN I FIRST ARRIVED IN PARIS IN 1636, TO SERVE UNDER CARDINAL RICHELIEU, HIS EMINENCE WAS STILL THE LORD'S MOST HUMBLE AND LOYAL SERVANT.
"HE WAS DEVOUT IN HIS BELIEFS AND ZEALOUS IN THE PURSUIT AND PUNISHMENT OF THOSE HE DEEMED ENEMIES OF CHURCH AND STATE...
"ALCHEMISTS, BRIGANDS, CORRUPT NOBLES, PHILOSOPHERS, REVOLUTIONARIES, SPIES.
"HE CREATED AN INFALLIBLE INTELLIGENCE NETWORK, THE CABINET NOIR, THAT INTERCEPTED ALL SUSPICIOUS CORRESPONDENCE.
"THERE WASN'T A LETTER OPENED IN PARIS THAT THE CARDINAL HADN'T READ FIRST."

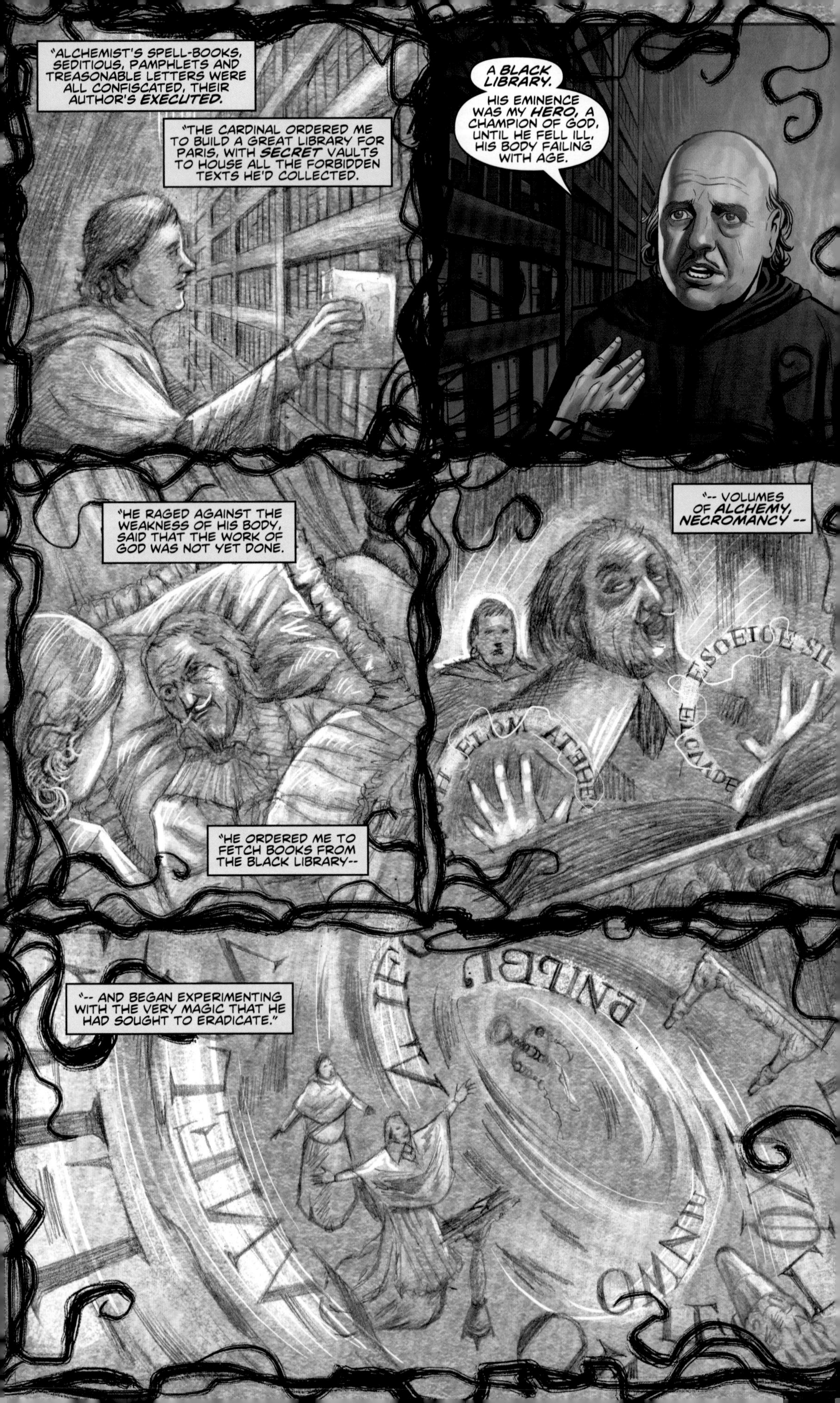
"ALCHEMIST'S SPELL-BOOKS, SEDITIOUS, PAMPHLETS AND TREASONABLE LETTERS WERE ALL CONFISCATED, THEIR AUTHOR'S EXECUTED.
"THE CARDINAL ORDERED ME TO BUILD A GREAT LIBRARY FOR PARIS, WITH SECRET VAULTS TO HOUSE ALL THE FORBIDDEN TEXTS HE'D COLLECTED.
A BLACK LIBRARY.
HIS EMINENCE WAS MY HERO, A CHAMPION OF GOD, UNTIL HE FELL ILL, HIS BODY FAILING WITH AGE.
"HE RAGED AGAINST THE WEAKNESS OF HIS BODY, SAID THAT THE WORK OF GOD WAS NOT YET DONE.
"HE ORDERED ME TO FETCH BOOKS FROM THE BLACK LIBRARY--
"-- VOLUMES OF ALCHEMY, NECROMANCY --
"-- AND BEGAN EXPERIMENTING WITH THE VERY MAGIC THAT HE HAD SOUGHT TO ERADICATE."

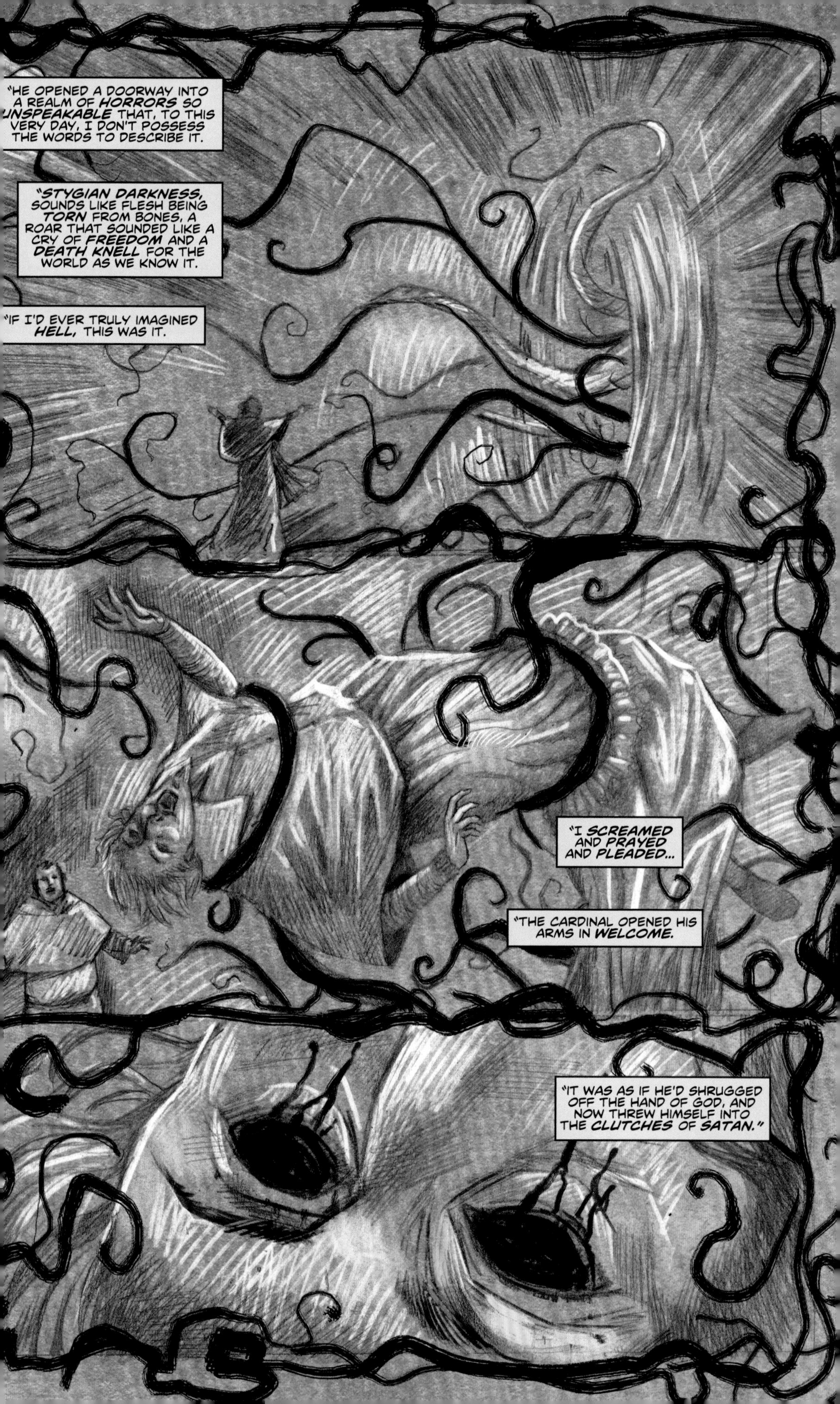
"HE OPENED A DOORWAY INTO A REALM OF HORRORS SO UNSPEAKABLE THAT, TO THIS VERY DAY, I DON'T POSSESS THE WORDS TO DESCRIBE IT.
"STYGIAN DARKNESS, SOUNDS LIKE FLESH BEING TORN FROM BONES, A ROAR THAT SOUNDED LIKE A CRY OF FREEDOM AND A DEATH KNELL FOR THE WORLD AS WE KNOW IT.
"IF I'D EVER TRULY IMAGINED HELL, THIS WAS IT.
"I SCREAMED AND PRAYED AND PLEADED...
"THE CARDINAL OPENED HIS ARMS IN WELCOME.
"IT WAS AS IF HE'D SHRUGGED OFF THE HAND OF GOD, AND NOW THREW HIMSELF INTO THE CLUTCHES OF SATAN."

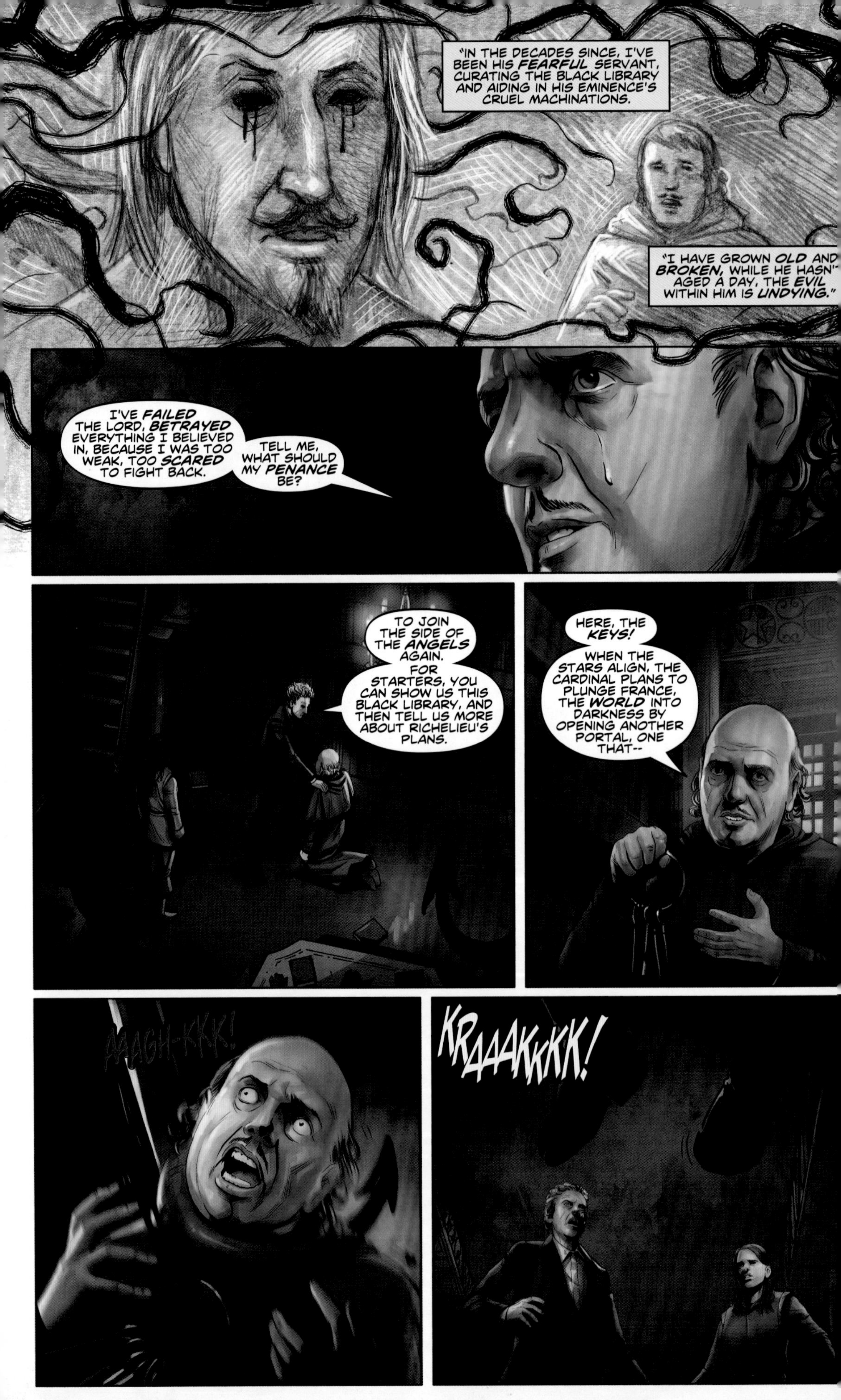
"IN THE DECADES SINCE, I'VE BEEN HIS FEARFUL SERVANT, CURATING THE BLACK LIBRARY AND AIDING IN HIS EMINENCE'S CRUEL MACHINATIONS.
"I HAVE GROWN OLD AND BROKEN, WHILE HE HASN'T AGED A DAY. THE EVIL WITHIN HIM IS UNDYING."
I'VE FAILED THE LORD, BETRAYED EVERYTHING I BELIEVED IN, BECAUSE I WAS TOO WEAK, TOO SCARED TO FIGHT BACK.
TELL ME, WHAT SHOULD MY PENANCE BE?
TO JOIN THE SIDE OF THE ANGELS AGAIN.
FOR STARTERS, YOU CAN SHOW US THIS BLACK LIBRARY, AND THEN TELL US MORE ABOUT RICHELIEU'S PLANS.
HERE, THE KEYS!
WHEN THE STARS ALIGN, THE CARDINAL PLANS TO PLUNGE FRANCE, THE WORLD INTO DARKNESS BY OPENING ANOTHER PORTAL, ONE THAT--
AAAGH-KKK!
KRAAAKKKK!

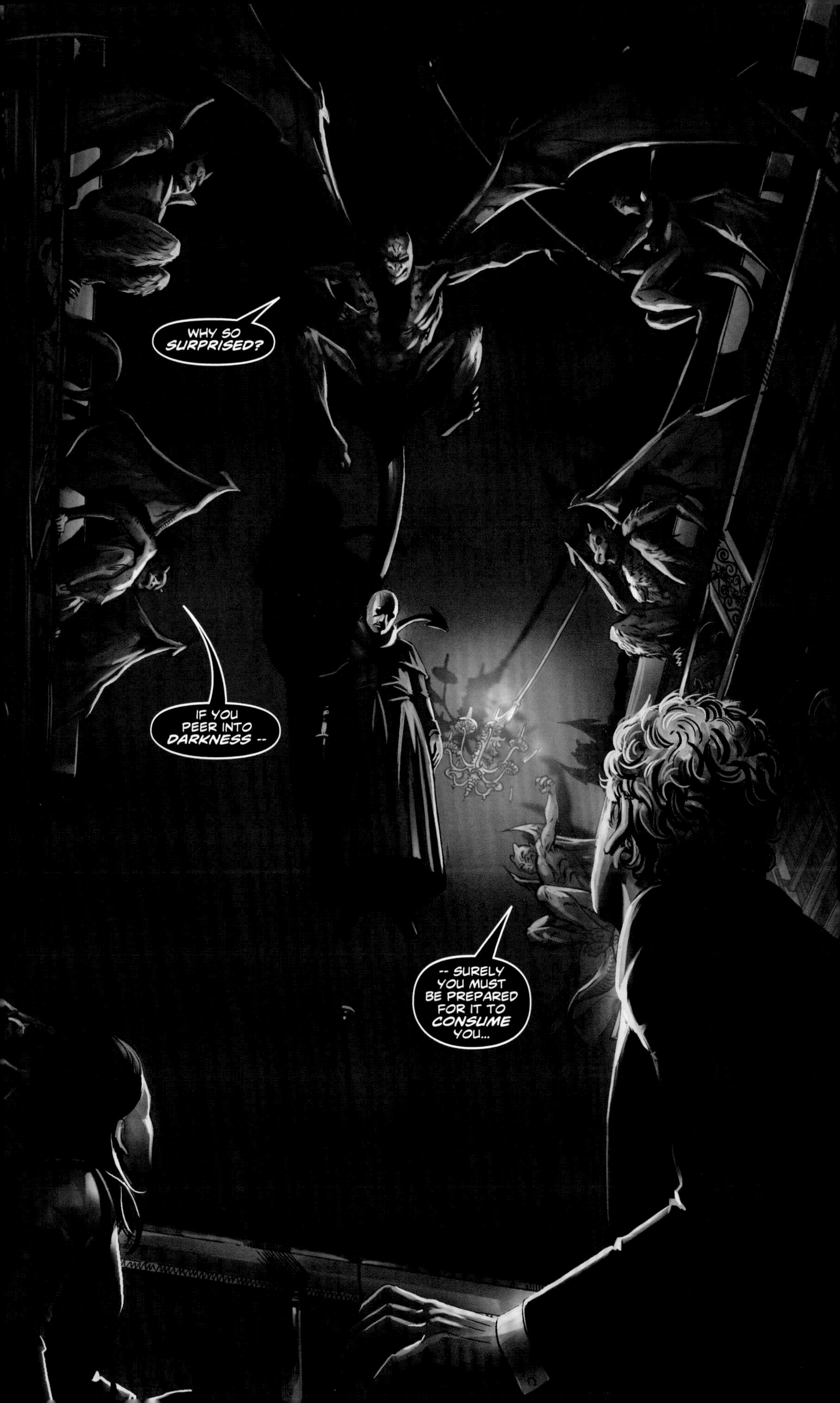
WHY SO SURPRISED?
IF YOU PEER INTO DARKNESS --
-- SURELY YOU MUST BE PREPARED FOR IT TO CONSUME YOU...

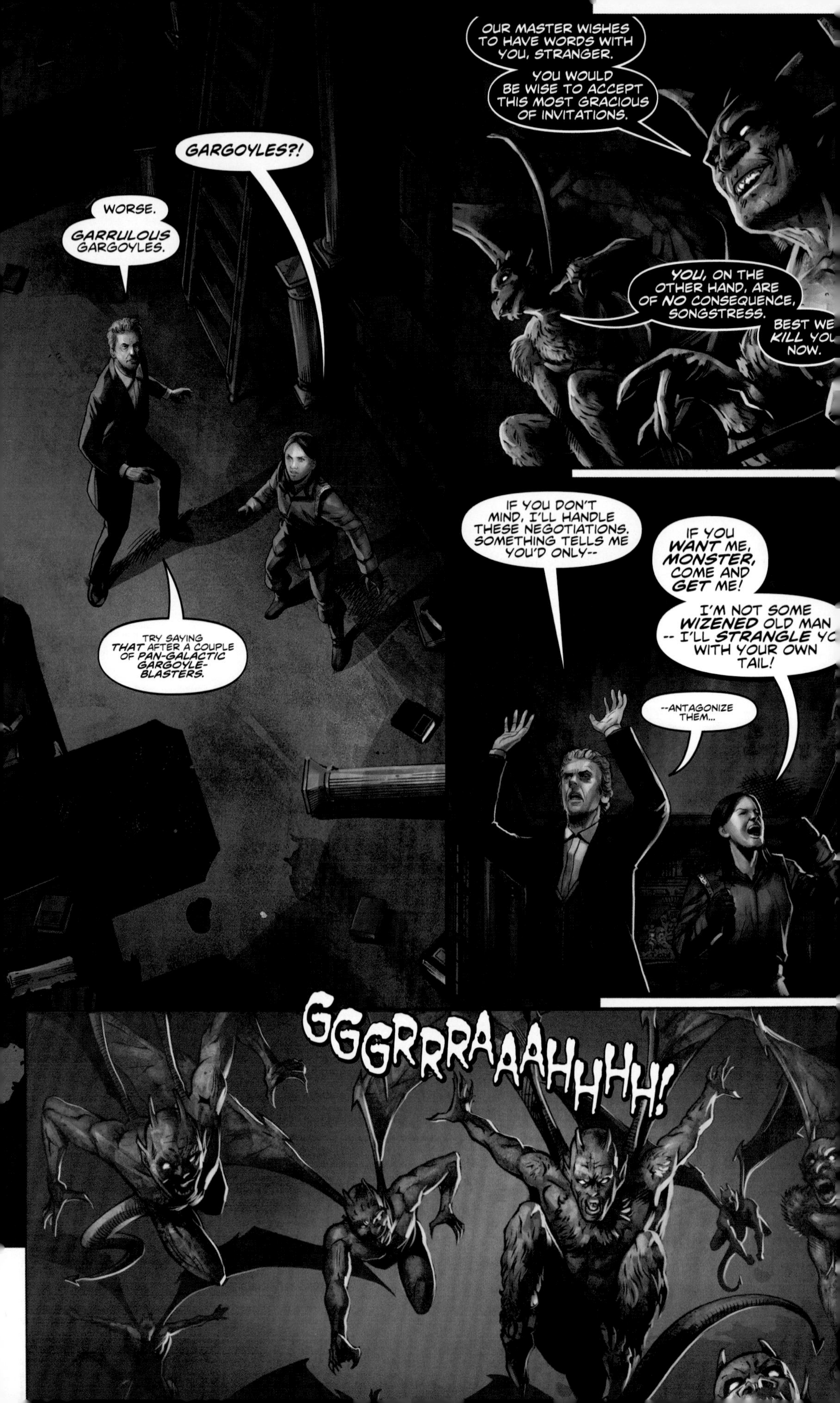
GARGOYLES?!
WORSE.
GARRULOUS GARGOYLES.
TRY SAYING THAT AFTER A COUPLE OF PAN-GALACTIC GARGOYLE-BLASTERS.
OUR MASTER WISHES TO HAVE WORDS WITH YOU, STRANGER.
YOU WOULD BE WISE TO ACCEPT THIS MOST GRACIOUS OF INVITATIONS.
YOU, ON THE OTHER HAND, ARE OF NO CONSEQUENCE, SONGSTRESS.
BEST WE KILL YOU NOW.
IF YOU DON'T MIND, I'LL HANDLE THESE NEGOTIATIONS. SOMETHING TELLS ME YOU'D ONLY--
IF YOU WANT ME, MONSTER, COME AND GET ME!
I'M NOT SOME WIZENED OLD MAN -- I'LL STRANGLE YOU WITH YOUR OWN TAIL!
--ANTAGONIZE THEM...
GGGRRRAAAHHHH!

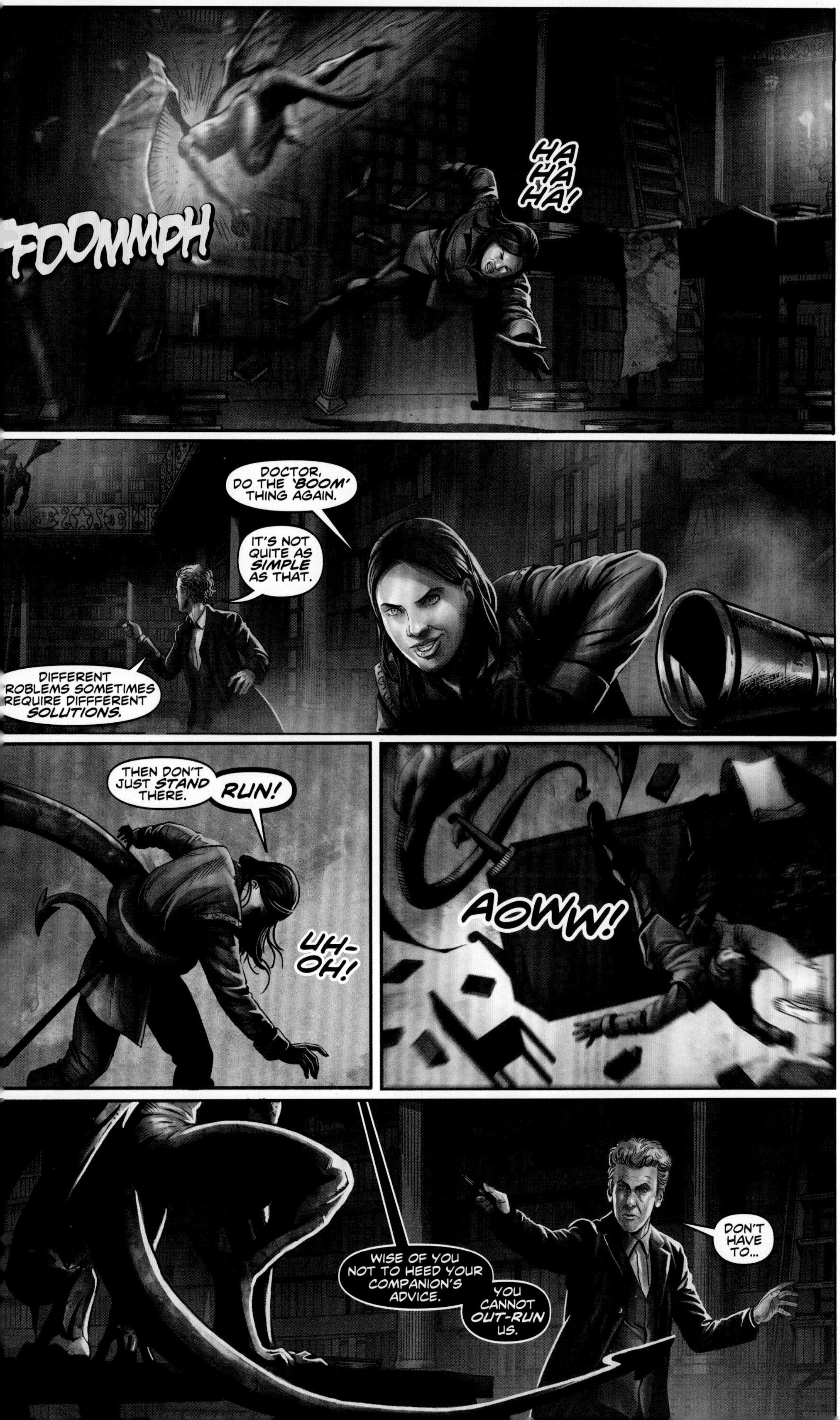

FOOMMPH
HA HA HA HA!
DOCTOR, DO THE 'BOOM' THING AGAIN.
IT'S NOT QUITE AS SIMPLE AS THAT.
DIFFERENT PROBLEMS SOMETIMES REQUIRE DIFFFERENT SOLUTIONS.
THEN DON'T JUST STAND THERE.
RUN!
UH-OH!
AOWW!
WISE OF YOU NOT TO HEED YOUR COMPANION'S ADVICE.
YOU CANNOT OUT-RUN US.
DON'T HAVE TO...

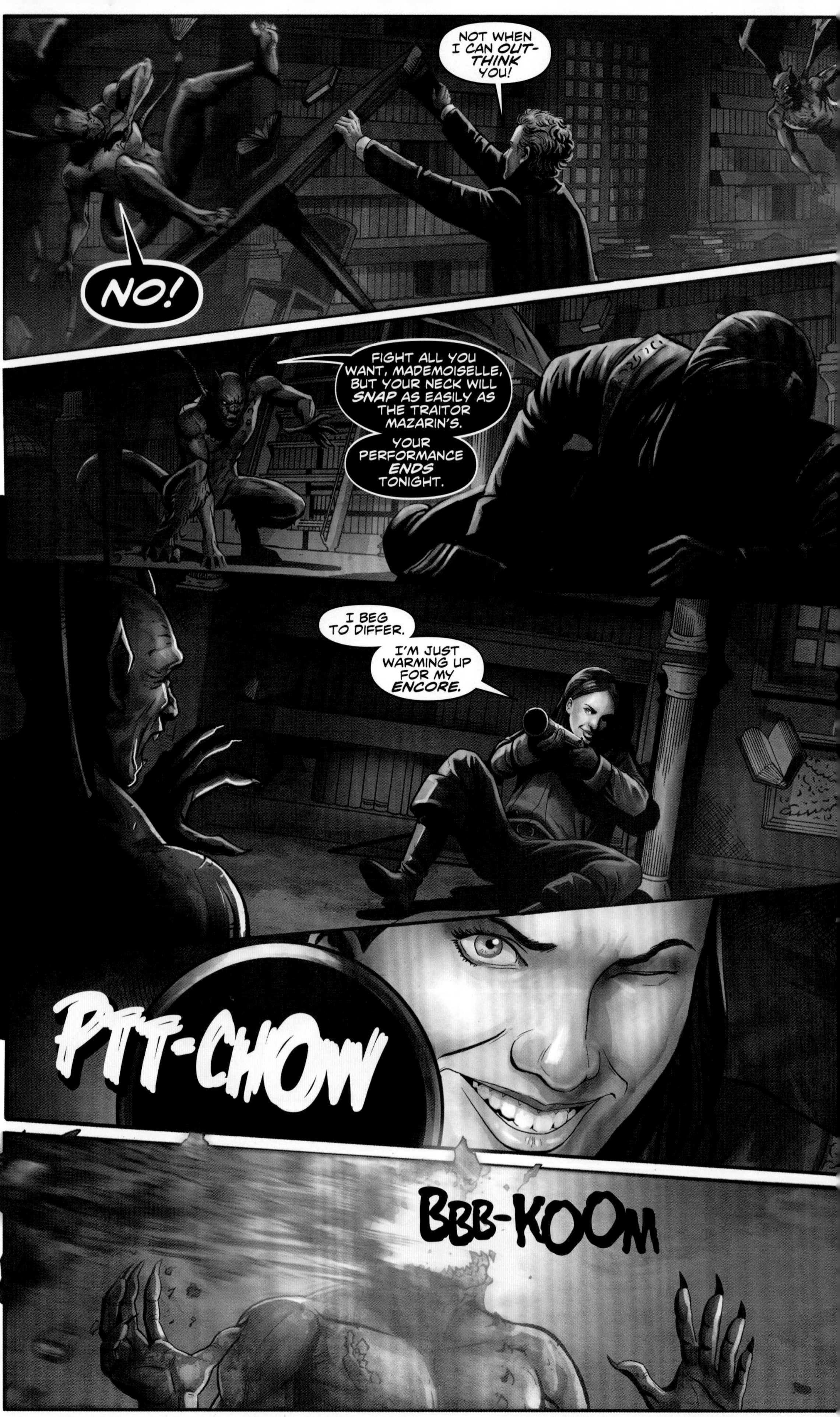
NOT WHEN I CAN OUT-THINK YOU!
NO!
FIGHT ALL YOU WANT, MADEMOISELLE, BUT YOUR NECK WILL SNAP AS EASILY AS THE TRAITOR MAZARIN'S.
YOUR PERFORMANCE ENDS TONIGHT.
I BEG TO DIFFER.
I'M JUST WARMING UP FOR MY ENCORE.
PTT-CHOW
BBB-KOOM

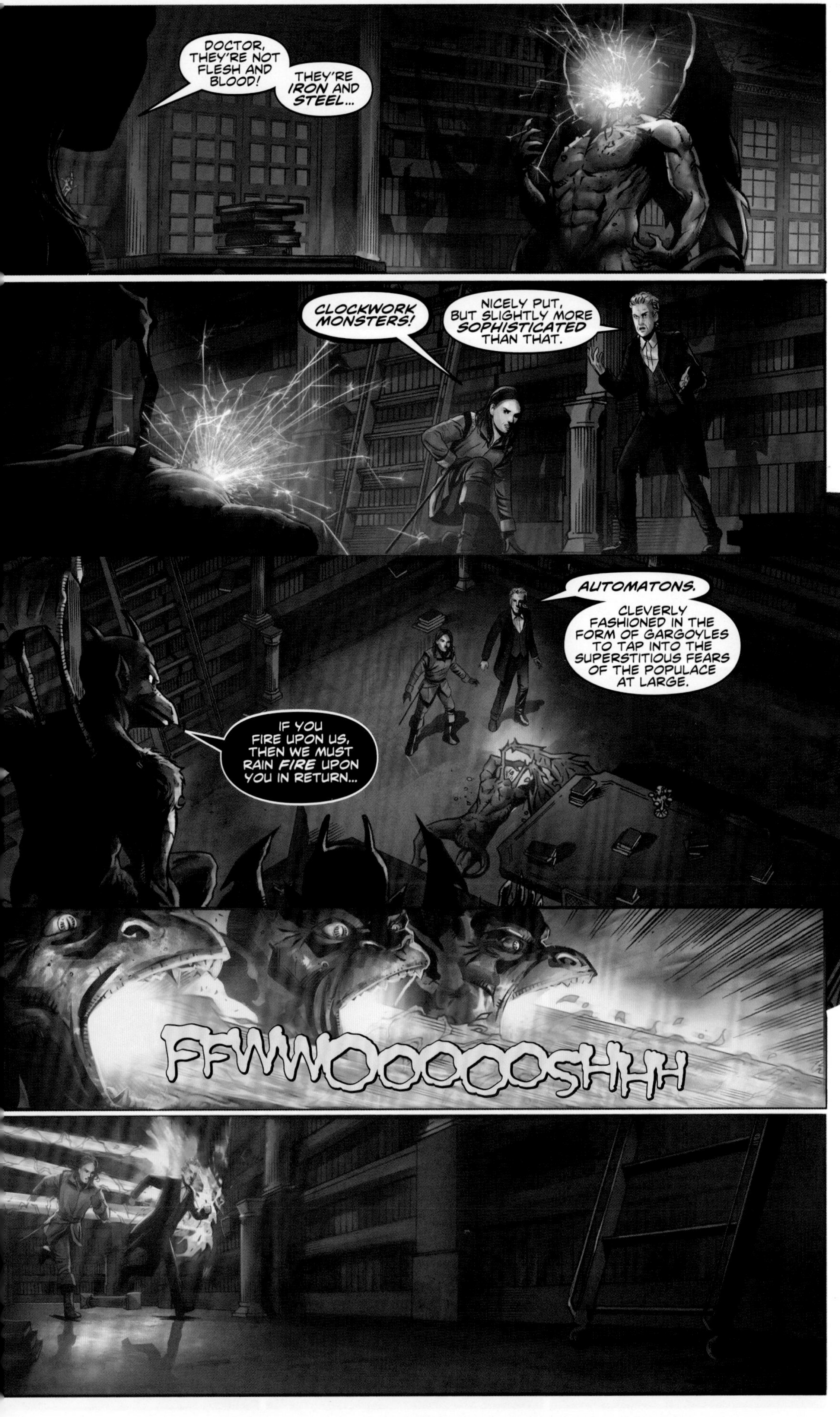
DOCTOR, THEY'RE NOT FLESH AND BLOOD!
THEY'RE IRON AND STEEL...
CLOCKWORK MONSTERS!
NICELY PUT, BUT SLIGHTLY MORE SOPHISTICATED THAN THAT.
AUTOMATONS.
CLEVERLY FASHIONED IN THE FORM OF GARGOYLES TO TAP INTO THE SUPERSTITIOUS FEARS OF THE POPULACE AT LARGE.
IF YOU FIRE UPON US, THEN WE MUST RAIN FIRE UPON YOU IN RETURN...
FFWWOOOOOOSHHH

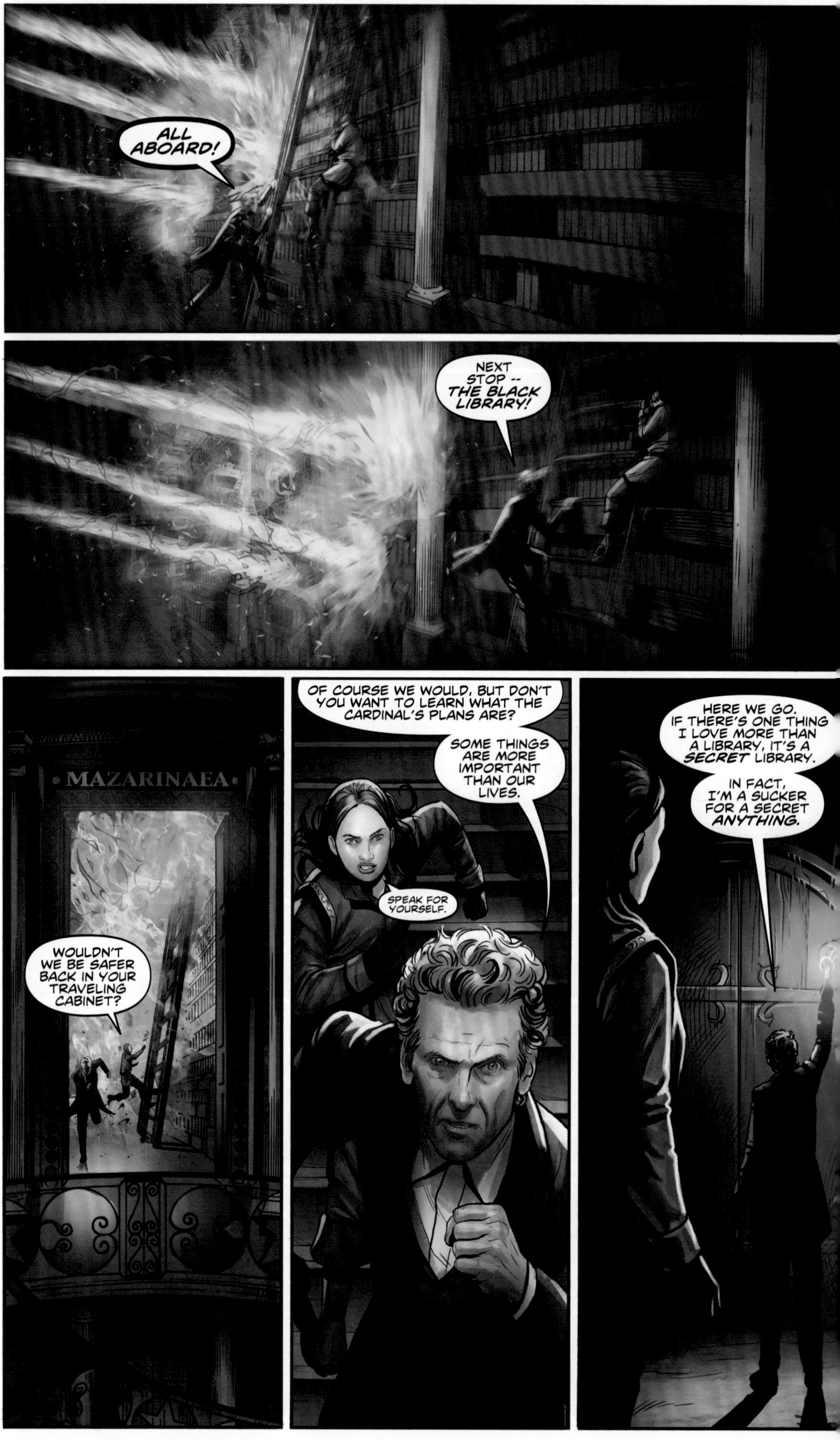

ALL ABOARD!
NEXT STOP -- THE BLACK LIBRARY!
MAZARINAEA
WOULDN'T WE BE SAFER BACK IN YOUR TRAVELING CABINET?
OF COURSE WE WOULD, BUT DON'T YOU WANT TO LEARN WHAT THE CARDINAL'S PLANS ARE?
SOME THINGS ARE MORE IMPORTANT THAN OUR LIVES.
SPEAK FOR YOURSELF.
HERE WE GO. IF THERE'S ONE THING I LOVE MORE THAN A LIBRARY, IT'S A SECRET LIBRARY.
IN FACT, I'M A SUCKER FOR A SECRET ANYTHING.

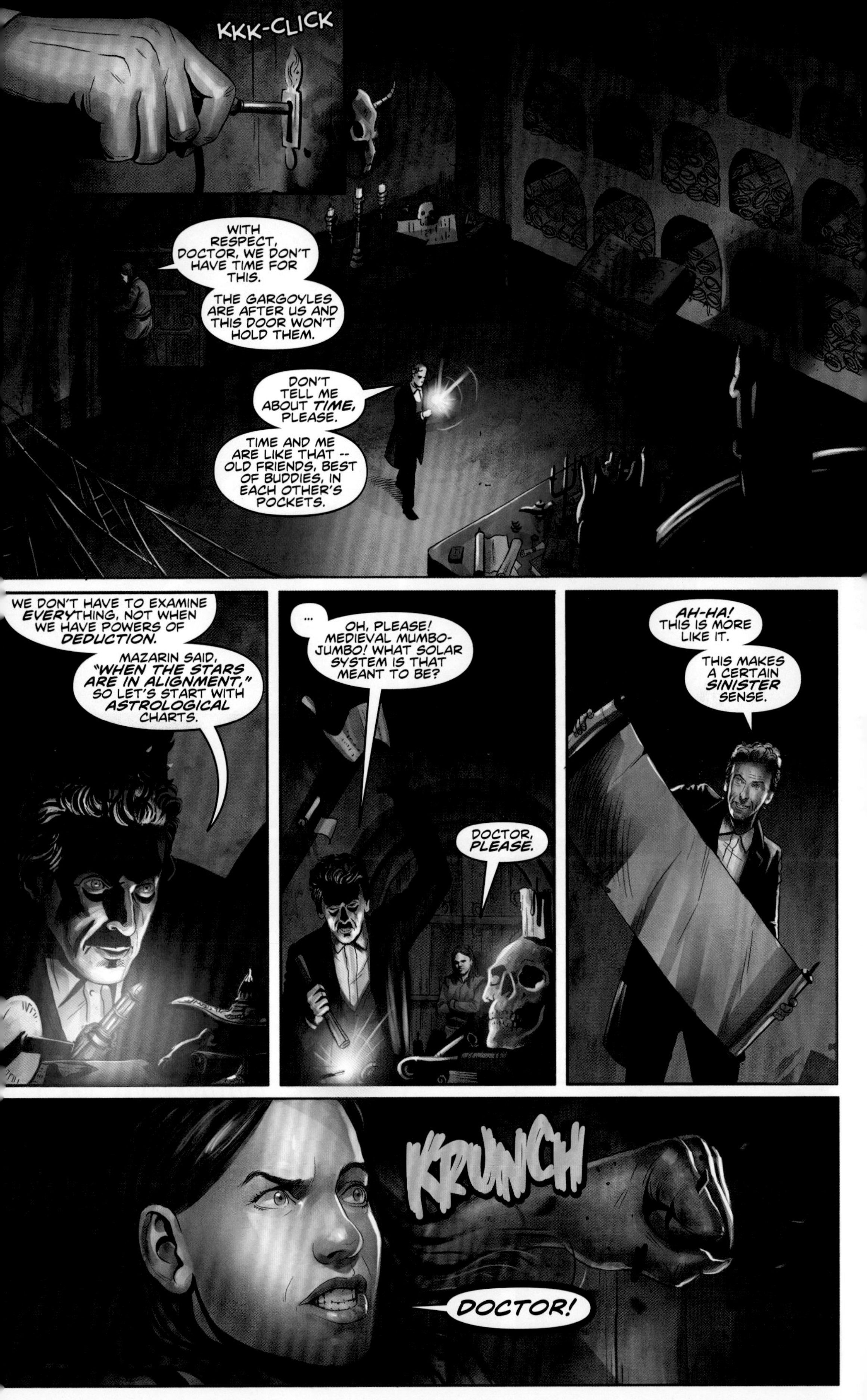
KKK-CLICK
WITH RESPECT, DOCTOR, WE DON'T HAVE TIME FOR THIS.
THE GARGOYLES ARE AFTER US AND THIS DOOR WON'T HOLD THEM.
DON'T TELL ME ABOUT TIME, PLEASE.
TIME AND ME ARE LIKE THAT -- OLD FRIENDS, BEST OF BUDDIES, IN EACH OTHER'S POCKETS.
WE DON'T HAVE TO EXAMINE EVERYTHING, NOT WHEN WE HAVE POWERS OF DEDUCTION.
MAZARIN SAID, "WHEN THE STARS ARE IN ALIGNMENT," SO LET'S START WITH ASTROLOGICAL CHARTS.
... OH, PLEASE! MEDIEVAL MUMBO-JUMBO! WHAT SOLAR SYSTEM IS THAT MEANT TO BE?
DOCTOR, PLEASE.
AH-HA! THIS IS MORE LIKE IT.
THIS MAKES A CERTAIN SINISTER SENSE.
KRUNCH
DOCTOR!

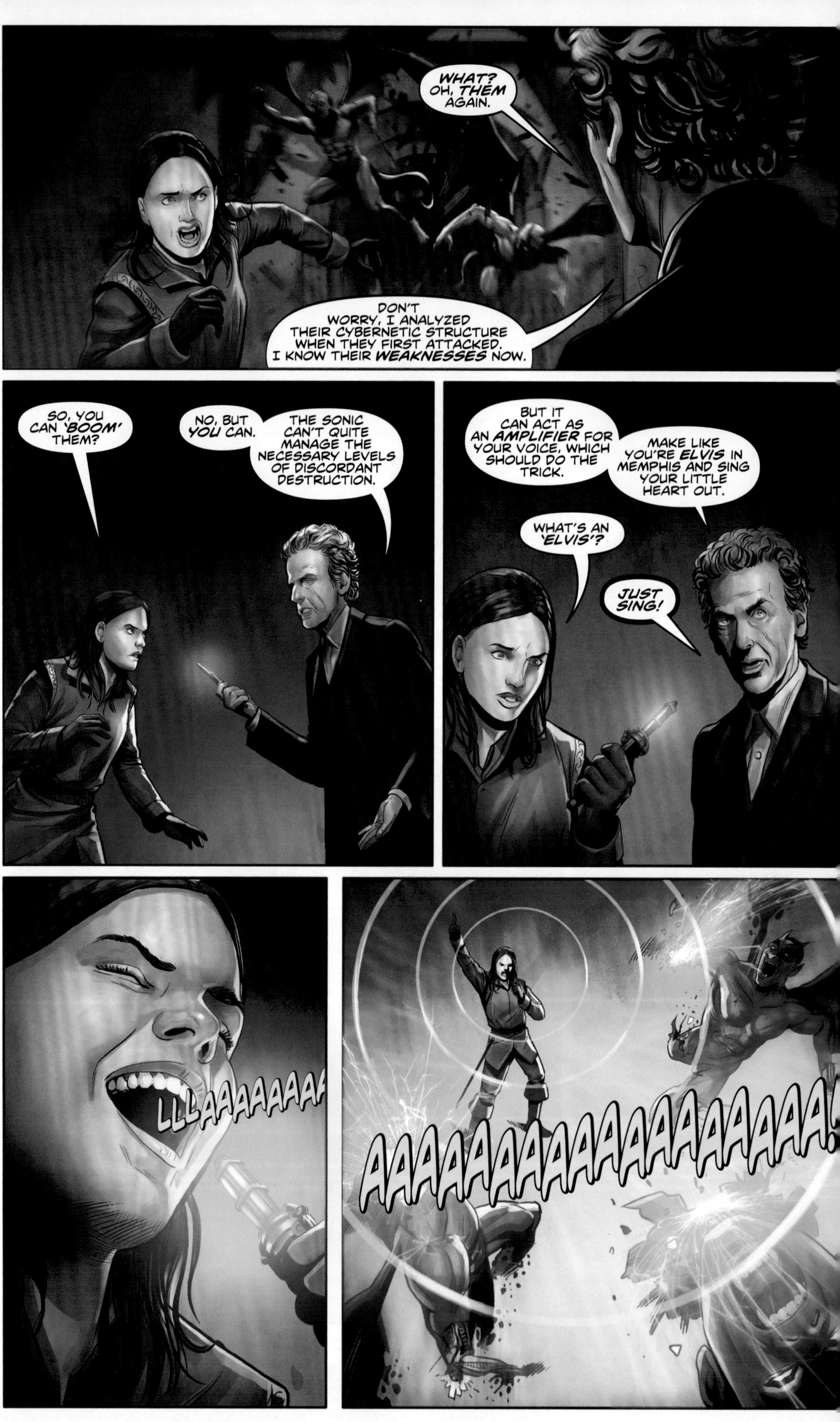
WHAT? OH, THEM AGAIN.
DON'T WORRY, I ANALYZED THEIR CYBERNETIC STRUCTURE WHEN THEY FIRST ATTACKED. I KNOW THEIR WEAKNESSES NOW.
SO, YOU CAN 'BOOM' THEM?
NO, BUT YOU CAN.
THE SONIC CAN'T QUITE MANAGE THE NECESSARY LEVELS OF DISCORDANT DESTRUCTION.
BUT IT CAN ACT AS AN AMPLIFIER FOR YOUR VOICE, WHICH SHOULD DO THE TRICK.
MAKE LIKE YOU'RE ELVIS IN MEMPHIS AND SING YOUR LITTLE HEART OUT.
WHAT'S AN 'ELVIS'?
JUST SING!
LLLAAAAAAA
AAAAAAAAAAAAAAAAAAAAAA!

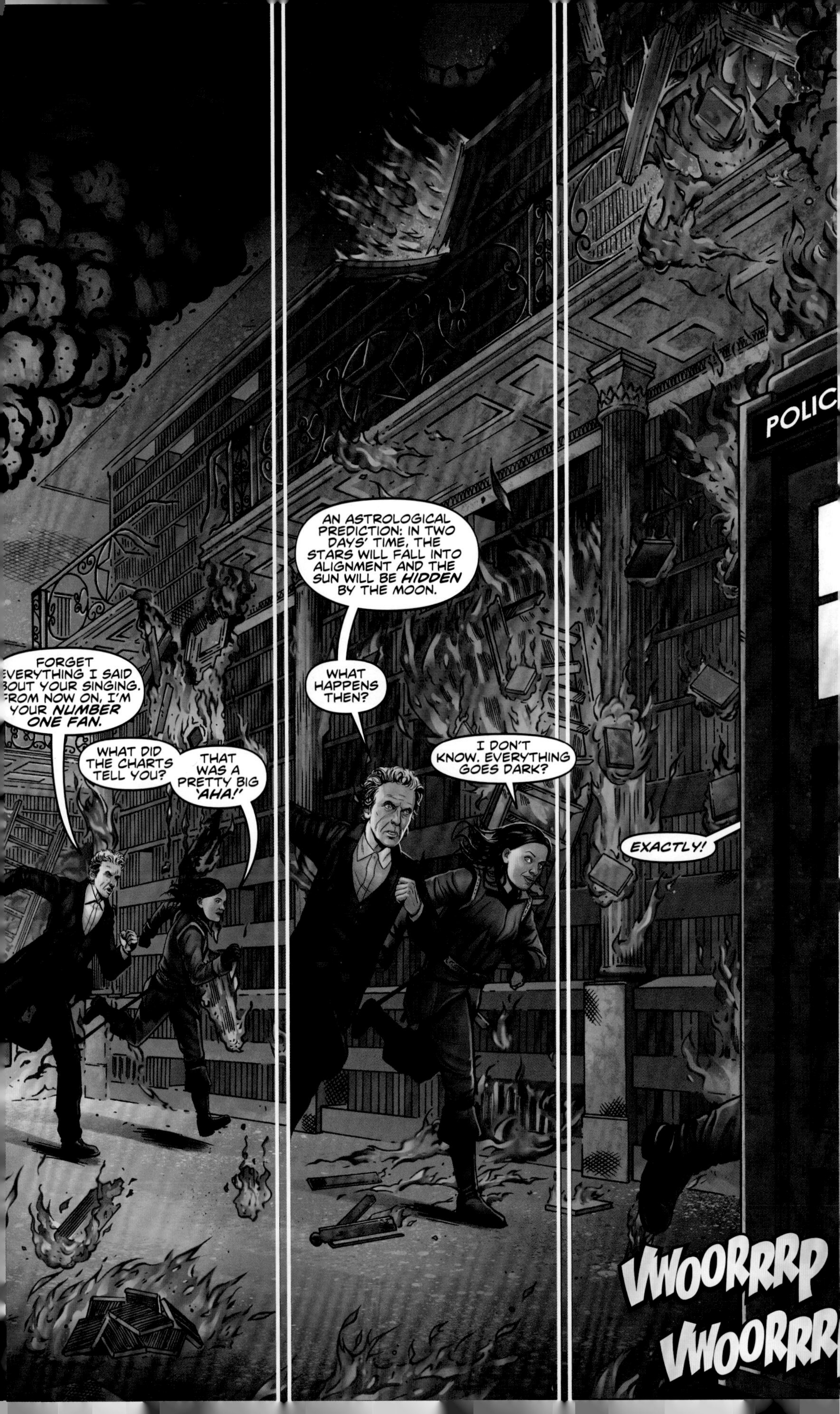
FORGET EVERYTHING I SAID BOUT YOUR SINGING. FROM NOW ON, I'M YOUR **NUMBER ONE FAN.**
WHAT DID THE CHARTS TELL YOU?
THAT WAS A PRETTY BIG ***'AHA!'***
AN ASTROLOGICAL PREDICTION: IN TWO DAYS' TIME, THE STARS WILL FALL INTO ALIGNMENT AND THE SUN WILL BE ***HIDDEN*** BY THE MOON.
WHAT HAPPENS THEN?
I DON'T KNOW. EVERYTHING GOES DARK?
EXACTLY!
POLIC
VWOORRRP
VWOORRR

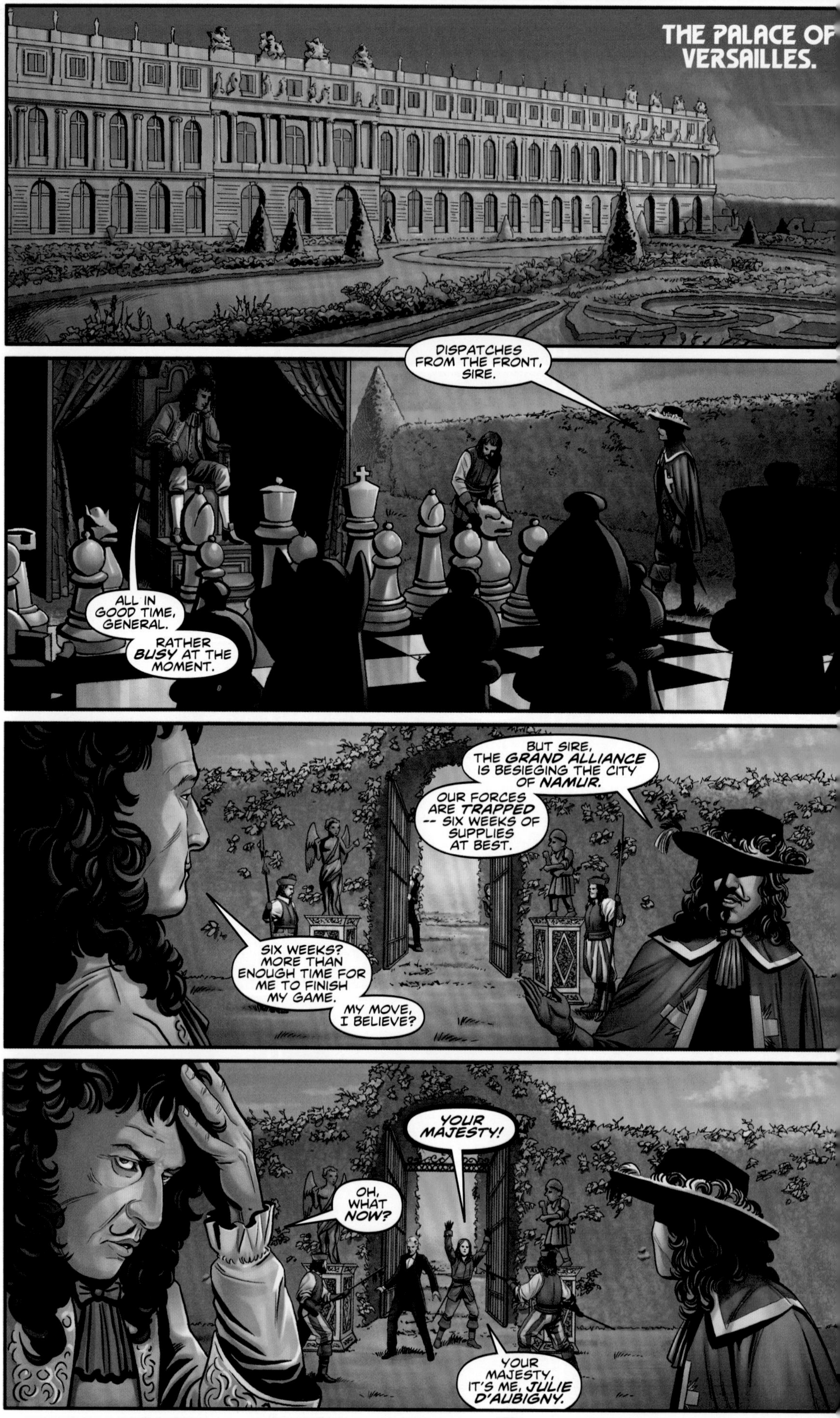
THE PALACE OF VERSAILLES.
DISPATCHES FROM THE FRONT, SIRE.
ALL IN GOOD TIME, GENERAL.
RATHER BUSY AT THE MOMENT.
BUT SIRE, THE GRAND ALLIANCE IS BESIEGING THE CITY OF NAMUR.
OUR FORCES ARE TRAPPED -- SIX WEEKS OF SUPPLIES AT BEST.
SIX WEEKS? MORE THAN ENOUGH TIME FOR ME TO FINISH MY GAME.
MY MOVE, I BELIEVE?
YOUR MAJESTY!
OH, WHAT NOW?
YOUR MAJESTY, IT'S ME, JULIE D'AUBIGNY.

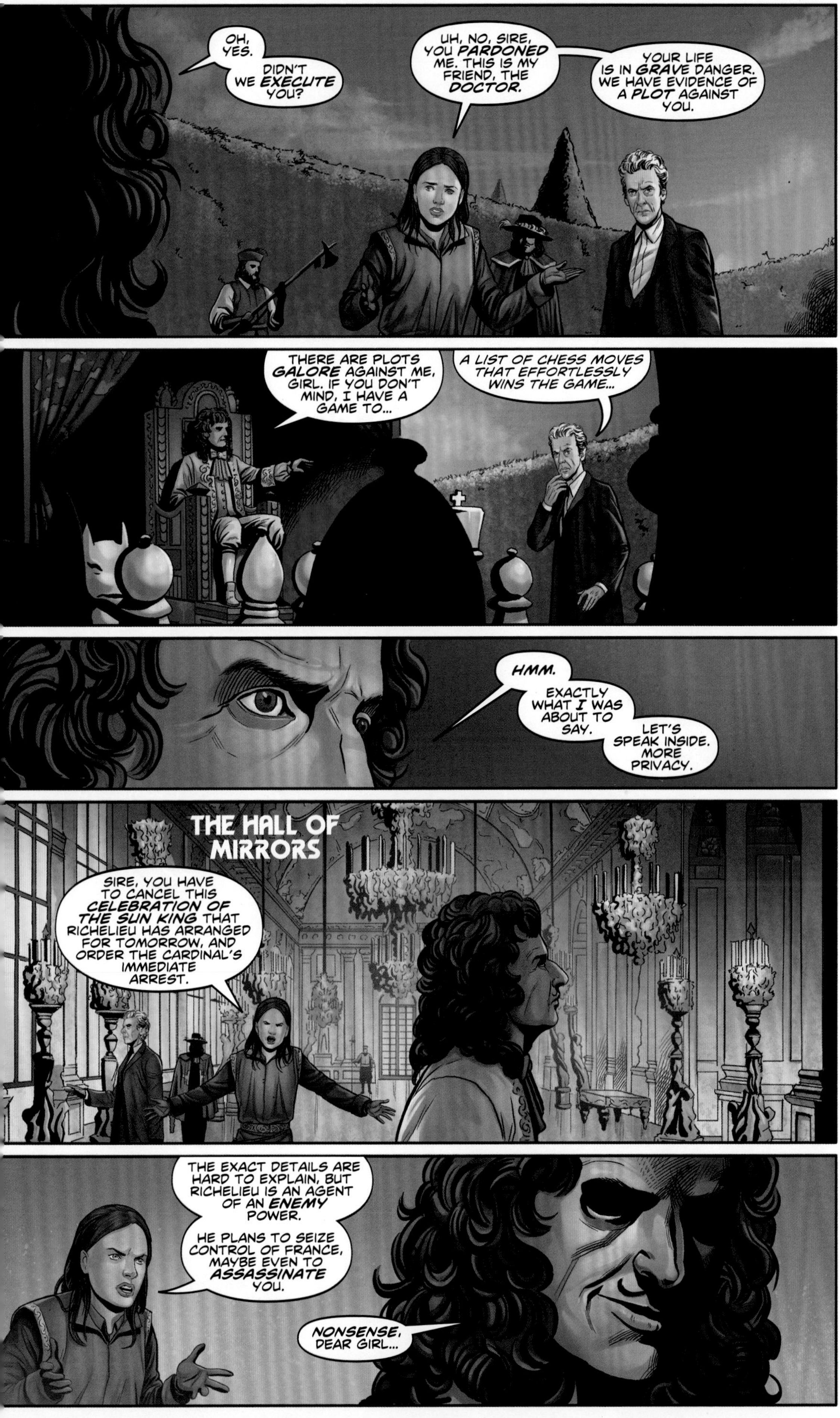
OH, YES.
DIDN'T WE EXECUTE YOU?
UH, NO, SIRE, YOU PARDONED ME. THIS IS MY FRIEND, THE DOCTOR.
YOUR LIFE IS IN GRAVE DANGER. WE HAVE EVIDENCE OF A PLOT AGAINST YOU.
THERE ARE PLOTS GALORE AGAINST ME, GIRL. IF YOU DON'T MIND, I HAVE A GAME TO...
A LIST OF CHESS MOVES THAT EFFORTLESSLY WINS THE GAME...
HMM.
EXACTLY WHAT I WAS ABOUT TO SAY.
LET'S SPEAK INSIDE. MORE PRIVACY.
THE HALL OF MIRRORS
SIRE, YOU HAVE TO CANCEL THIS CELEBRATION OF THE SUN KING THAT RICHELIEU HAS ARRANGED FOR TOMORROW, AND ORDER THE CARDINAL'S IMMEDIATE ARREST.
THE EXACT DETAILS ARE HARD TO EXPLAIN, BUT RICHELIEU IS AN AGENT OF AN ENEMY POWER.
HE PLANS TO SEIZE CONTROL OF FRANCE, MAYBE EVEN TO ASSASSINATE YOU.
NONSENSE, DEAR GIRL...

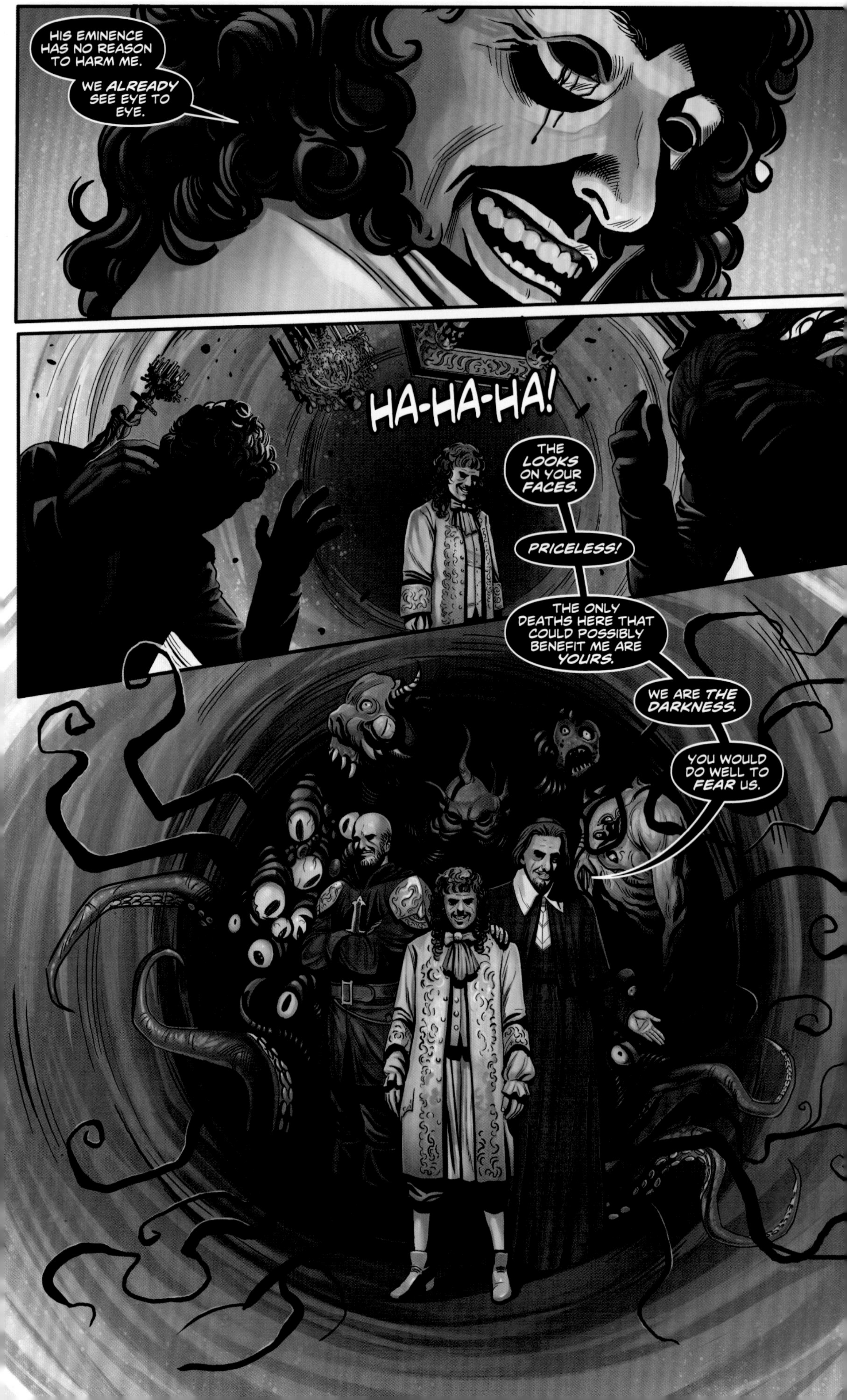
HIS EMINENCE HAS NO REASON TO HARM ME.
WE ALREADY SEE EYE TO EYE.
HA-HA-HA!
THE LOOKS ON YOUR FACES.
PRICELESS!
THE ONLY DEATHS HERE THAT COULD POSSIBLY BENEFIT ME ARE YOURS.
WE ARE THE DARKNESS.
YOU WOULD DO WELL TO FEAR US.

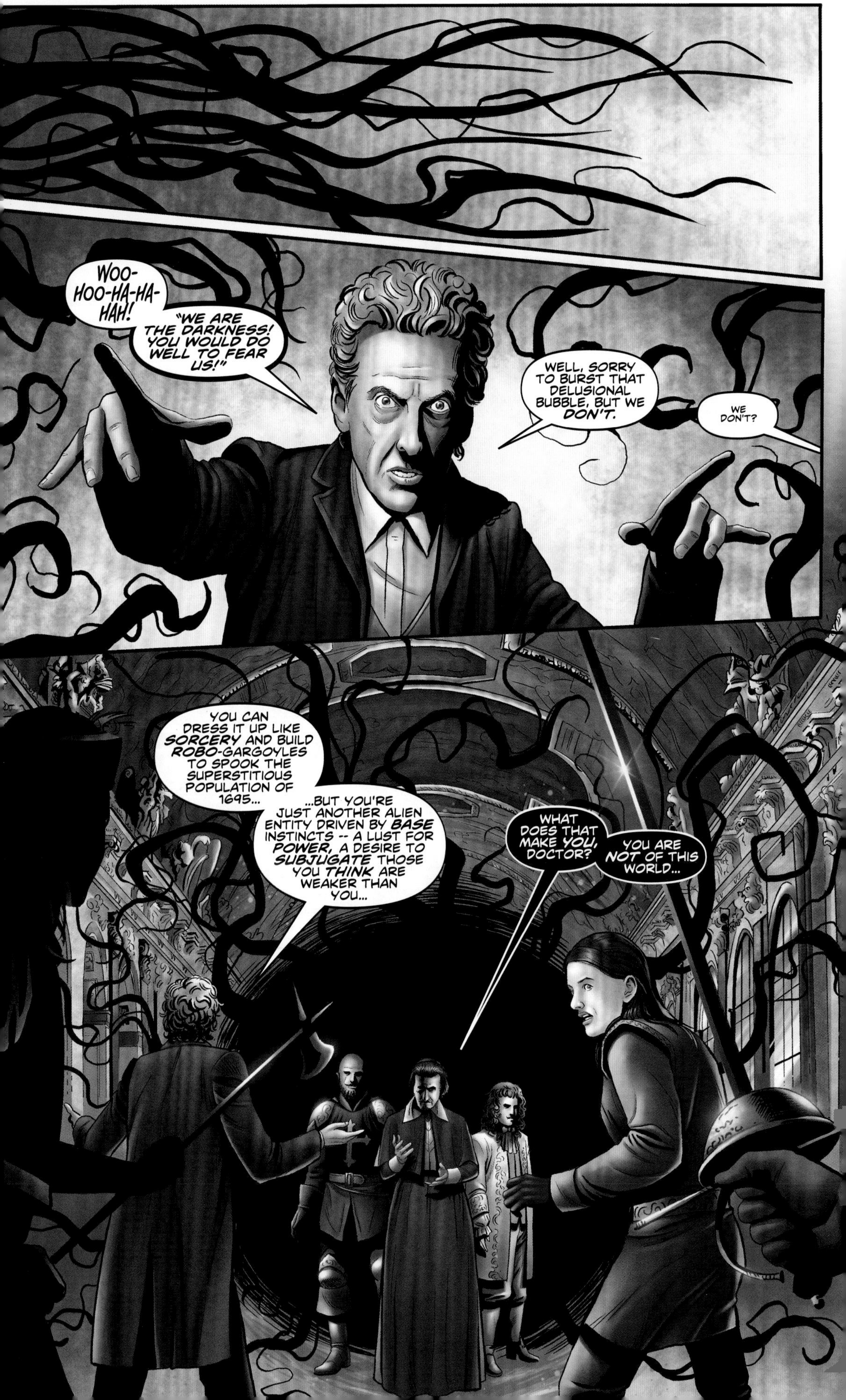
WOO-HOO-HA-HA-HAH!
"WE ARE THE DARKNESS! YOU WOULD DO WELL TO FEAR US!"
WELL, SORRY TO BURST THAT DELUSIONAL BUBBLE, BUT WE DON'T.
WE DON'T?
YOU CAN DRESS IT UP LIKE SORCERY AND BUILD ROBO-GARGOYLES TO SPOOK THE SUPERSTITIOUS POPULATION OF 1695...
...BUT YOU'RE JUST ANOTHER ALIEN ENTITY DRIVEN BY BASE INSTINCTS -- A LUST FOR POWER, A DESIRE TO SUBJUGATE THOSE YOU THINK ARE WEAKER THAN YOU...
WHAT DOES THAT MAKE YOU, DOCTOR?
YOU ARE NOT OF THIS WORLD...

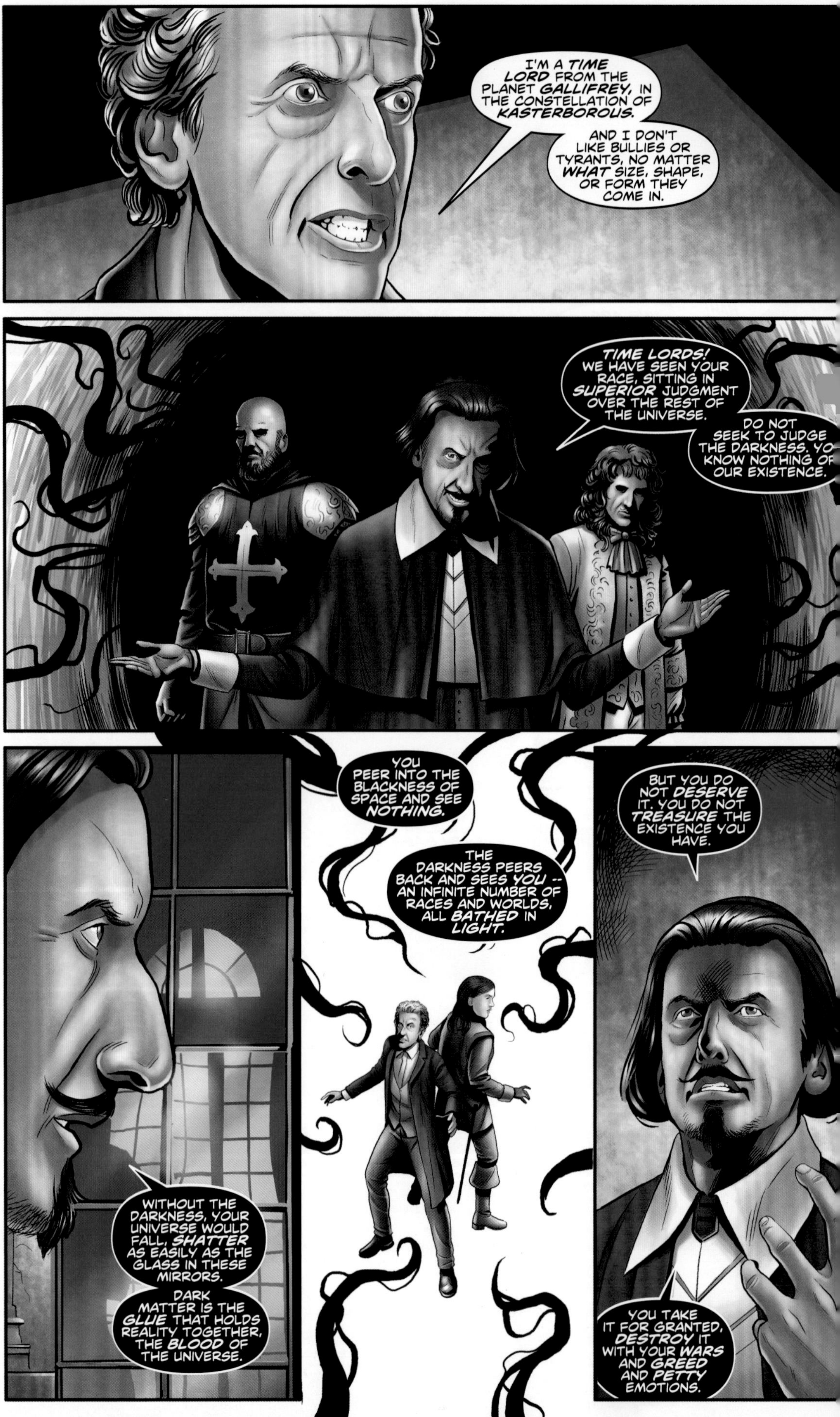
I'M A TIME LORD FROM THE PLANET GALLIFREY, IN THE CONSTELLATION OF KASTERBOROUS.
AND I DON'T LIKE BULLIES OR TYRANTS, NO MATTER WHAT SIZE, SHAPE, OR FORM THEY COME IN.
TIME LORDS! WE HAVE SEEN YOUR RACE, SITTING IN SUPERIOR JUDGMENT OVER THE REST OF THE UNIVERSE.
DO NOT SEEK TO JUDGE THE DARKNESS. YOU KNOW NOTHING OF OUR EXISTENCE.
YOU PEER INTO THE BLACKNESS OF SPACE AND SEE NOTHING.
THE DARKNESS PEERS BACK AND SEES YOU -- AN INFINITE NUMBER OF RACES AND WORLDS, ALL BATHED IN LIGHT.
WITHOUT THE DARKNESS, YOUR UNIVERSE WOULD FALL, SHATTER AS EASILY AS THE GLASS IN THESE MIRRORS.
DARK MATTER IS THE GLUE THAT HOLDS REALITY TOGETHER, THE BLOOD OF THE UNIVERSE.
BUT YOU DO NOT DESERVE IT. YOU DO NOT TREASURE THE EXISTENCE YOU HAVE.
YOU TAKE IT FOR GRANTED, DESTROY IT WITH YOUR WARS AND GREED AND PETTY EMOTIONS.

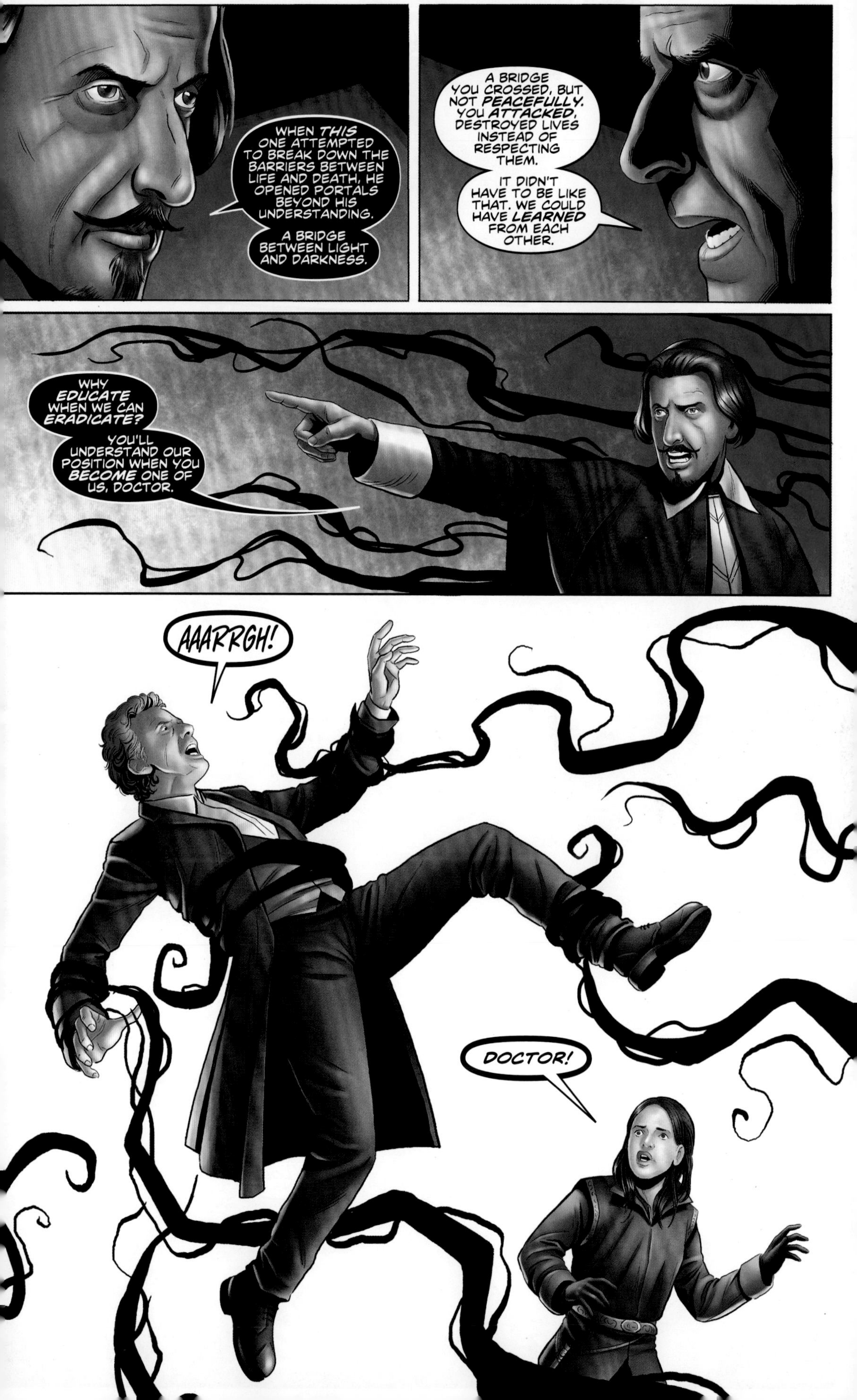
WHEN THIS ONE ATTEMPTED TO BREAK DOWN THE BARRIERS BETWEEN LIFE AND DEATH, HE OPENED PORTALS BEYOND HIS UNDERSTANDING.
A BRIDGE BETWEEN LIGHT AND DARKNESS.
A BRIDGE YOU CROSSED, BUT NOT PEACEFULLY. YOU ATTACKED, DESTROYED LIVES INSTEAD OF RESPECTING THEM.
IT DIDN'T HAVE TO BE LIKE THAT. WE COULD HAVE LEARNED FROM EACH OTHER.
WHY EDUCATE WHEN WE CAN ERADICATE?
YOU'LL UNDERSTAND OUR POSITION WHEN YOU BECOME ONE OF US, DOCTOR.
AAARRGH!
DOCTOR!

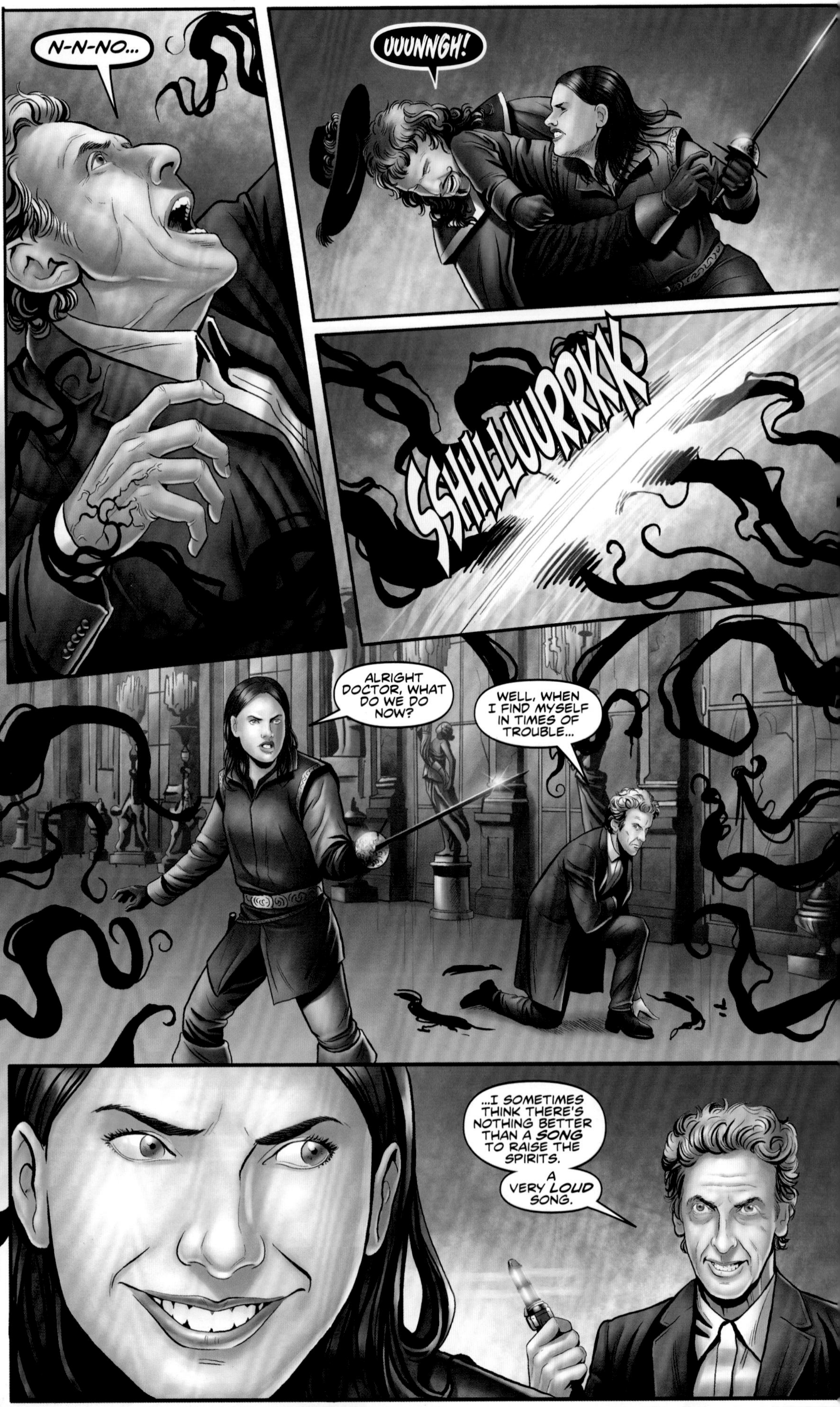
N-N-NO...
UUUNNGH!
SSHHLUURKK
ALRIGHT DOCTOR, WHAT DO WE DO NOW?
WELL, WHEN I FIND MYSELF IN TIMES OF TROUBLE...
...I SOMETIMES THINK THERE'S NOTHING BETTER THAN A SONG TO RAISE THE SPIRITS.
A VERY LOUD SONG.

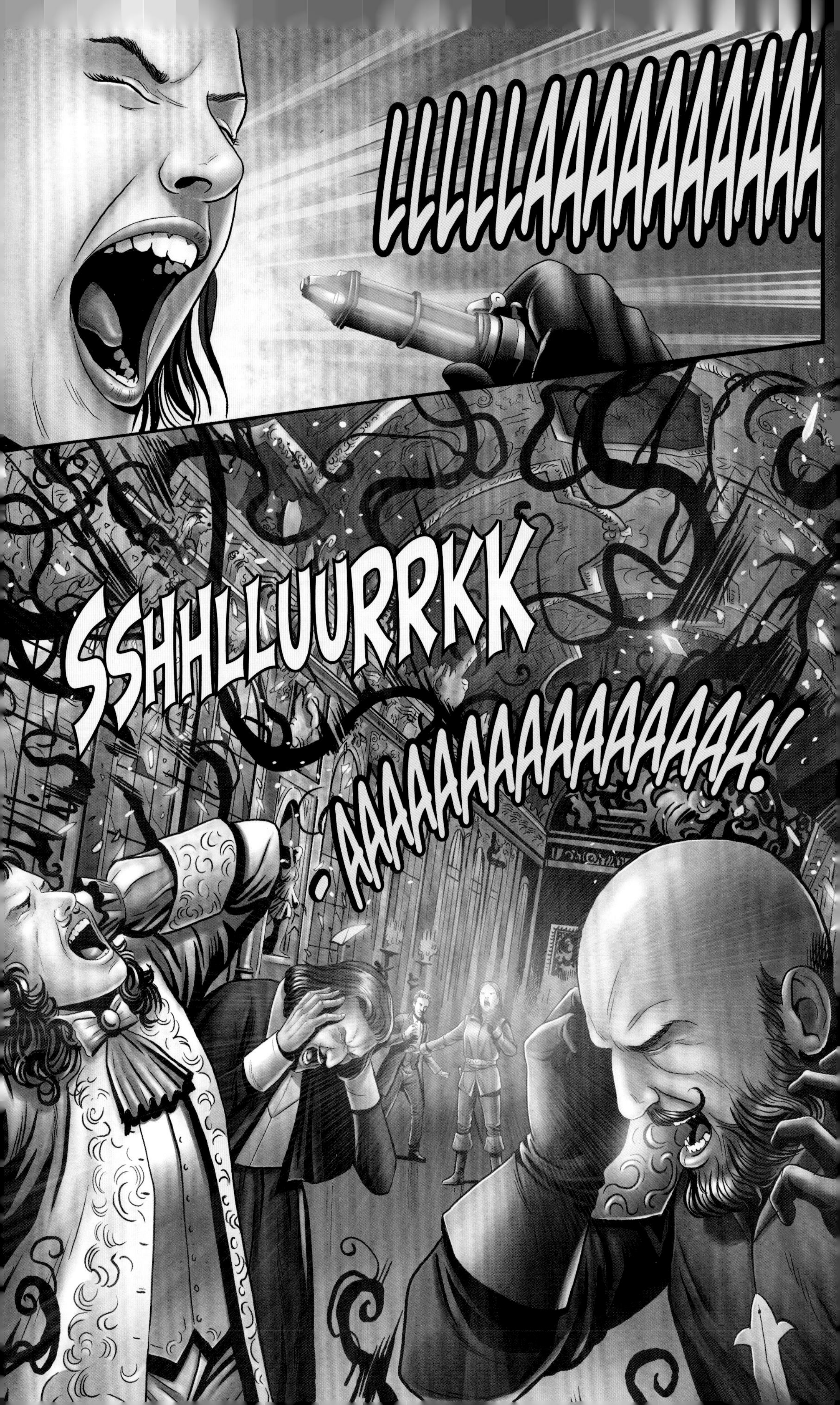
LLLLLAAAAAAAAAA
SSHLLUURRKK
AAAAAAAAAAAAAA!

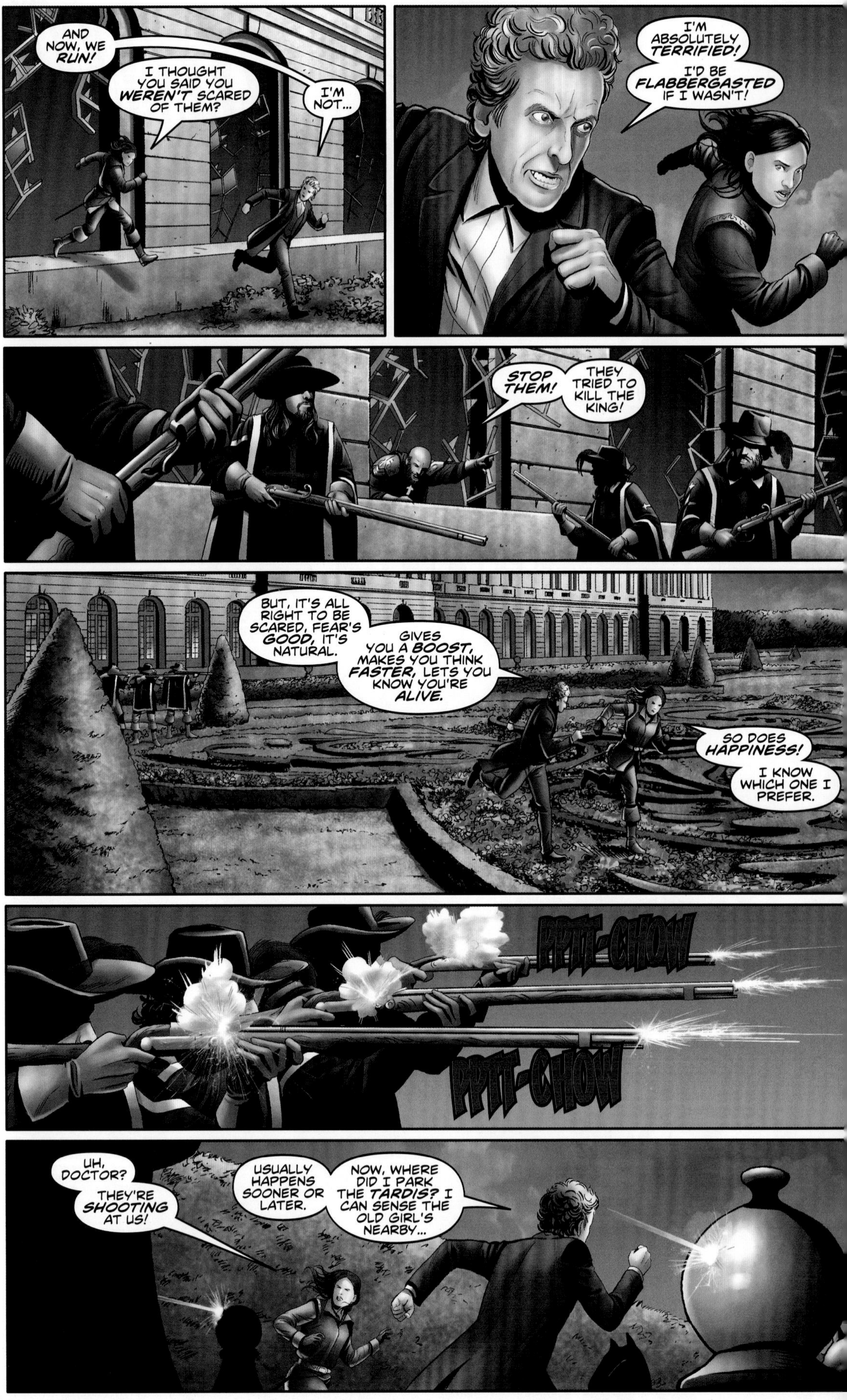
AND NOW, WE RUN!
I THOUGHT YOU SAID YOU WEREN'T SCARED OF THEM?
I'M NOT...
I'M ABSOLUTELY TERRIFIED!
I'D BE FLABBERGASTED IF I WASN'T!
STOP THEM!
THEY TRIED TO KILL THE KING!
BUT, IT'S ALL RIGHT TO BE SCARED, FEAR'S GOOD, IT'S NATURAL.
GIVES YOU A BOOST, MAKES YOU THINK FASTER, LETS YOU KNOW YOU'RE ALIVE.
SO DOES HAPPINESS!
I KNOW WHICH ONE I PREFER.
PPTT-CHOW
PPTT-CHOW
UH, DOCTOR?
THEY'RE SHOOTING AT US!
USUALLY HAPPENS SOONER OR LATER.
NOW, WHERE DID I PARK THE TARDIS? I CAN SENSE THE OLD GIRL'S NEARBY...

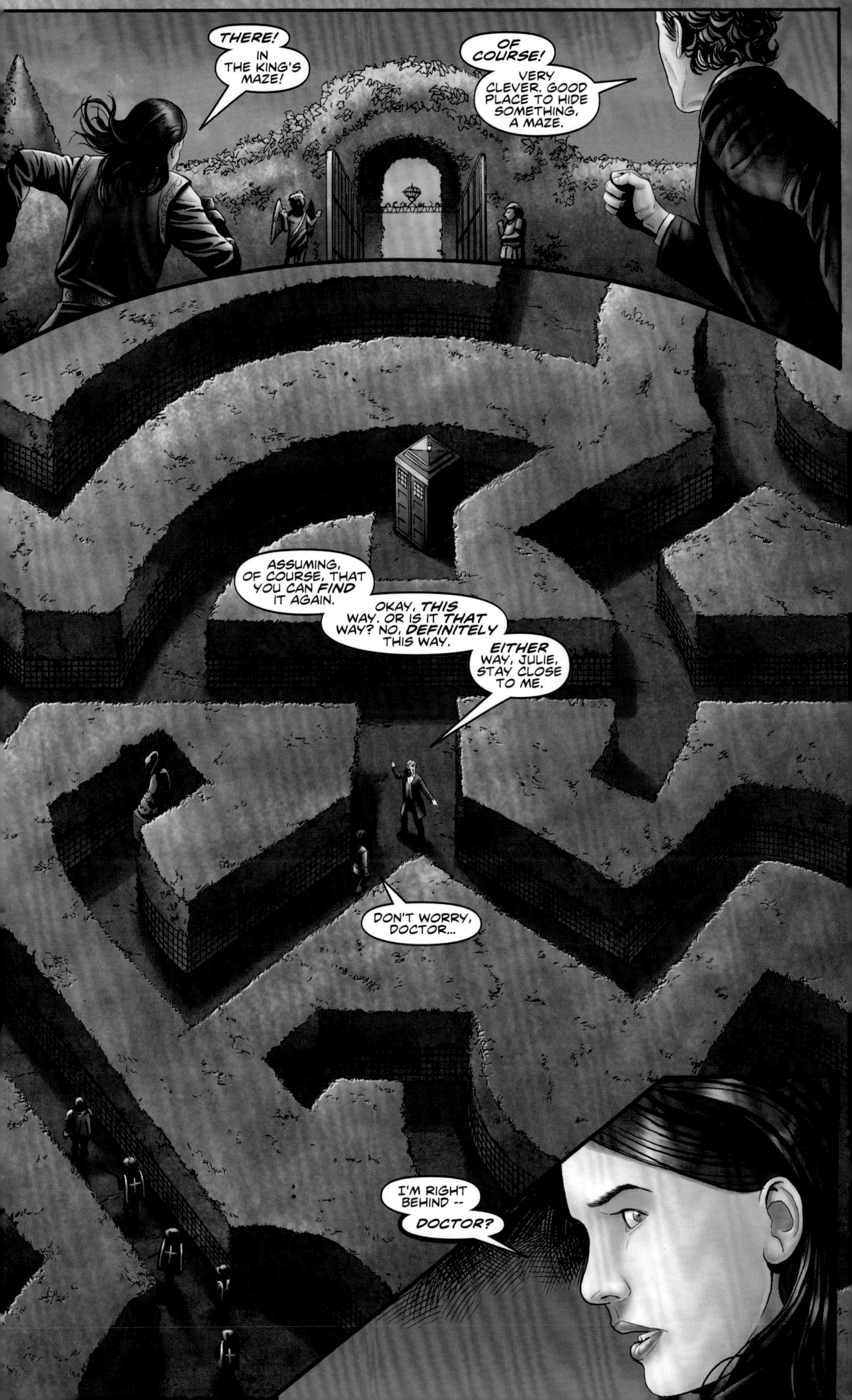
THERE! IN THE KING'S MAZE!
OF COURSE! VERY CLEVER. GOOD PLACE TO HIDE SOMETHING, A MAZE.
ASSUMING, OF COURSE, THAT YOU CAN FIND IT AGAIN.
OKAY, THIS WAY. OR IS IT THAT WAY? NO, DEFINITELY THIS WAY.
EITHER WAY, JULIE, STAY CLOSE TO ME.
DON'T WORRY, DOCTOR...
I'M RIGHT BEHIND -- DOCTOR?

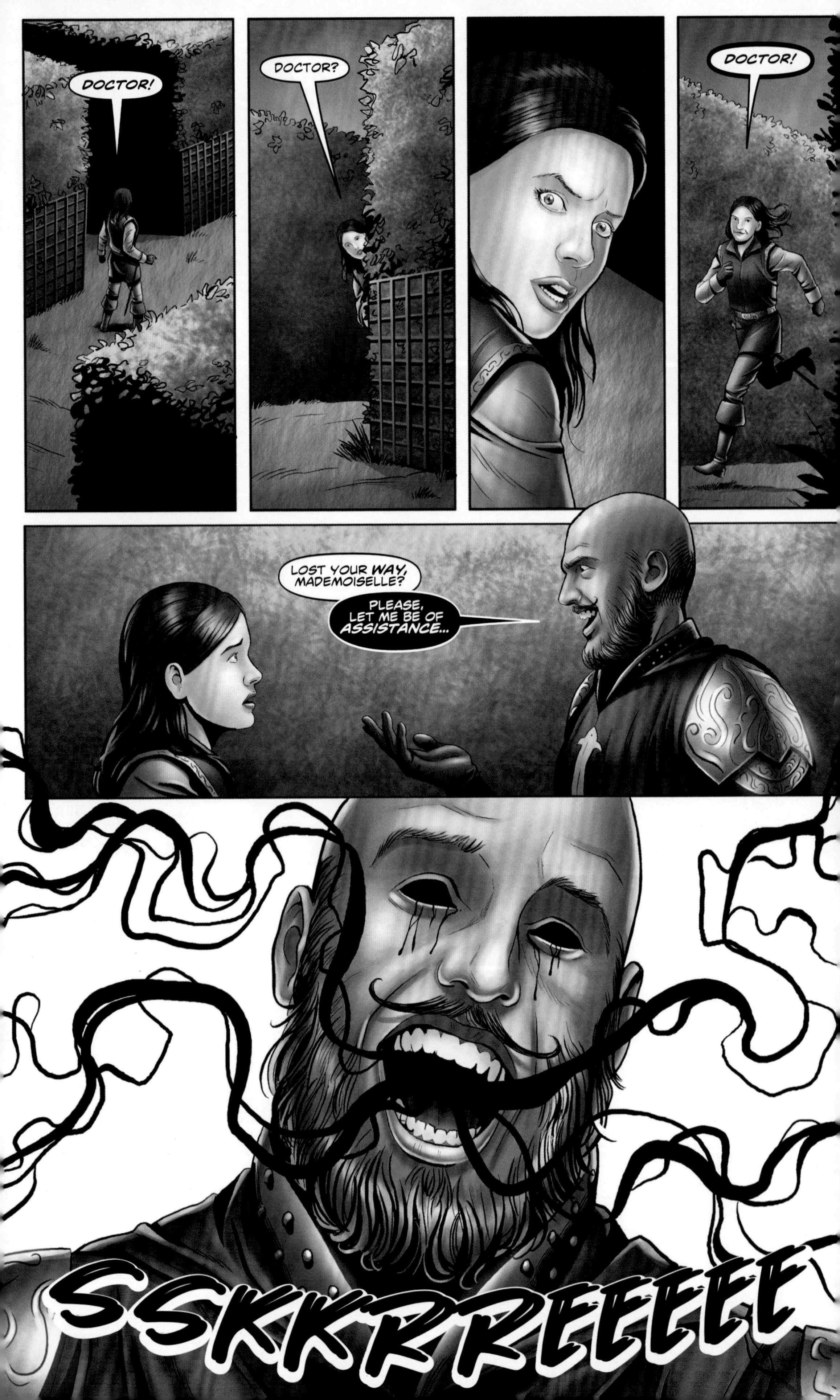
DOCTOR!
DOCTOR?
DOCTOR!
LOST YOUR WAY, MADEMOISELLE?
PLEASE, LET ME BE OF ASSISTANCE...
SSKKRREEEEEE

’S AMAZING!

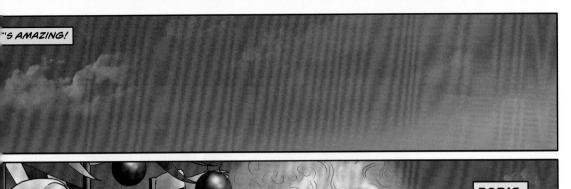

PARIS.

"THE *WHOLE* OF PARIS HAS COME OUT TO PLAY, MORE BECAUSE OF THE FREE *WINE* THE CARDINAL HAS SUPPLIED THAN IN HONOR OF THE KING, I SUSPECT.

THE BASTILLE PRISON.

"ƎSIGHE IF ONLY YOU COULD *SEE* IT.

"YOU'D BE THE LIFE AND SOUL OF THE PARTY."

I DIDN'T WANT TO SAY ANYTHING, BUT BEFORE YOUR *LATEST* ESCAPADE, I WAS NEGOTIATING FOR YOU TO PLAY A MAJOR PART IN THE FESTIVITIES, TO PERFORM BEFORE THE KING.

I *AM* PART OF IT, GABRIEL.

I'M THE *OPENING* ACT.

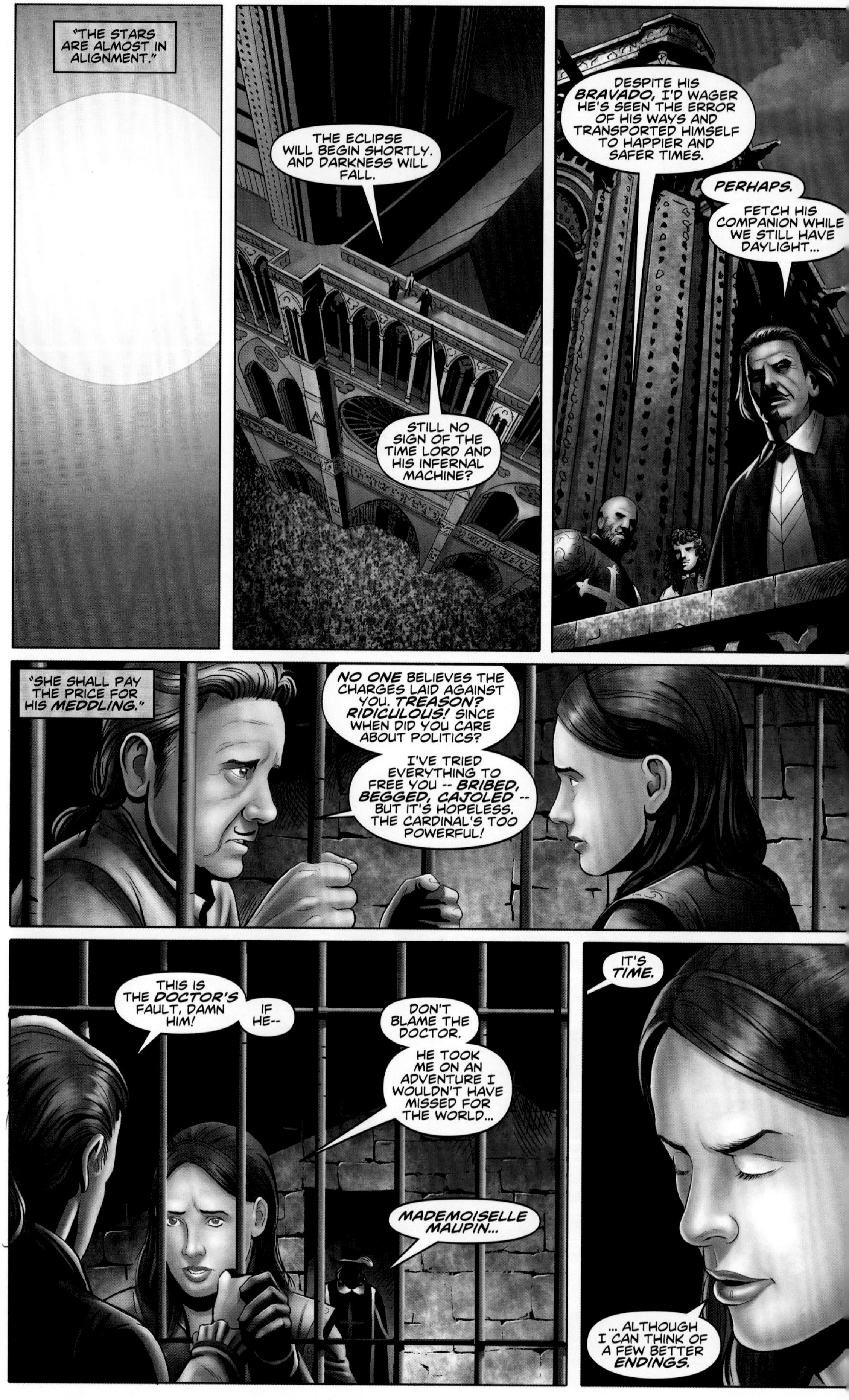
"THE STARS ARE ALMOST IN ALIGNMENT."
THE ECLIPSE WILL BEGIN SHORTLY. AND DARKNESS WILL FALL.
STILL NO SIGN OF THE TIME LORD AND HIS INFERNAL MACHINE?
DESPITE HIS BRAVADO, I'D WAGER HE'S SEEN THE ERROR OF HIS WAYS AND TRANSPORTED HIMSELF TO HAPPIER AND SAFER TIMES.
PERHAPS.
FETCH HIS COMPANION WHILE WE STILL HAVE DAYLIGHT...
"SHE SHALL PAY THE PRICE FOR HIS MEDDLING."
NO ONE BELIEVES THE CHARGES LAID AGAINST YOU. TREASON? RIDICULOUS! SINCE WHEN DID YOU CARE ABOUT POLITICS?
I'VE TRIED EVERYTHING TO FREE YOU -- BRIBED, BEGGED, CAJOLED -- BUT IT'S HOPELESS. THE CARDINAL'S TOO POWERFUL!
THIS IS THE DOCTOR'S FAULT, DAMN HIM!
IF HE--
DON'T BLAME THE DOCTOR.
HE TOOK ME ON AN ADVENTURE I WOULDN'T HAVE MISSED FOR THE WORLD...
MADEMOISELLE MAUPIN...
IT'S TIME.
... ALTHOUGH I CAN THINK OF A FEW BETTER ENDINGS.

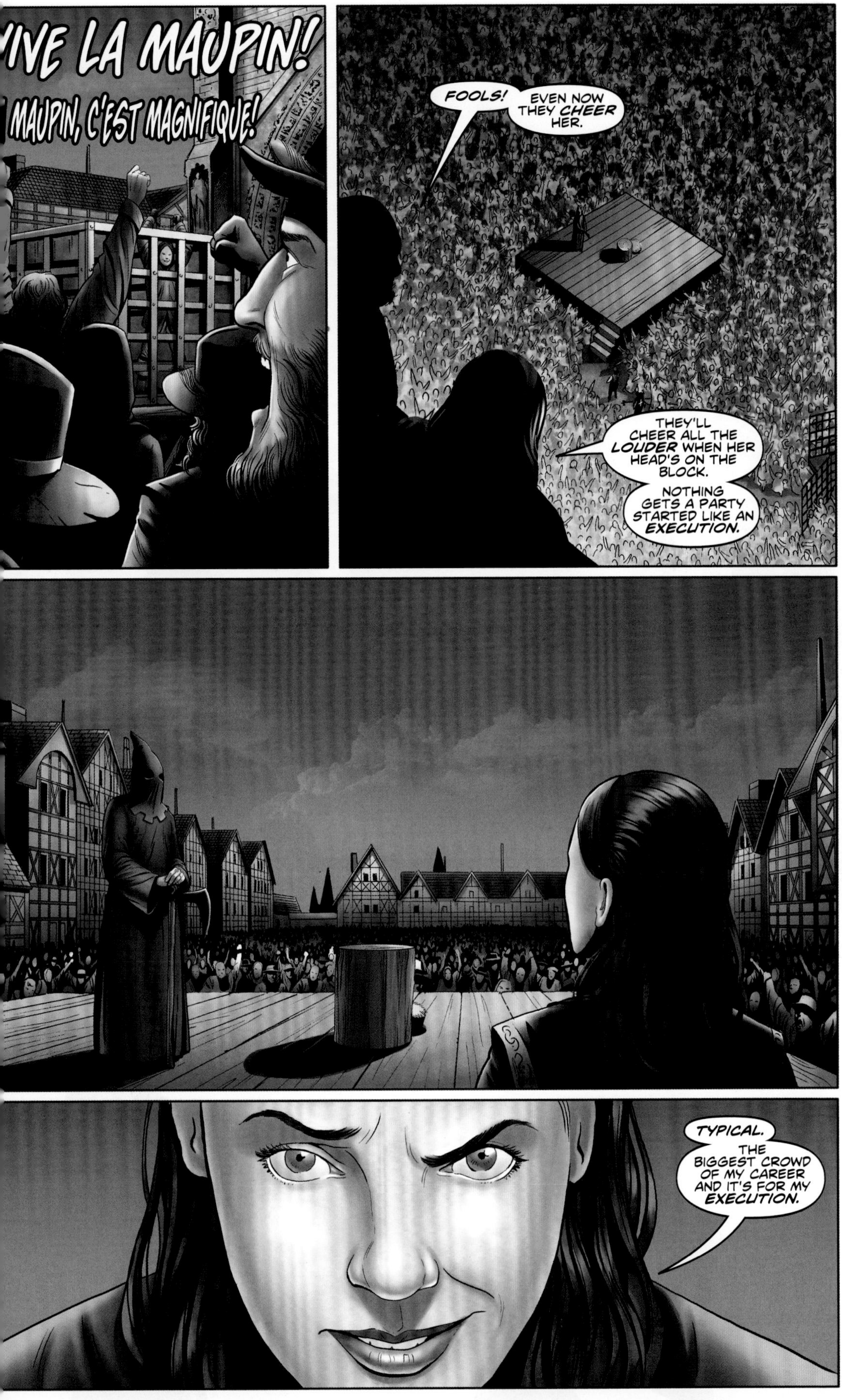

VIVE LA MAUPIN!
MAUPIN, C'EST MAGNIFIQUE!
FOOLS!
EVEN NOW THEY CHEER HER.
THEY'LL CHEER ALL THE LOUDER WHEN HER HEAD'S ON THE BLOCK.
NOTHING GETS A PARTY STARTED LIKE AN EXECUTION.
TYPICAL.
THE BIGGEST CROWD OF MY CAREER AND IT'S FOR MY EXECUTION.

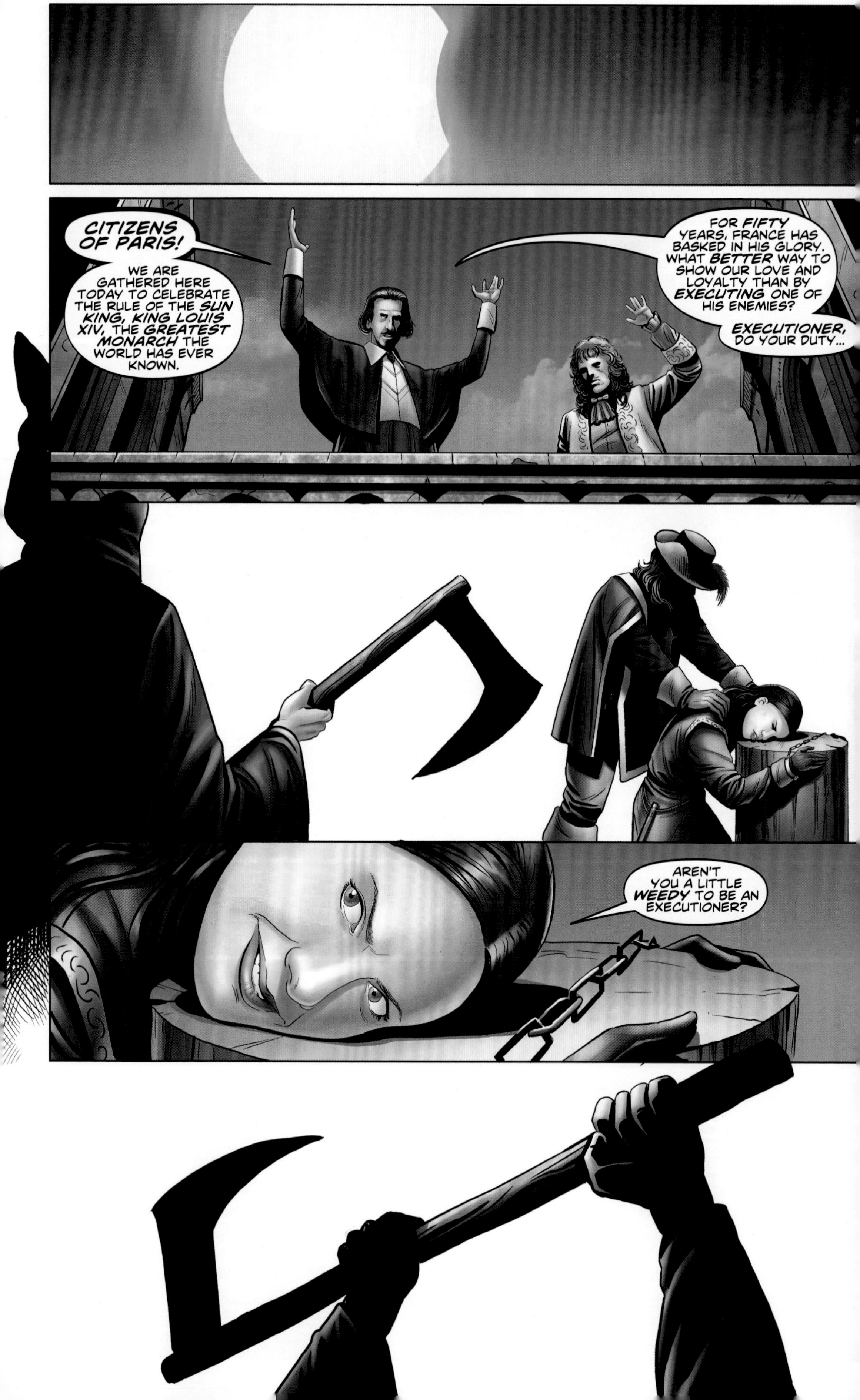
CITIZENS OF PARIS!
WE ARE GATHERED HERE TODAY TO CELEBRATE THE RULE OF THE SUN KING, KING LOUIS XIV, THE GREATEST MONARCH THE WORLD HAS EVER KNOWN.
FOR FIFTY YEARS, FRANCE HAS BASKED IN HIS GLORY. WHAT BETTER WAY TO SHOW OUR LOVE AND LOYALTY THAN BY EXECUTING ONE OF HIS ENEMIES?
EXECUTIONER, DO YOUR DUTY...
AREN'T YOU A LITTLE WEEDY TO BE AN EXECUTIONER?

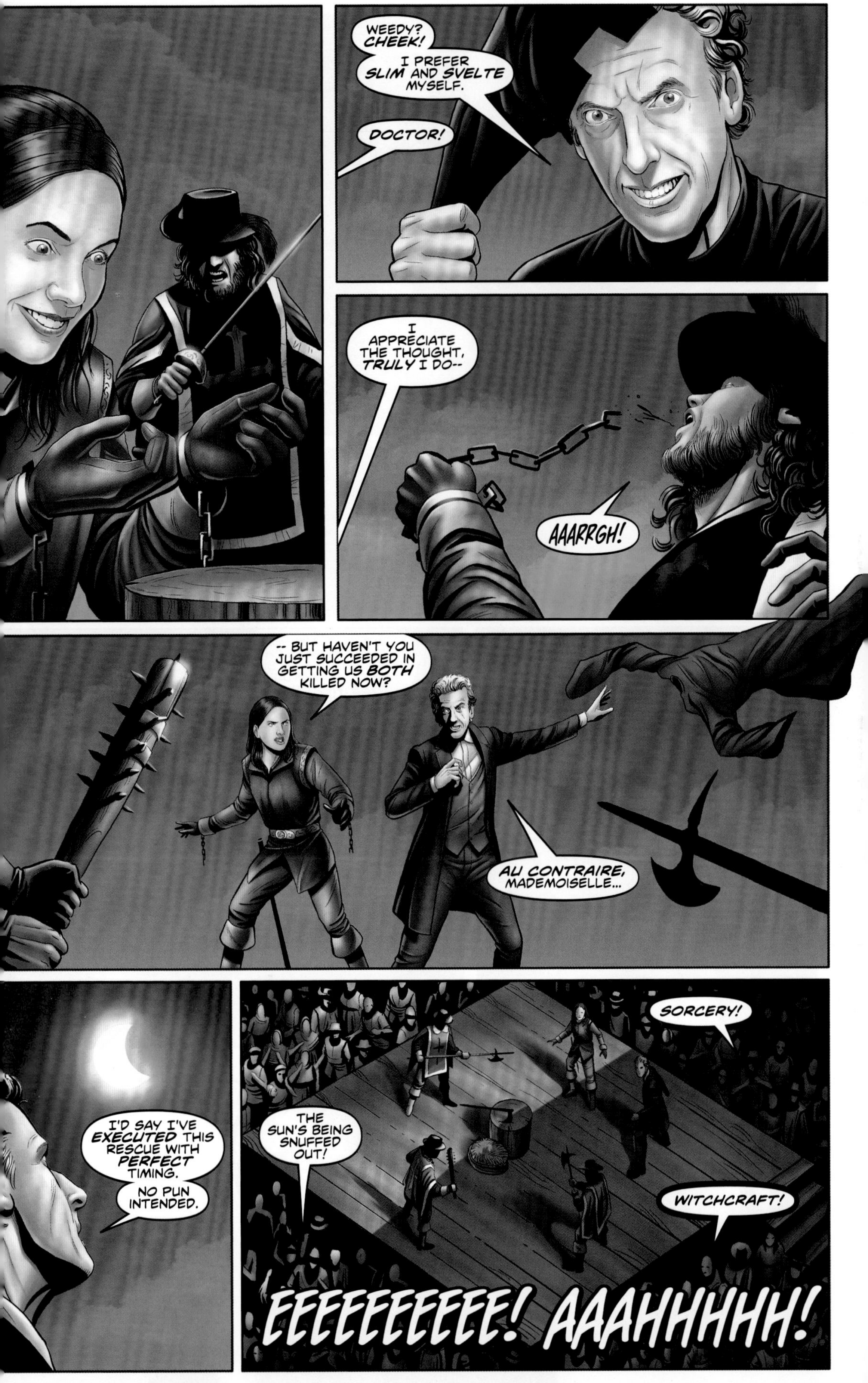
WEEDY? CHEEK!
I PREFER SLIM AND SVELTE MYSELF.
DOCTOR!
I APPRECIATE THE THOUGHT, TRULY I DO--
AAARRGH!
-- BUT HAVEN'T YOU JUST SUCCEEDED IN GETTING US BOTH KILLED NOW?
AU CONTRAIRE, MADEMOISELLE...
I'D SAY I'VE EXECUTED THIS RESCUE WITH PERFECT TIMING.
NO PUN INTENDED.
SORCERY!
THE SUN'S BEING SNUFFED OUT!
WITCHCRAFT!
EEEEEEEEEEEE! AAAHHHHH!

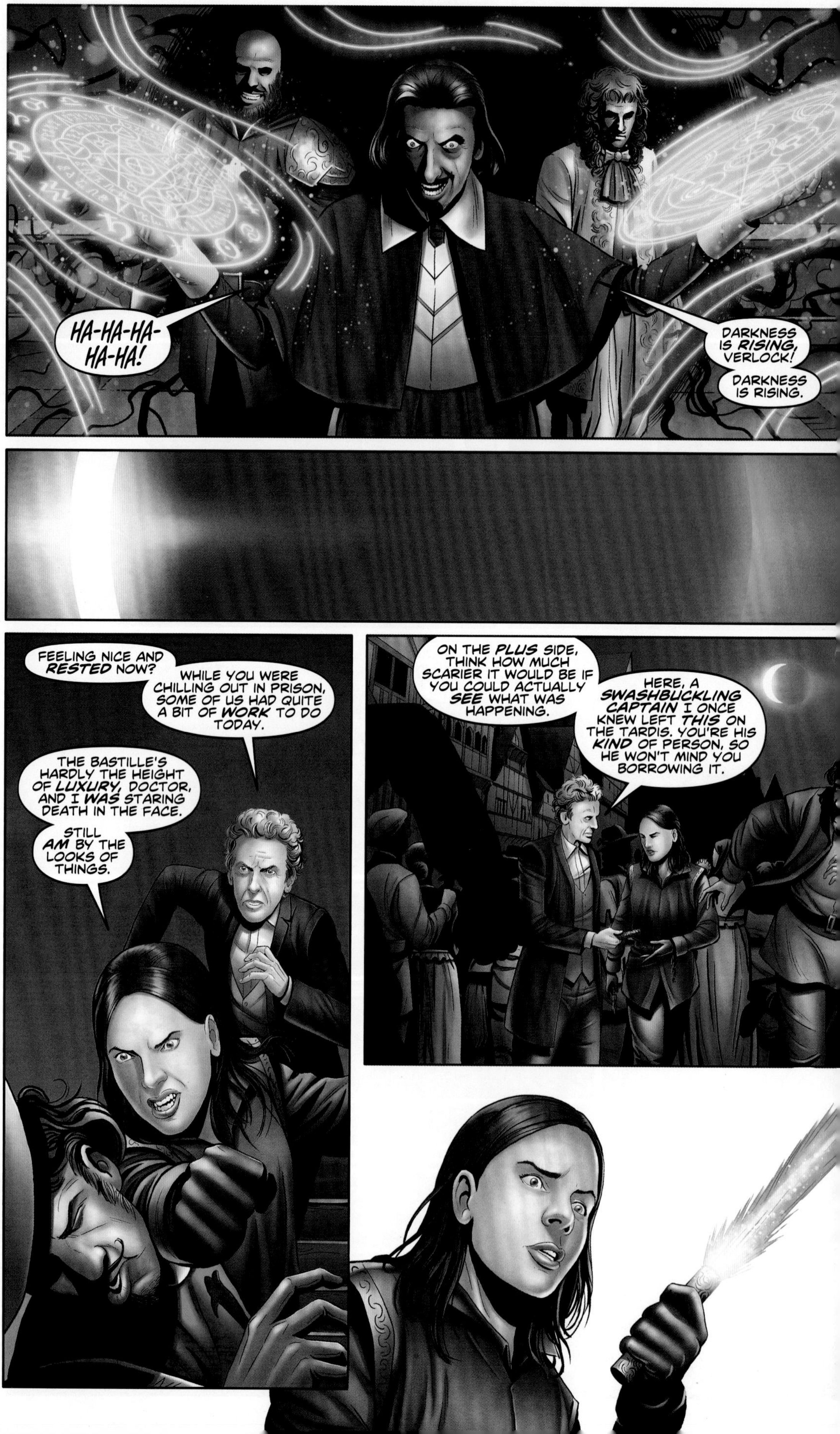

HA-HA-HA-HA-HA!
DARKNESS IS RISING, VERLOCK!
DARKNESS IS RISING.
FEELING NICE AND RESTED NOW?
WHILE YOU WERE CHILLING OUT IN PRISON, SOME OF US HAD QUITE A BIT OF WORK TO DO TODAY.
THE BASTILLE'S HARDLY THE HEIGHT OF LUXURY, DOCTOR, AND I WAS STARING DEATH IN THE FACE.
STILL AM BY THE LOOKS OF THINGS.
ON THE PLUS SIDE, THINK HOW MUCH SCARIER IT WOULD BE IF YOU COULD ACTUALLY SEE WHAT WAS HAPPENING.
HERE, A SWASHBUCKLING CAPTAIN I ONCE KNEW LEFT THIS ON THE TARDIS. YOU'RE HIS KIND OF PERSON, SO HE WON'T MIND YOU BORROWING IT.

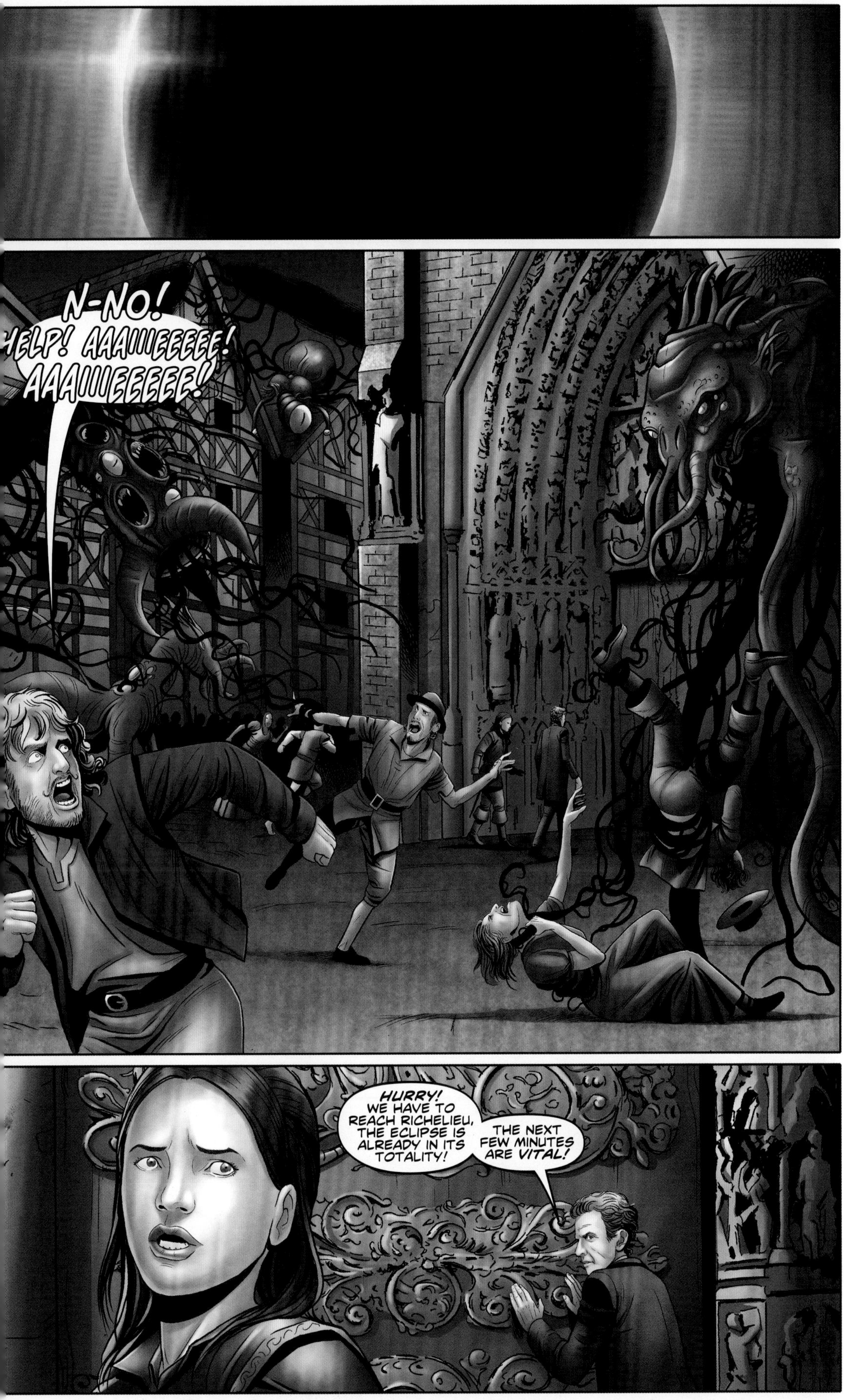

N-NO!
HELP! AAAIIIEEEEE!
AAAIIIEEEEE!
HURRY! WE HAVE TO REACH RICHELIEU, THE ECLIPSE IS ALREADY IN ITS TOTALITY!
THE NEXT FEW MINUTES ARE VITAL!

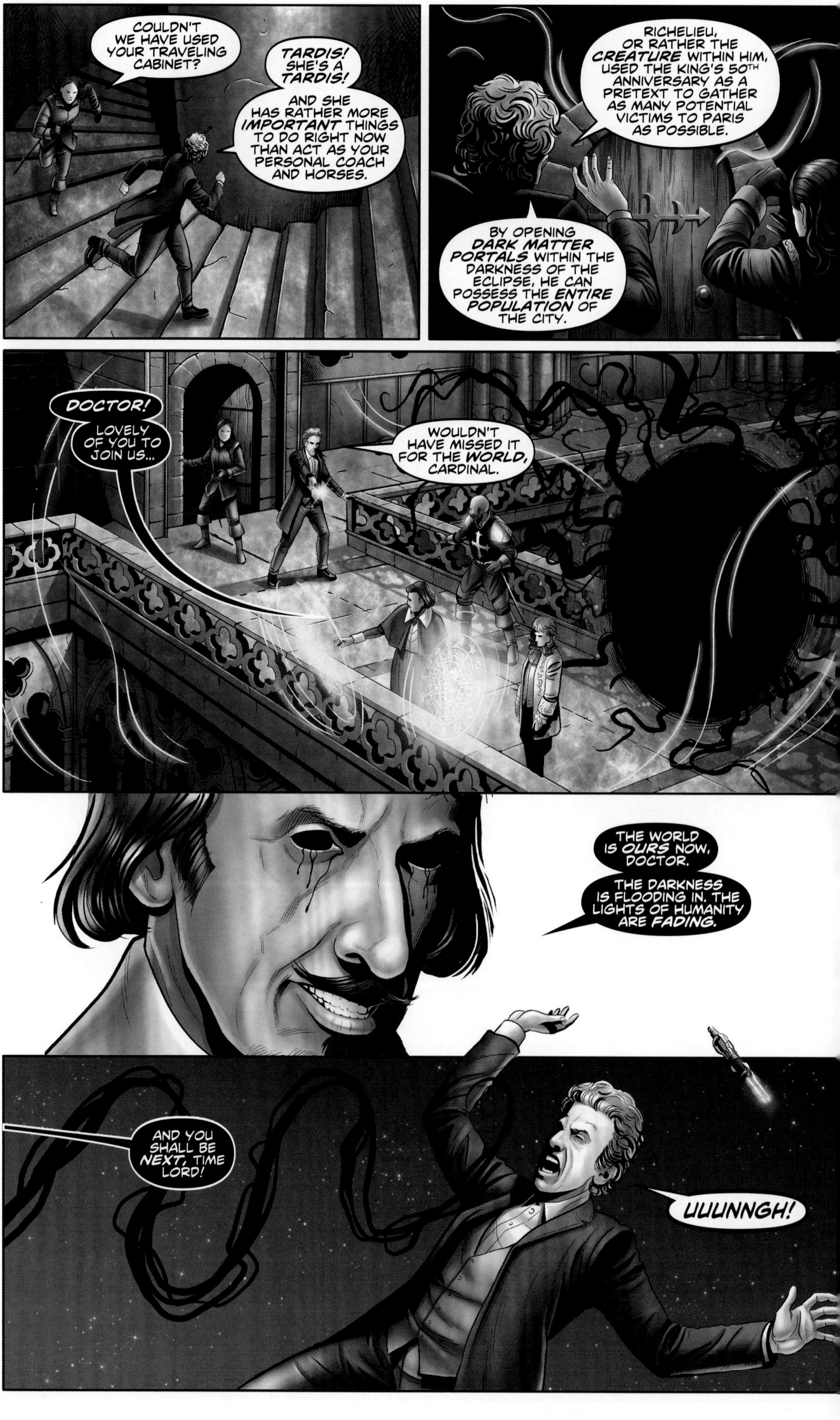

COULDN'T WE HAVE USED YOUR TRAVELING CABINET?
TARDIS! SHE'S A TARDIS!
AND SHE HAS RATHER MORE IMPORTANT THINGS TO DO RIGHT NOW THAN ACT AS YOUR PERSONAL COACH AND HORSES.
RICHELIEU, OR RATHER THE CREATURE WITHIN HIM, USED THE KING'S 50TH ANNIVERSARY AS A PRETEXT TO GATHER AS MANY POTENTIAL VICTIMS TO PARIS AS POSSIBLE.
BY OPENING DARK MATTER PORTALS WITHIN THE DARKNESS OF THE ECLIPSE, HE CAN POSSESS THE ENTIRE POPULATION OF THE CITY.
DOCTOR!
LOVELY OF YOU TO JOIN US...
WOULDN'T HAVE MISSED IT FOR THE WORLD, CARDINAL.
THE WORLD IS OURS NOW, DOCTOR.
THE DARKNESS IS FLOODING IN. THE LIGHTS OF HUMANITY ARE FADING.
AND YOU SHALL BE NEXT, TIME LORD!
UUUNNGH!

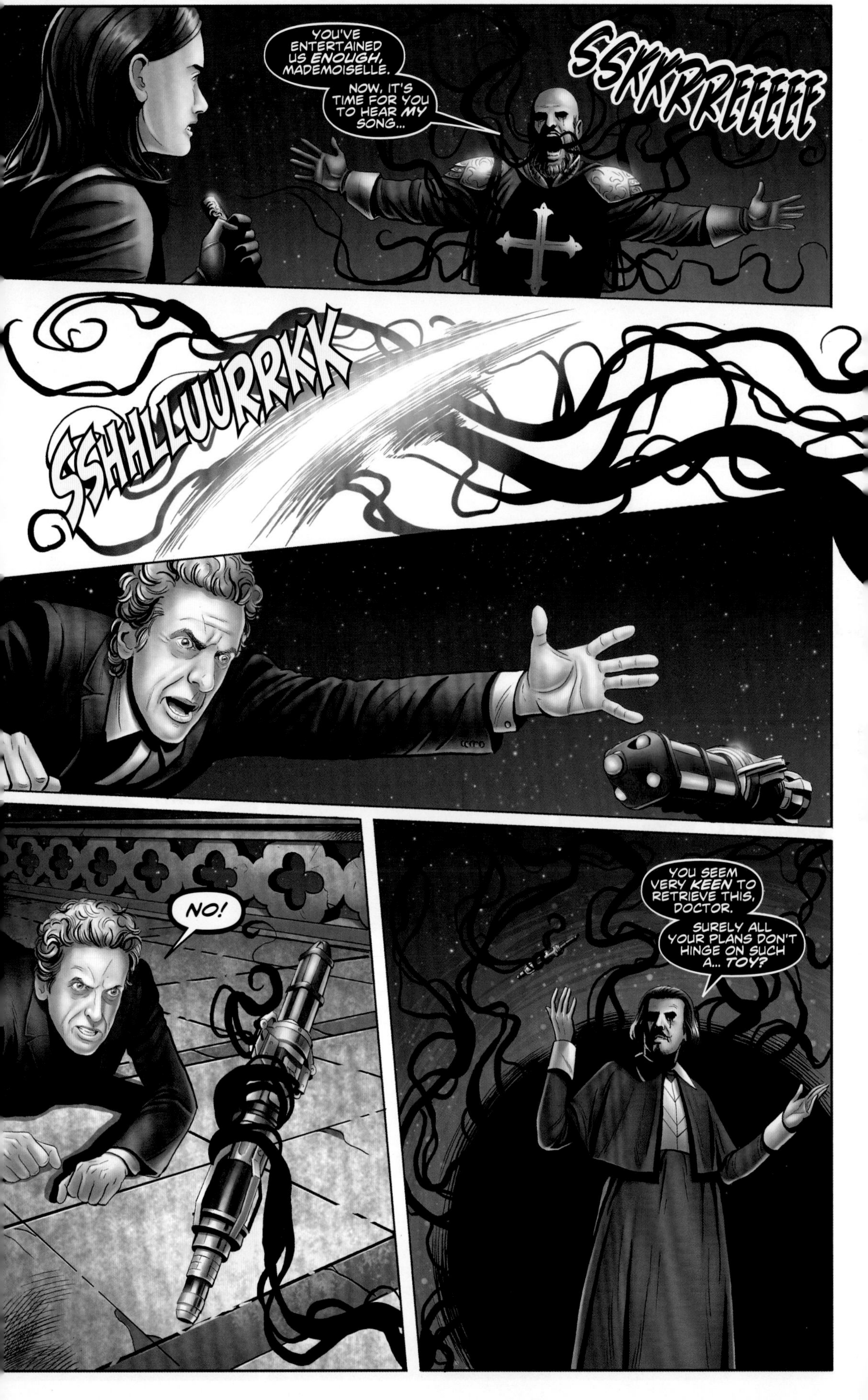
YOU'VE ENTERTAINED US ENOUGH, MADEMOISELLE.
NOW, IT'S TIME FOR YOU TO HEAR MY SONG...
SSKKRREEEEE
SSHHLLUURRKK
NO!
YOU SEEM VERY KEEN TO RETRIEVE THIS, DOCTOR.
SURELY ALL YOUR PLANS DON'T HINGE ON SUCH A... TOY?

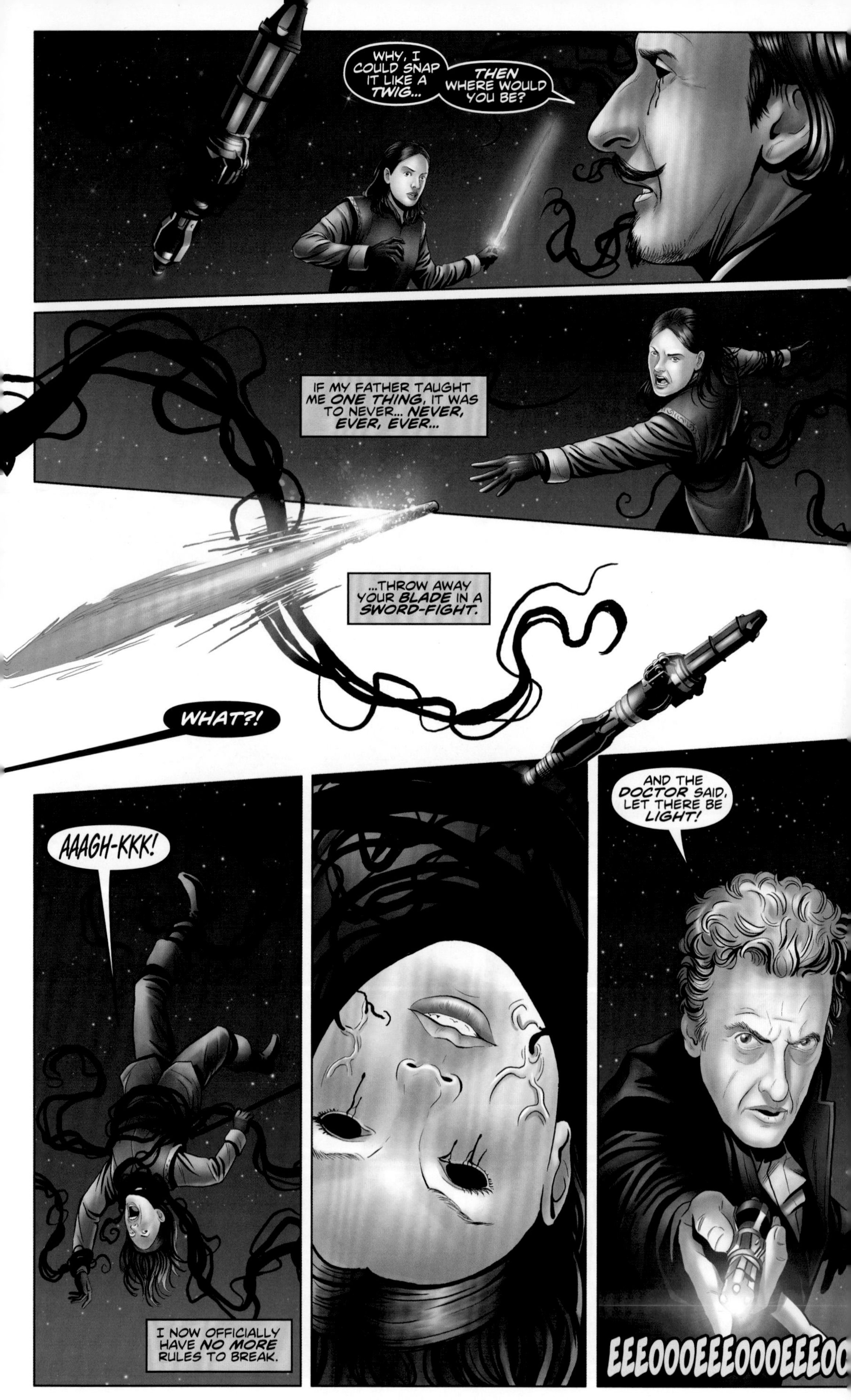
WHY, I COULD SNAP IT LIKE A TWIG...
THEN WHERE WOULD YOU BE?
IF MY FATHER TAUGHT ME ONE THING, IT WAS TO NEVER... NEVER, EVER, EVER...
...THROW AWAY YOUR BLADE IN A SWORD-FIGHT.
WHAT?!
AAAGH-KKK!
I NOW OFFICIALLY HAVE NO MORE RULES TO BREAK.
AND THE DOCTOR SAID, LET THERE BE LIGHT!
EEEOOOEEEOOOEEEOO

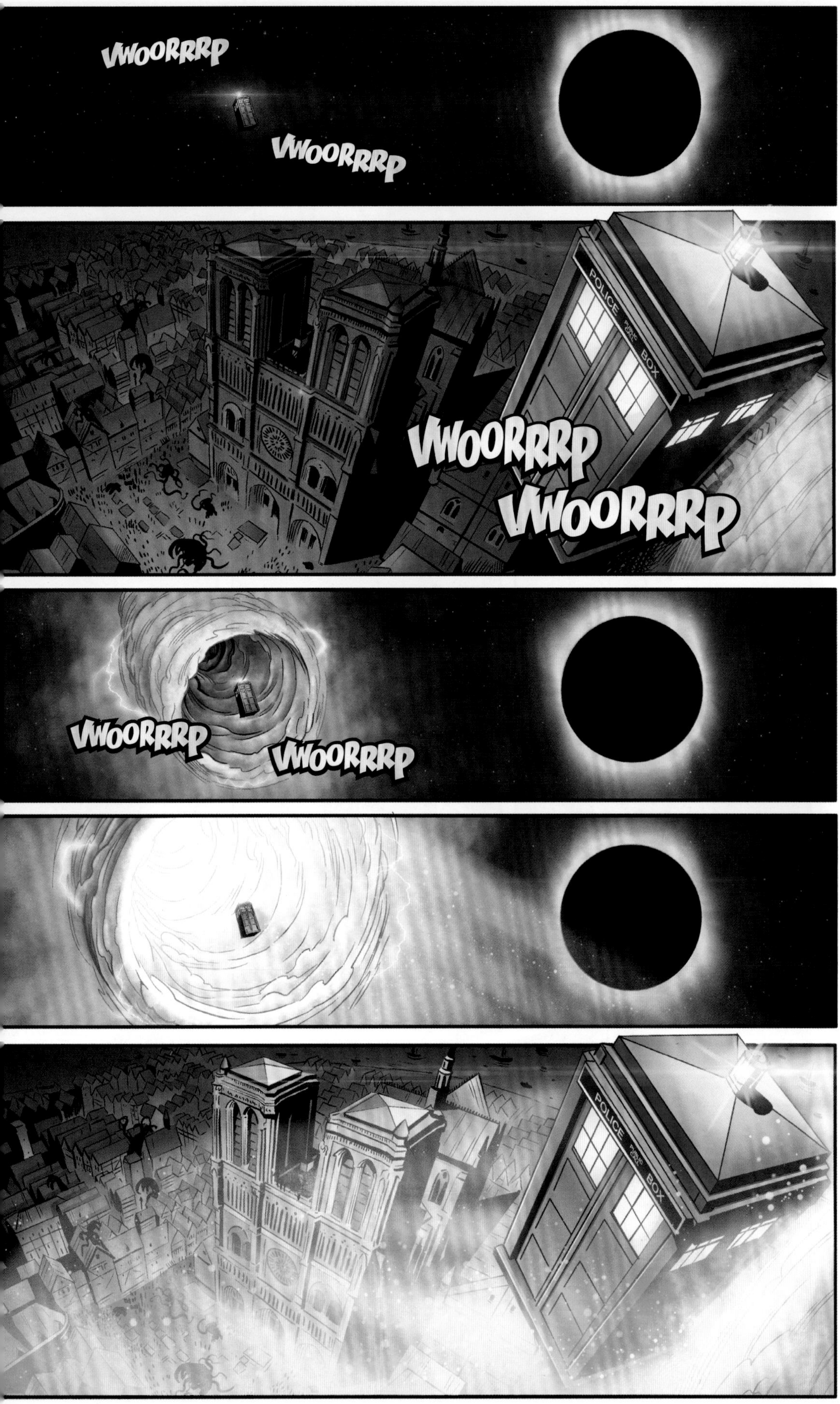

VWOORRRP
VWOORRRP
POLICE BOX
VWOORRRP
VWOORRRP
VWOORRRP
VWOORRRP
POLICE BOX

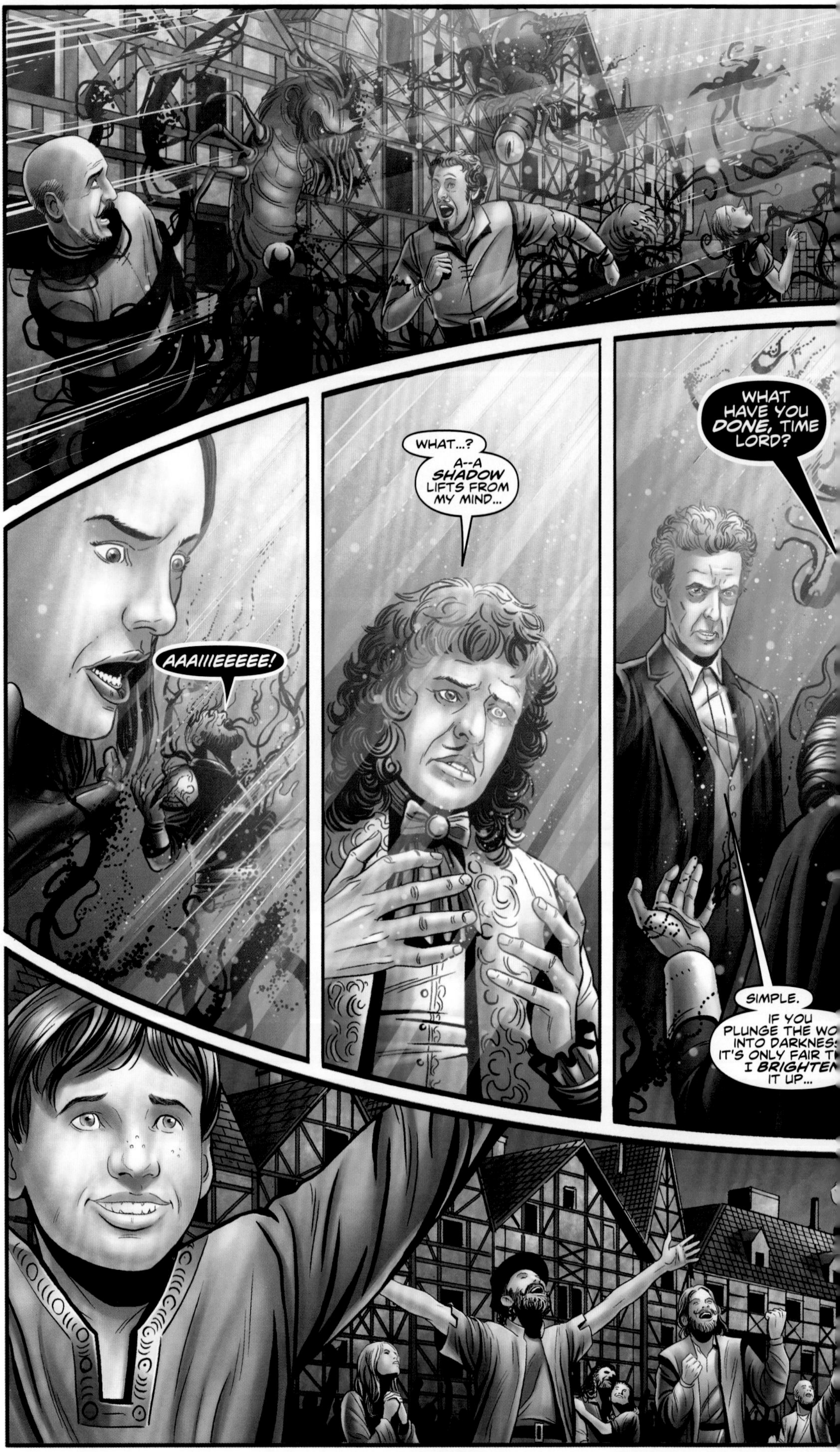
WHAT...?
A--A SHADOW LIFTS FROM MY MIND...
WHAT HAVE YOU DONE, TIME LORD?
AAAIIIEEEEE!
SIMPLE.
IF YOU PLUNGE THE WO INTO DARKNES IT'S ONLY FAIR T I BRIGHTEN IT UP...

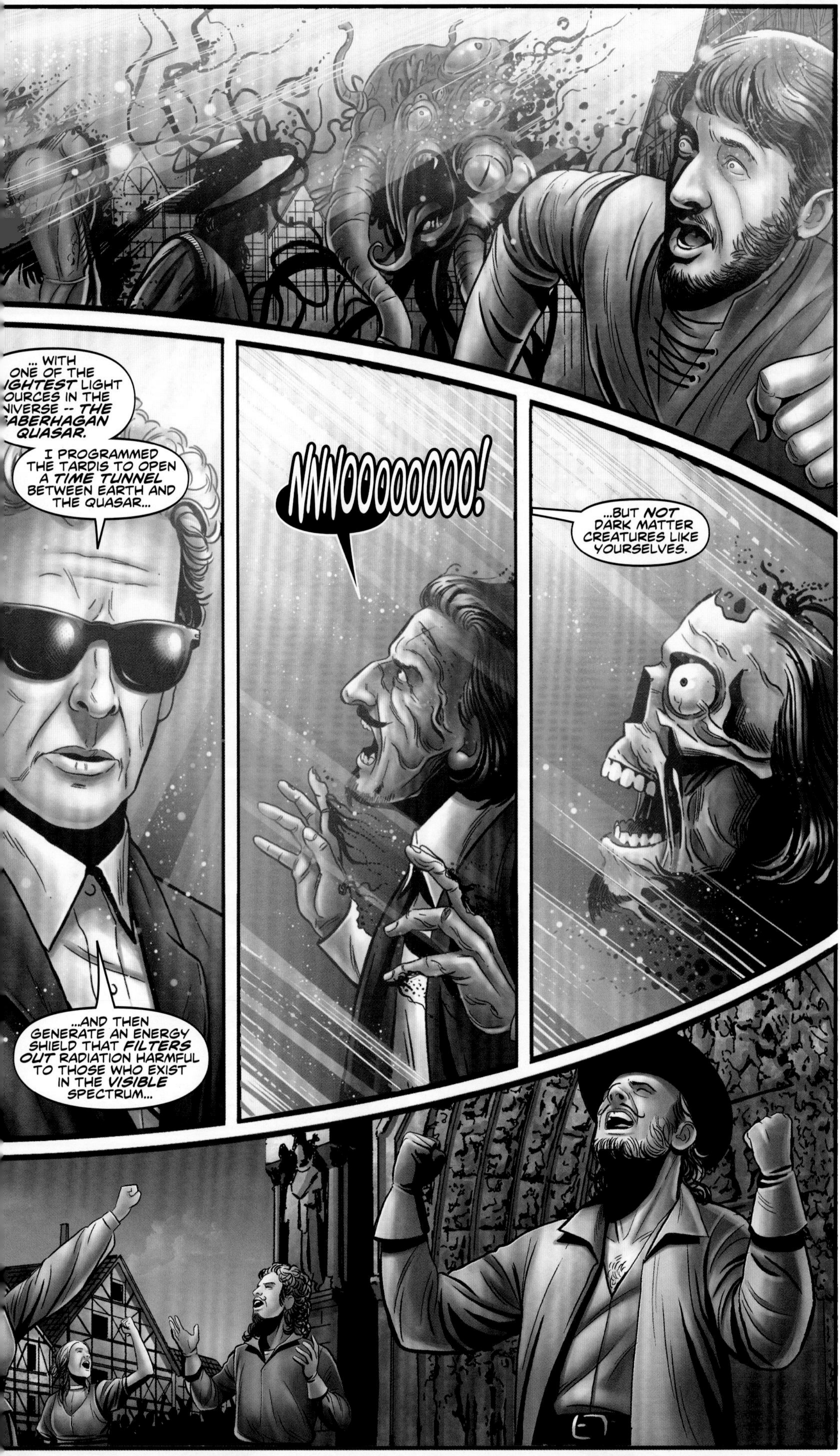

... WITH ONE OF THE IGHTEST LIGHT OURCES IN THE NIVERSE -- THE ABERHAGAN QUASAR.
I PROGRAMMED THE TARDIS TO OPEN A TIME TUNNEL BETWEEN EARTH AND THE QUASAR...
...AND THEN GENERATE AN ENERGY SHIELD THAT FILTERS OUT RADIATION HARMFUL TO THOSE WHO EXIST IN THE VISIBLE SPECTRUM...
NNNOOOOOOOO!
...BUT NOT DARK MATTER CREATURES LIKE YOURSELVES.

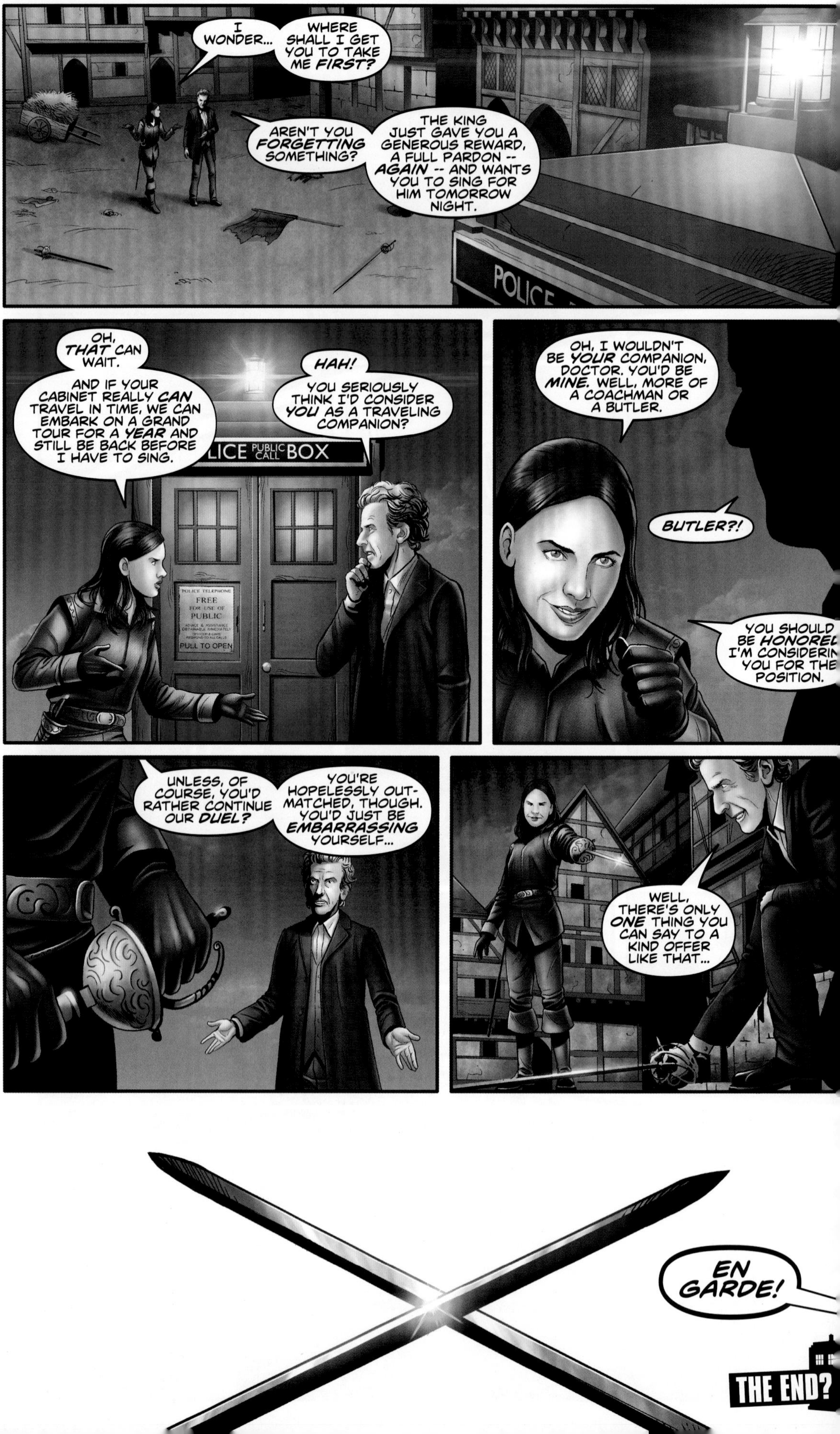

I WONDER...
WHERE SHALL I GET YOU TO TAKE ME *FIRST?*
AREN'T YOU *FORGETTING* SOMETHING?
THE KING JUST GAVE YOU A GENEROUS REWARD, A FULL PARDON -- *AGAIN* -- AND WANTS YOU TO SING FOR HIM TOMORROW NIGHT.
POLICE
OH, *THAT* CAN WAIT.
AND IF YOUR CABINET REALLY *CAN* TRAVEL IN TIME, WE CAN EMBARK ON A GRAND TOUR FOR A *YEAR* AND STILL BE BACK BEFORE I HAVE TO SING.
HAH!
YOU SERIOUSLY THINK I'D CONSIDER *YOU* AS A TRAVELING COMPANION?
LICE PUBLIC CALL BOX
POLICE TELEPHONE
FREE
FOR USE OF
PUBLIC
PULL TO OPEN
OH, I WOULDN'T BE *YOUR* COMPANION, DOCTOR. YOU'D BE *MINE.* WELL, MORE OF A COACHMAN OR A BUTLER.
BUTLER?!
YOU SHOULD BE *HONOREL* I'M CONSIDERIN YOU FOR THE POSITION.
UNLESS, OF COURSE, YOU'D RATHER CONTINUE OUR *DUEL?*
YOU'RE HOPELESSLY OUT-MATCHED, THOUGH. YOU'D JUST BE *EMBARRASSING* YOURSELF...
WELL, THERE'S ONLY *ONE* THING YOU CAN SAY TO A KIND OFFER LIKE THAT...
EN GARDE!
THE END?

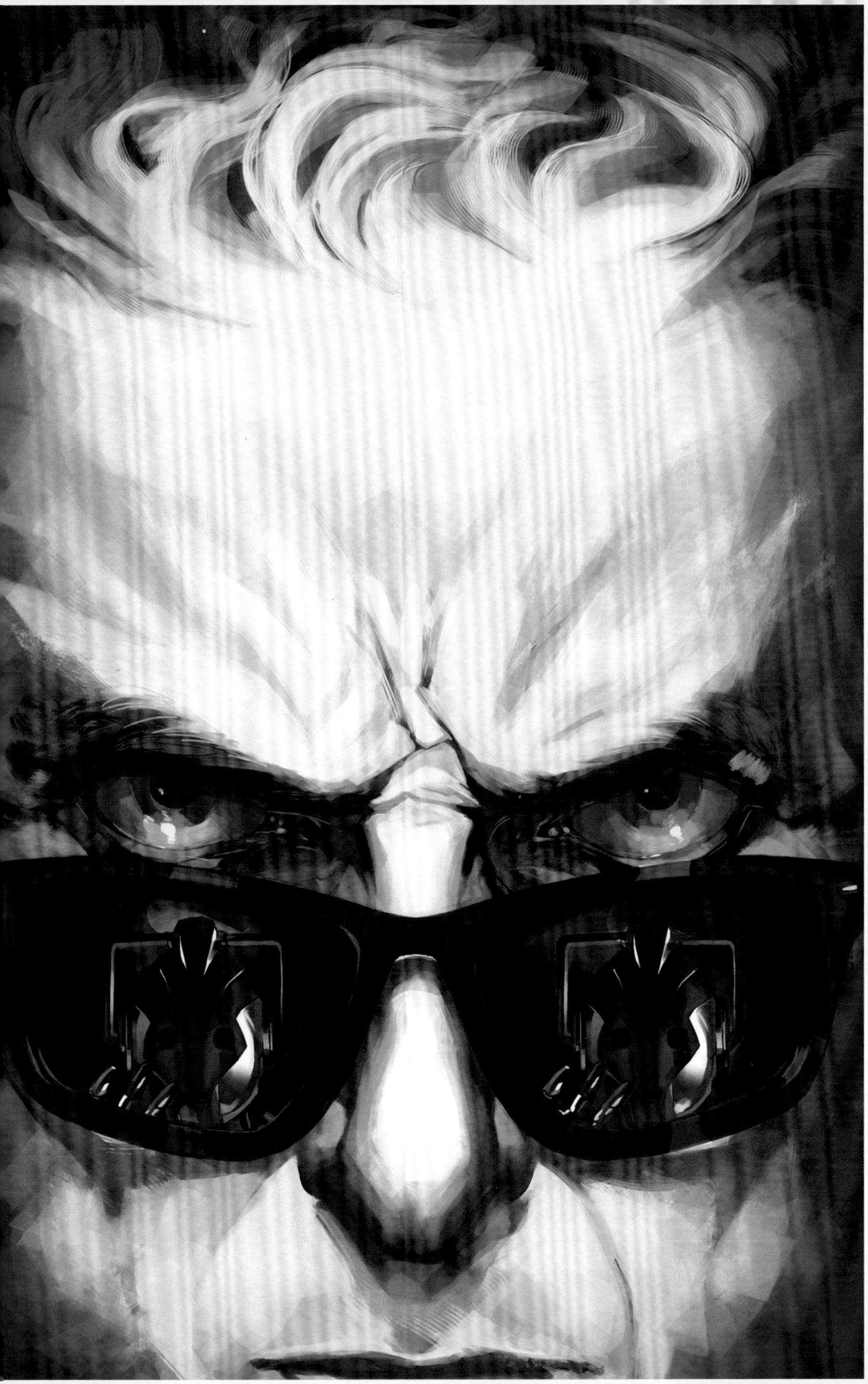

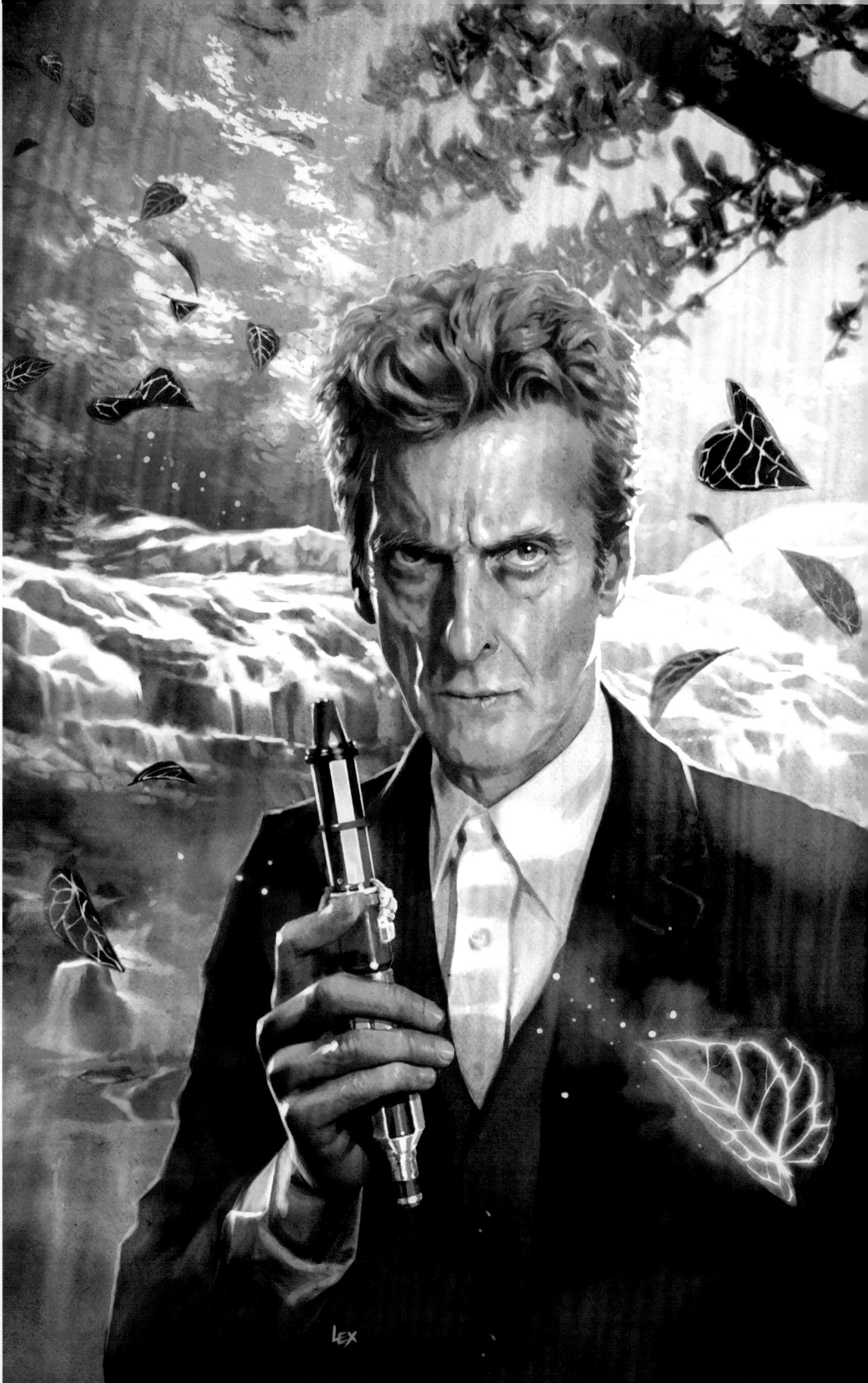
LEX

Cover: ALEX RONA

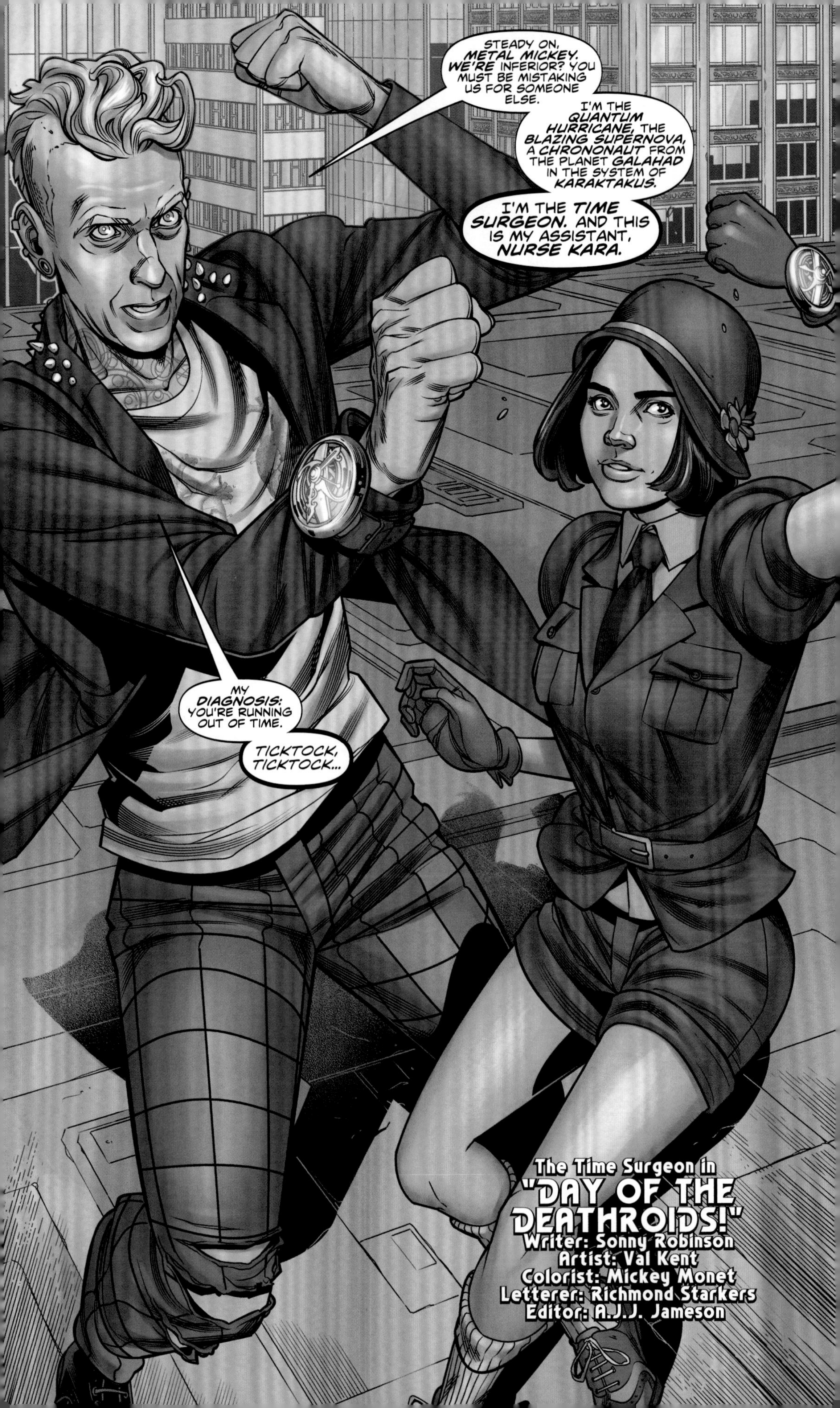
STEADY ON, METAL MICKEY. WE'RE INFERIOR? YOU MUST BE MISTAKING US FOR SOMEONE ELSE.
I'M THE QUANTUM HURRICANE, THE BLAZING SUPERNOVA, A CHRONONAUT FROM THE PLANET GALAHAD IN THE SYSTEM OF KARAKTAKUS.
I'M THE TIME SURGEON. AND THIS IS MY ASSISTANT, NURSE KARA.
MY DIAGNOSIS: YOU'RE RUNNING OUT OF TIME.
TICKTOCK, TICKTOCK...
The Time Surgeon in
"DAY OF THE DEATHROIDS!"
Writer: Sonny Robinson
Artist: Val Kent
Colorist: Mickey Monet
Letterer: Richmond Starkers
Editor: A.J.J. Jameson

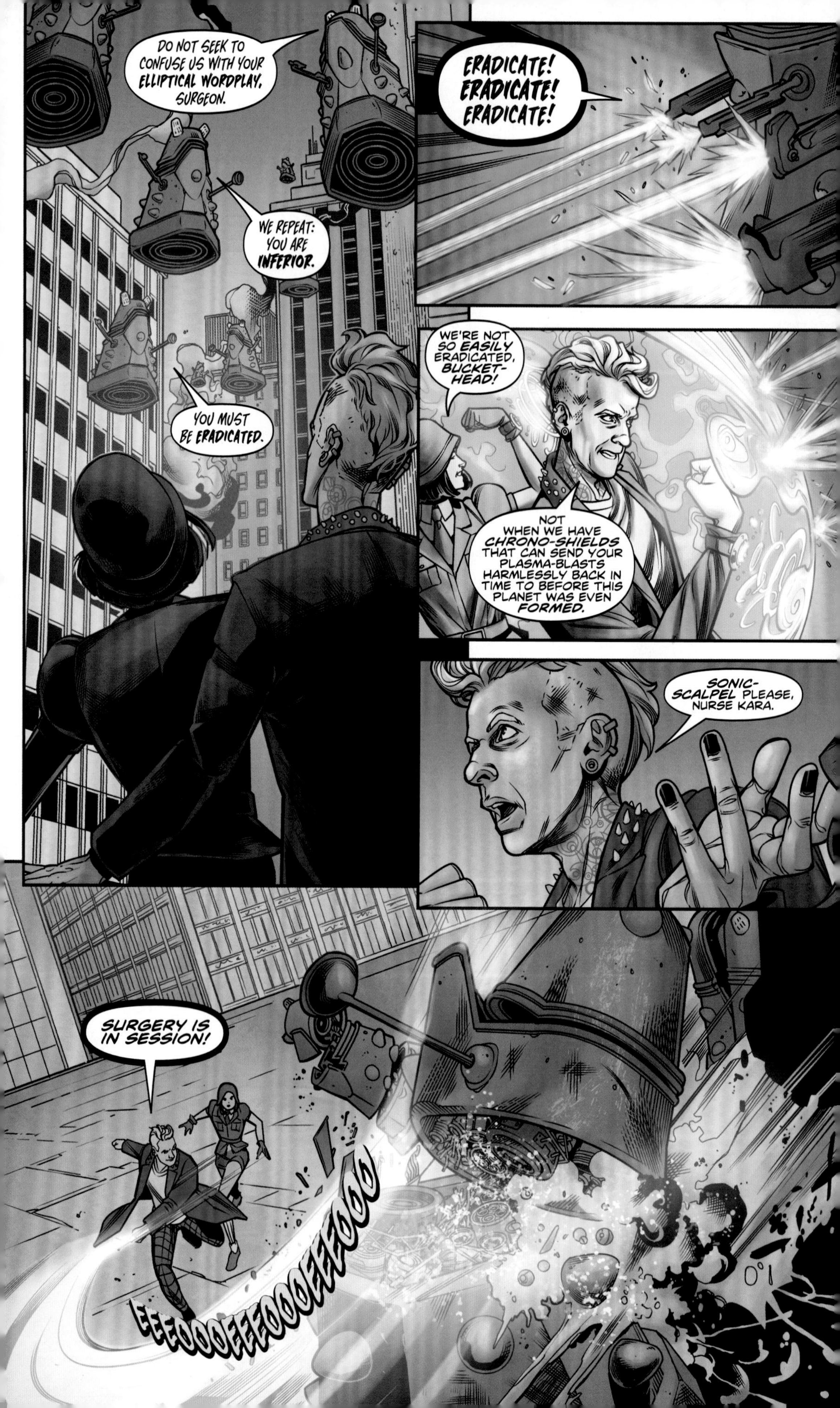
DO NOT SEEK TO CONFUSE US WITH YOUR ELLIPTICAL WORDPLAY, SURGEON.
WE REPEAT: YOU ARE INFERIOR.
YOU MUST BE ERADICATED.
ERADICATE! ERADICATE! ERADICATE!
WE'RE NOT SO EASILY ERADICATED, BUCKET-HEAD!
NOT WHEN WE HAVE CHRONO-SHIELDS THAT CAN SEND YOUR PLASMA-BLASTS HARMLESSLY BACK IN TIME TO BEFORE THIS PLANET WAS EVEN FORMED.
SONIC-SCALPEL PLEASE, NURSE KARA.
SURGERY IS IN SESSION!
EEEOOOEEEOOOEEEOOO

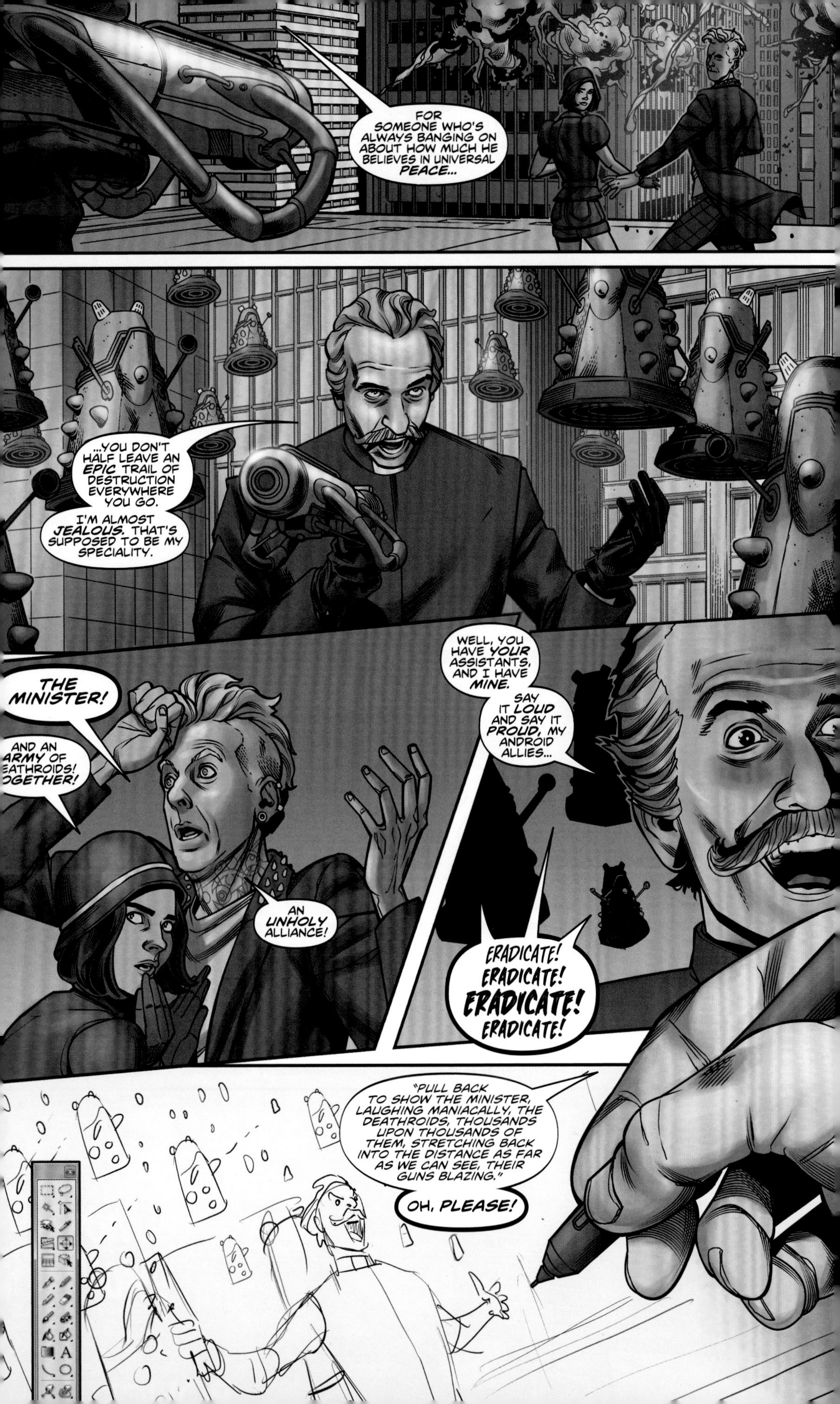
FOR SOMEONE WHO'S ALWAYS BANGING ON ABOUT HOW MUCH HE BELIEVES IN UNIVERSAL PEACE...
...YOU DON'T HALF LEAVE AN EPIC TRAIL OF DESTRUCTION EVERYWHERE YOU GO.
I'M ALMOST JEALOUS. THAT'S SUPPOSED TO BE MY SPECIALITY.
THE MINISTER!
AND AN ARMY OF DEATHROIDS! TOGETHER!
AN UNHOLY ALLIANCE!
WELL, YOU HAVE YOUR ASSISTANTS, AND I HAVE MINE.
SAY IT LOUD AND SAY IT PROUD, MY ANDROID ALLIES...
ERADICATE! ERADICATE! ERADICATE! ERADICATE!
"PULL BACK TO SHOW THE MINISTER, LAUGHING MANIACALLY, THE DEATHROIDS, THOUSANDS UPON THOUSANDS OF THEM, STRETCHING BACK INTO THE DISTANCE AS FAR AS WE CAN SEE, THEIR GUNS BLAZING."
OH, PLEASE!

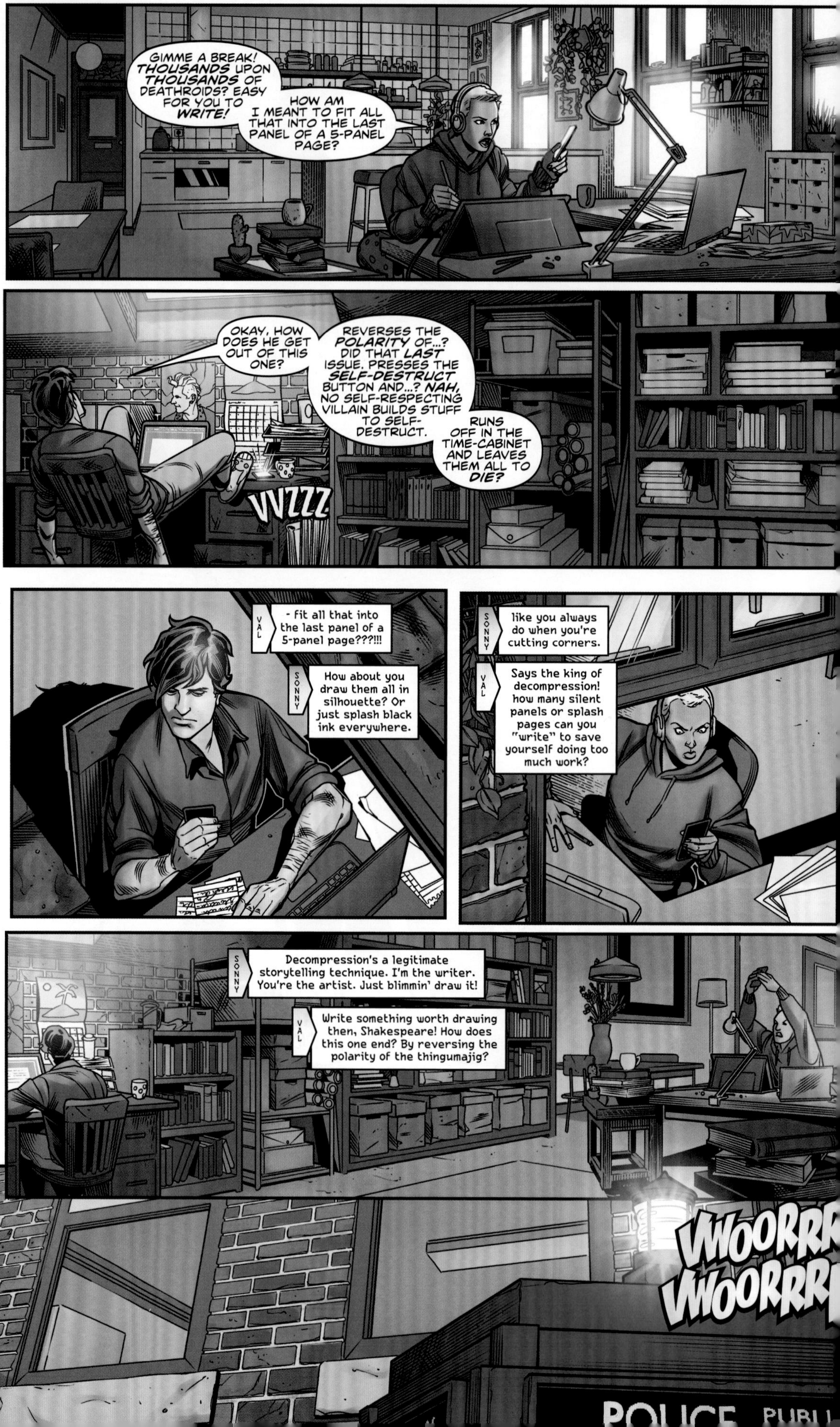

GIMME A BREAK! THOUSANDS UPON THOUSANDS OF DEATHROIDS? EASY FOR YOU TO WRITE!
HOW AM I MEANT TO FIT ALL THAT INTO THE LAST PANEL OF A 5-PANEL PAGE?
OKAY, HOW DOES HE GET OUT OF THIS ONE?
REVERSES THE POLARITY OF...? DID THAT LAST ISSUE. PRESSES THE SELF-DESTRUCT BUTTON AND...? NAH, NO SELF-RESPECTING VILLAIN BUILDS STUFF TO SELF-DESTRUCT.
RUNS OFF IN THE TIME-CABINET AND LEAVES THEM ALL TO DIE?
VVZZZ
VAL
- fit all that into the last panel of a 5-panel page???!!!
SONNY
How about you draw them all in silhouette? Or just splash black ink everywhere.
SONNY
like you always do when you're cutting corners.
VAL
Says the king of decompression! how many silent panels or splash pages can you "write" to save yourself doing too much work?
SONNY
Decompression's a legitimate storytelling technique. I'm the writer. You're the artist. Just blimmin' draw it!
VAL
Write something worth drawing then, Shakespeare! How does this one end? By reversing the polarity of the thingumajig?
VWOORRR
VWOORRR
POLICE PUBLI

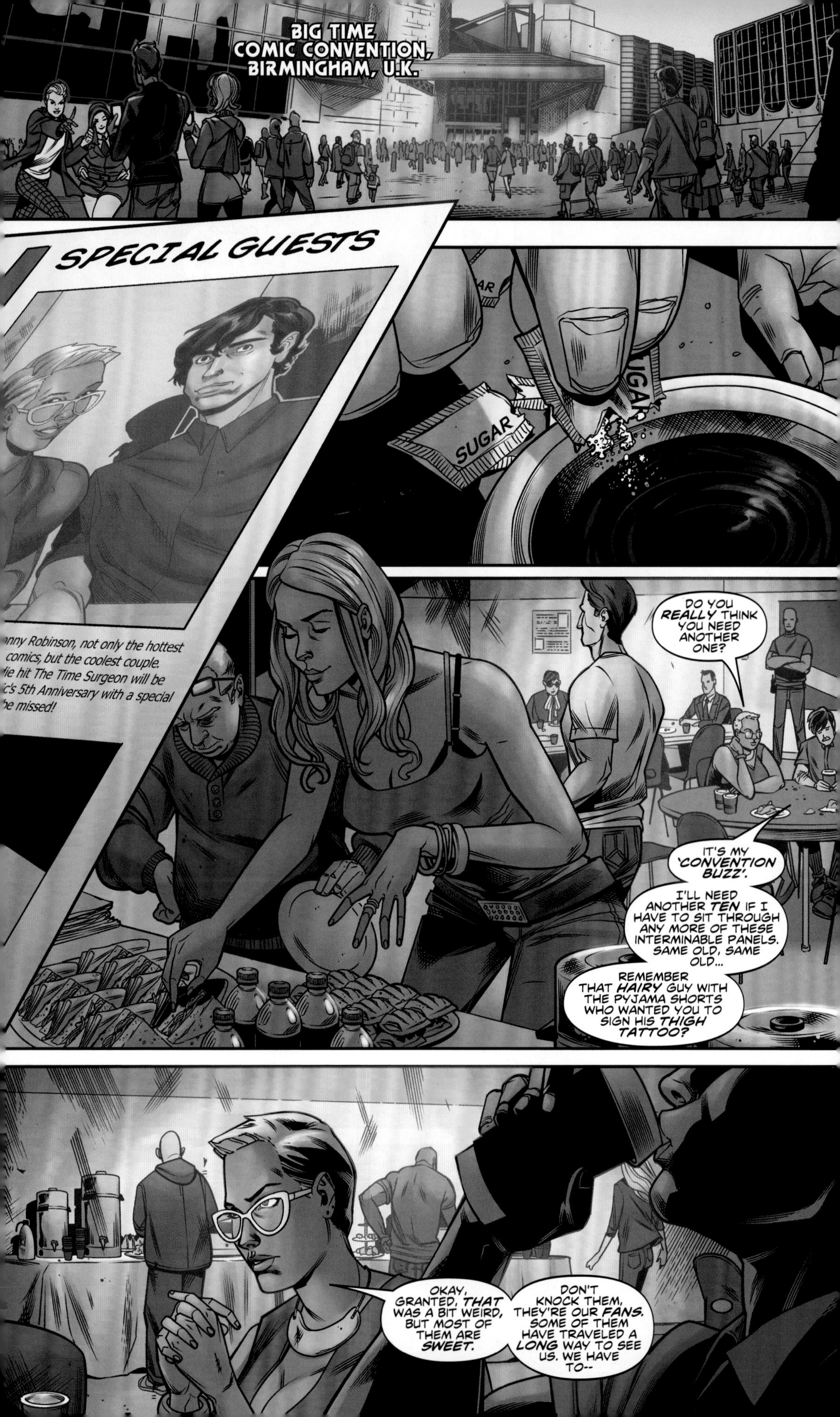
BIG TIME COMIC CONVENTION, BIRMINGHAM, U.K.
SPECIAL GUESTS
onny Robinson, not only the hottest
comics, but the coolest couple.
ie hit The Time Surgeon will be
c's 5th Anniversary with a special
be missed!
SUGAR
SUGAR
DO YOU REALLY THINK YOU NEED ANOTHER ONE?
IT'S MY 'CONVENTION BUZZ'.
I'LL NEED ANOTHER TEN IF I HAVE TO SIT THROUGH ANY MORE OF THESE INTERMINABLE PANELS. SAME OLD, SAME OLD...
REMEMBER THAT HAIRY GUY WITH THE PYJAMA SHORTS WHO WANTED YOU TO SIGN HIS THIGH TATTOO?
OKAY, GRANTED, THAT WAS A BIT WEIRD, BUT MOST OF THEM ARE SWEET.
DON'T KNOCK THEM, THEY'RE OUR FANS. SOME OF THEM HAVE TRAVELED A LONG WAY TO SEE US. WE HAVE TO--

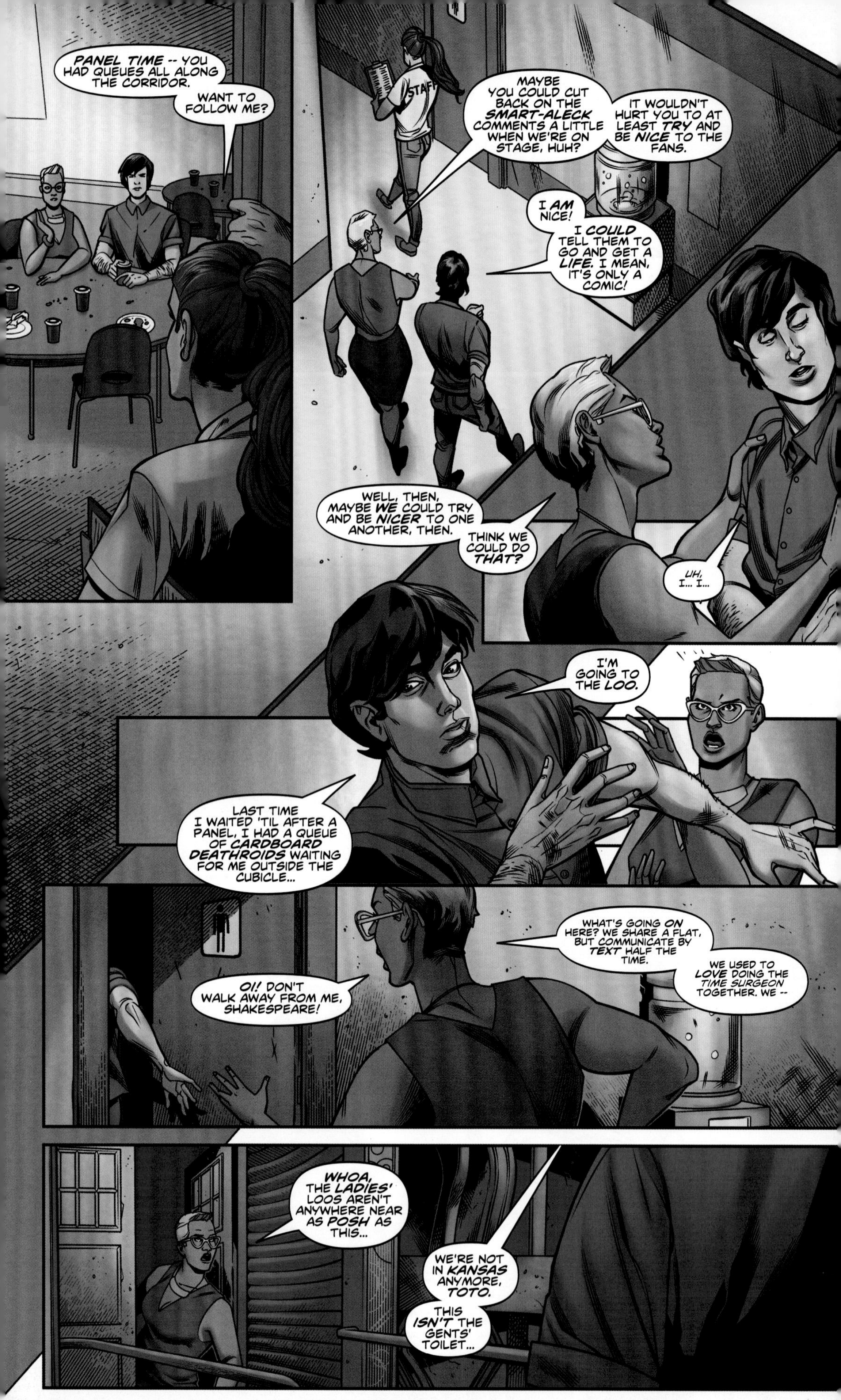
PANEL TIME -- YOU HAD QUEUES ALL ALONG THE CORRIDOR.
WANT TO FOLLOW ME?
STAFF
MAYBE YOU COULD CUT BACK ON THE SMART-ALECK COMMENTS A LITTLE WHEN WE'RE ON STAGE, HUH?
IT WOULDN'T HURT YOU TO AT LEAST TRY AND BE NICE TO THE FANS.
I AM NICE!
I COULD TELL THEM TO GO AND GET A LIFE. I MEAN, IT'S ONLY A COMIC!
WELL, THEN, MAYBE WE COULD TRY AND BE NICER TO ONE ANOTHER, THEN.
THINK WE COULD DO THAT?
UH, I... I...
I'M GOING TO THE LOO.
LAST TIME I WAITED 'TIL AFTER A PANEL, I HAD A QUEUE OF CARDBOARD DEATHROIDS WAITING FOR ME OUTSIDE THE CUBICLE...
WHAT'S GOING ON HERE? WE SHARE A FLAT, BUT COMMUNICATE BY TEXT HALF THE TIME.
WE USED TO LOVE DOING THE TIME SURGEON TOGETHER. WE --
OI! DON'T WALK AWAY FROM ME, SHAKESPEARE!
WHOA, THE LADIES' LOOS AREN'T ANYWHERE NEAR AS POSH AS THIS...
WE'RE NOT IN KANSAS ANYMORE, TOTO.
THIS ISN'T THE GENTS' TOILET...

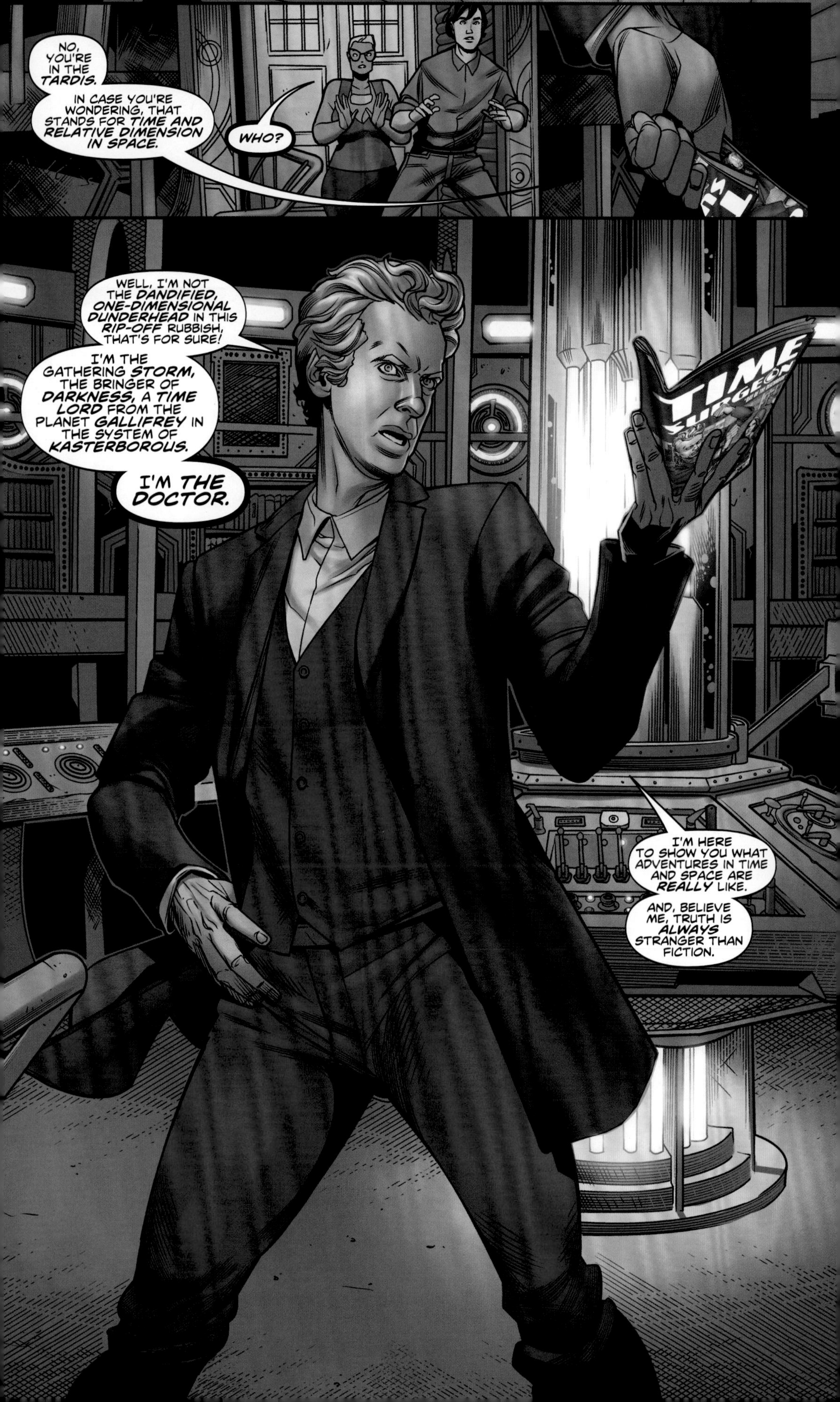
NO, YOU'RE IN THE TARDIS.
IN CASE YOU'RE WONDERING, THAT STANDS FOR TIME AND RELATIVE DIMENSION IN SPACE.
WHO?
WELL, I'M NOT THE DANDIFIED, ONE-DIMENSIONAL DUNDERHEAD IN THIS RIP-OFF RUBBISH, THAT'S FOR SURE!
I'M THE GATHERING STORM, THE BRINGER OF DARKNESS, A TIME LORD FROM THE PLANET GALLIFREY IN THE SYSTEM OF KASTERBOROUS.
I'M THE DOCTOR.
TIME SURGEON
I'M HERE TO SHOW YOU WHAT ADVENTURES IN TIME AND SPACE ARE REALLY LIKE.
AND, BELIEVE ME, TRUTH IS ALWAYS STRANGER THAN FICTION.

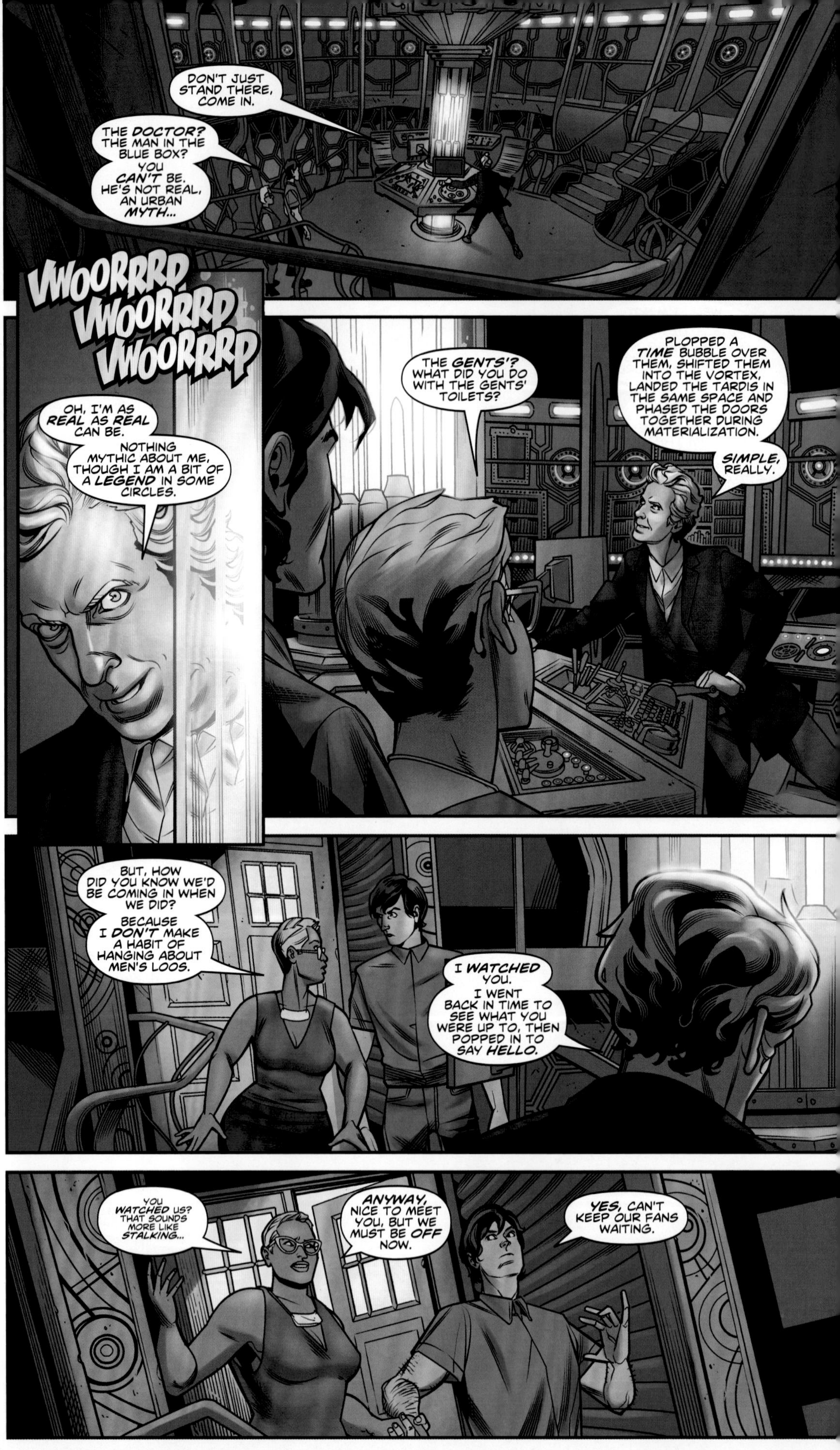
DON'T JUST STAND THERE, COME IN.
THE DOCTOR? THE MAN IN THE BLUE BOX? YOU CAN'T BE. HE'S NOT REAL, AN URBAN MYTH...
VWOORRRP VWOORRRP VWOORRRP
OH, I'M AS REAL AS REAL CAN BE.
NOTHING MYTHIC ABOUT ME, THOUGH I AM A BIT OF A LEGEND IN SOME CIRCLES.
THE GENTS'? WHAT DID YOU DO WITH THE GENTS' TOILETS?
PLOPPED A TIME BUBBLE OVER THEM, SHIFTED THEM INTO THE VORTEX, LANDED THE TARDIS IN THE SAME SPACE AND PHASED THE DOORS TOGETHER DURING MATERIALIZATION.
SIMPLE, REALLY.
BUT, HOW DID YOU KNOW WE'D BE COMING IN WHEN WE DID?
BECAUSE I DON'T MAKE A HABIT OF HANGING ABOUT MEN'S LOOS.
I WATCHED YOU.
I WENT BACK IN TIME TO SEE WHAT YOU WERE UP TO, THEN POPPED IN TO SAY HELLO.
YOU WATCHED US? THAT SOUNDS MORE LIKE STALKING...
ANYWAY, NICE TO MEET YOU, BUT WE MUST BE OFF NOW.
YES, CAN'T KEEP OUR FANS WAITING.

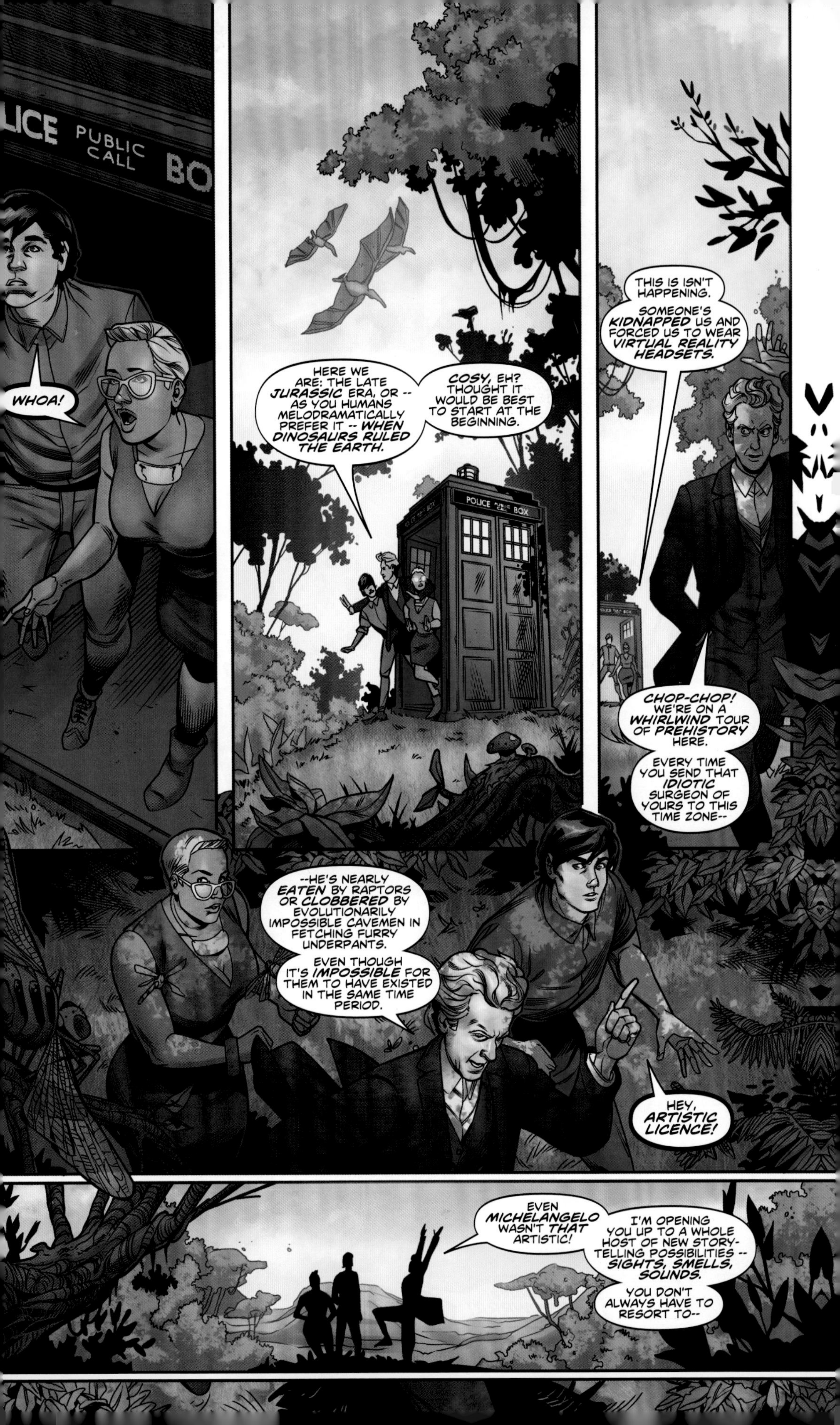
LICE PUBLIC CALL BO
WHOA!
HERE WE ARE: THE LATE JURASSIC ERA, OR -- AS YOU HUMANS MELODRAMATICALLY PREFER IT -- WHEN DINOSAURS RULED THE EARTH.
COSY, EH? THOUGHT IT WOULD BE BEST TO START AT THE BEGINNING.
POLICE PUBLIC CALL BOX
THIS IS ISN'T HAPPENING.
SOMEONE'S KIDNAPPED US AND FORCED US TO WEAR VIRTUAL REALITY HEADSETS.
CHOP-CHOP! WE'RE ON A WHIRLWIND TOUR OF PREHISTORY HERE.
EVERY TIME YOU SEND THAT IDIOTIC SURGEON OF YOURS TO THIS TIME ZONE--
--HE'S NEARLY EATEN BY RAPTORS OR CLOBBERED BY EVOLUTIONARILY IMPOSSIBLE CAVEMEN IN FETCHING FURRY UNDERPANTS.
EVEN THOUGH IT'S IMPOSSIBLE FOR THEM TO HAVE EXISTED IN THE SAME TIME PERIOD.
HEY, ARTISTIC LICENCE!
EVEN MICHELANGELO WASN'T THAT ARTISTIC!
I'M OPENING YOU UP TO A WHOLE HOST OF NEW STORY-TELLING POSSIBILITIES -- SIGHTS, SMELLS, SOUNDS.
YOU DON'T ALWAYS HAVE TO RESORT TO--

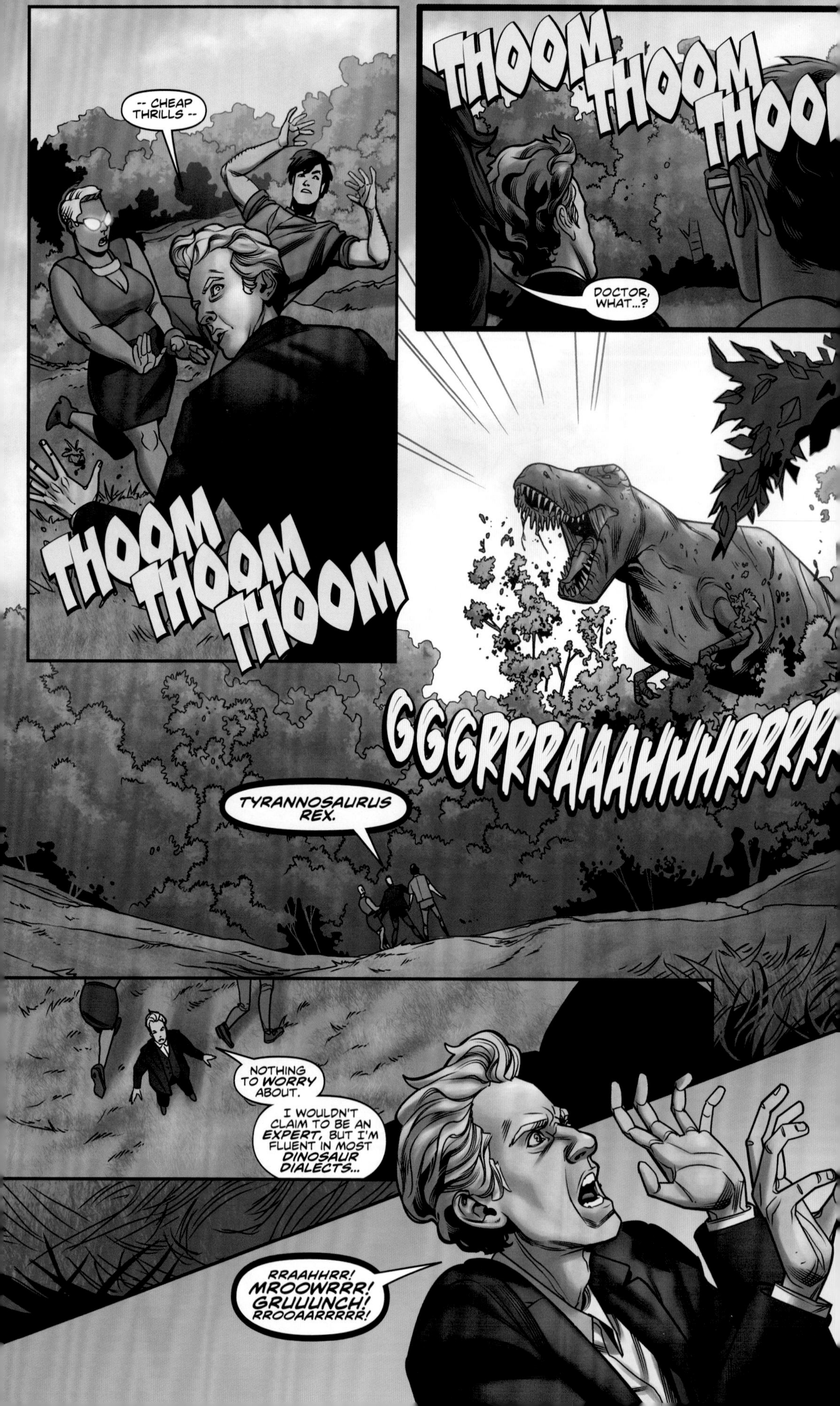
-- CHEAP THRILLS --
THOOM THOOM THOOM
THOOM THOOM THOO
DOCTOR, WHAT...?
GGGRRRAAAHHHRRR
TYRANNOSAURUS REX.
NOTHING TO WORRY ABOUT.
I WOULDN'T CLAIM TO BE AN EXPERT, BUT I'M FLUENT IN MOST DINOSAUR DIALECTS...
RRAAHHRR! MROOWRRR! GRUUUNCH! RROOAARRRRR!

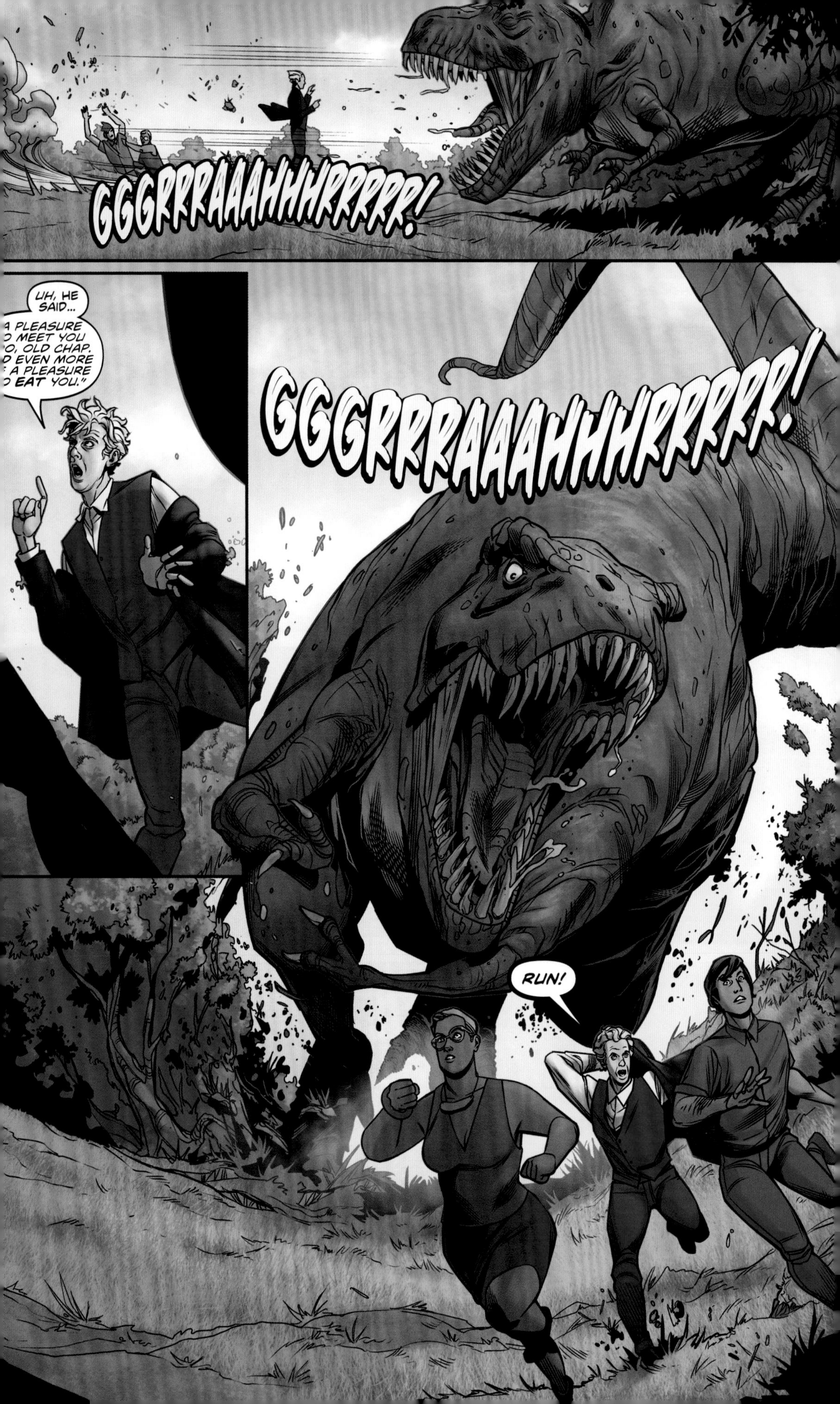
GGGRRRAAAHHHRRRRR!
UH, HE SAID...
A PLEASURE O MEET YOU O, OLD CHAP. D EVEN MORE F A PLEASURE O EAT YOU."
GGGRRRAAAHHHRRRRR!
RUN!

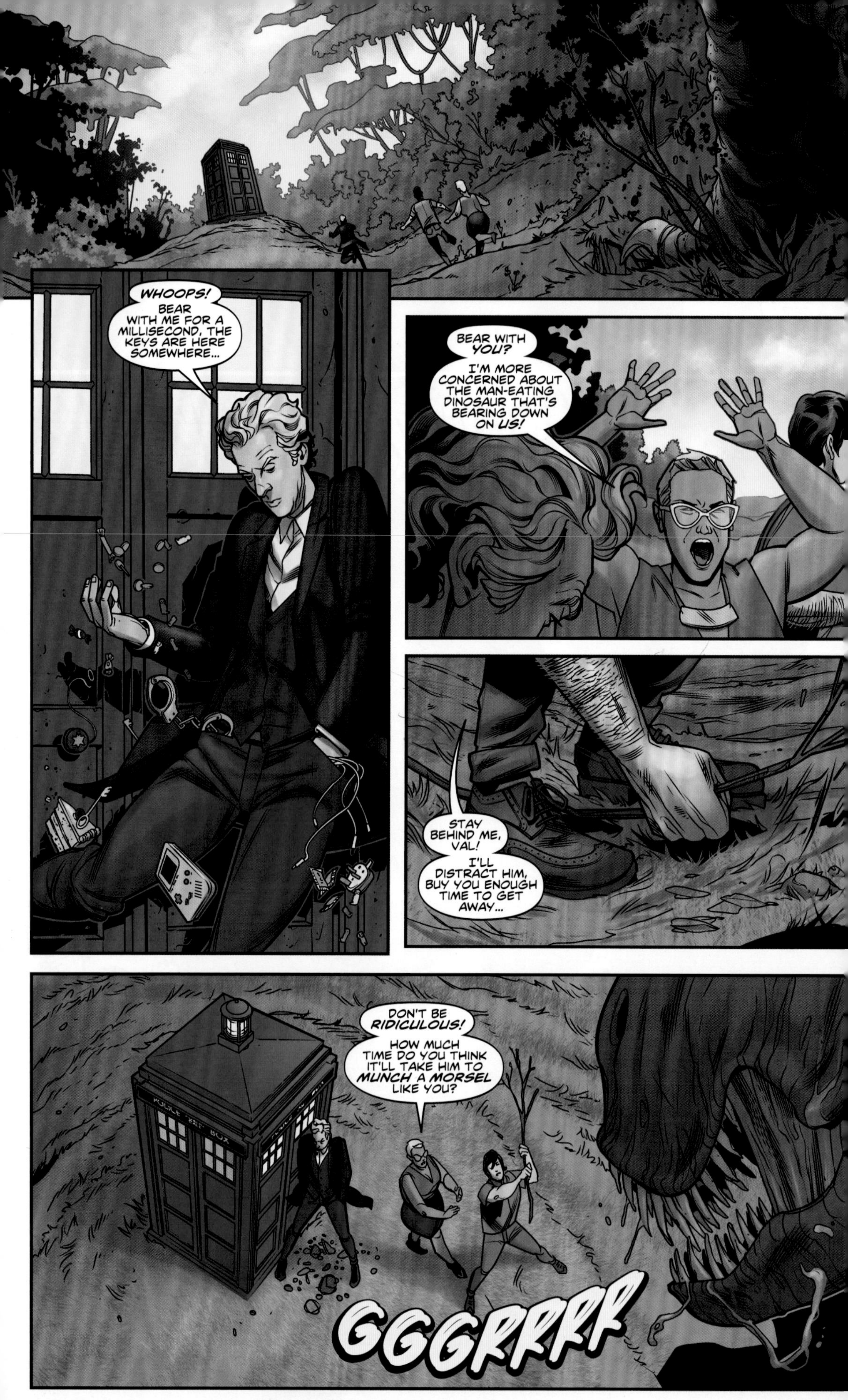
WHOOPS!
BEAR WITH ME FOR A MILLISECOND, THE KEYS ARE HERE SOMEWHERE...
BEAR WITH YOU?
I'M MORE CONCERNED ABOUT THE MAN-EATING DINOSAUR THAT'S BEARING DOWN ON US!
STAY BEHIND ME, VAL!
I'LL DISTRACT HIM, BUY YOU ENOUGH TIME TO GET AWAY...
DON'T BE RIDICULOUS!
HOW MUCH TIME DO YOU THINK IT'LL TAKE HIM TO MUNCH A MORSEL LIKE YOU?
POLICE BOX
GGGRRRR

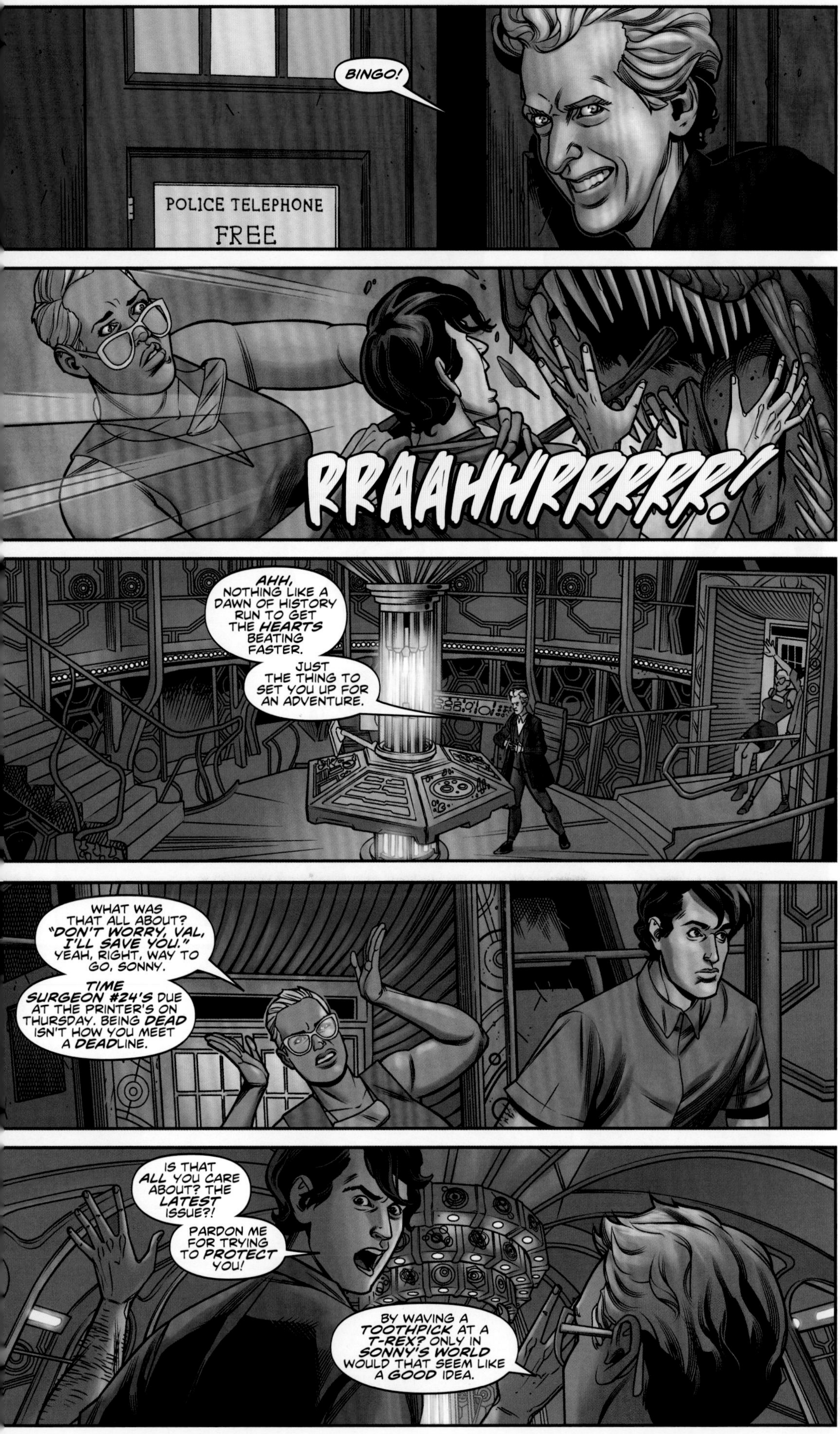

BINGO!
POLICE TELEPHONE
FREE
RRAAHHRRRRR!
AHH, NOTHING LIKE A DAWN OF HISTORY RUN TO GET THE HEARTS BEATING FASTER.
JUST THE THING TO SET YOU UP FOR AN ADVENTURE.
WHAT WAS THAT ALL ABOUT? "DON'T WORRY, VAL, I'LL SAVE YOU." YEAH, RIGHT, WAY TO GO, SONNY.
TIME SURGEON #24'S DUE AT THE PRINTER'S ON THURSDAY. BEING DEAD ISN'T HOW YOU MEET A DEADLINE.
IS THAT ALL YOU CARE ABOUT? THE LATEST ISSUE?!
PARDON ME FOR TRYING TO PROTECT YOU!
BY WAVING A TOOTHPICK AT A T-REX? ONLY IN SONNY'S WORLD WOULD THAT SEEM LIKE A GOOD IDEA.

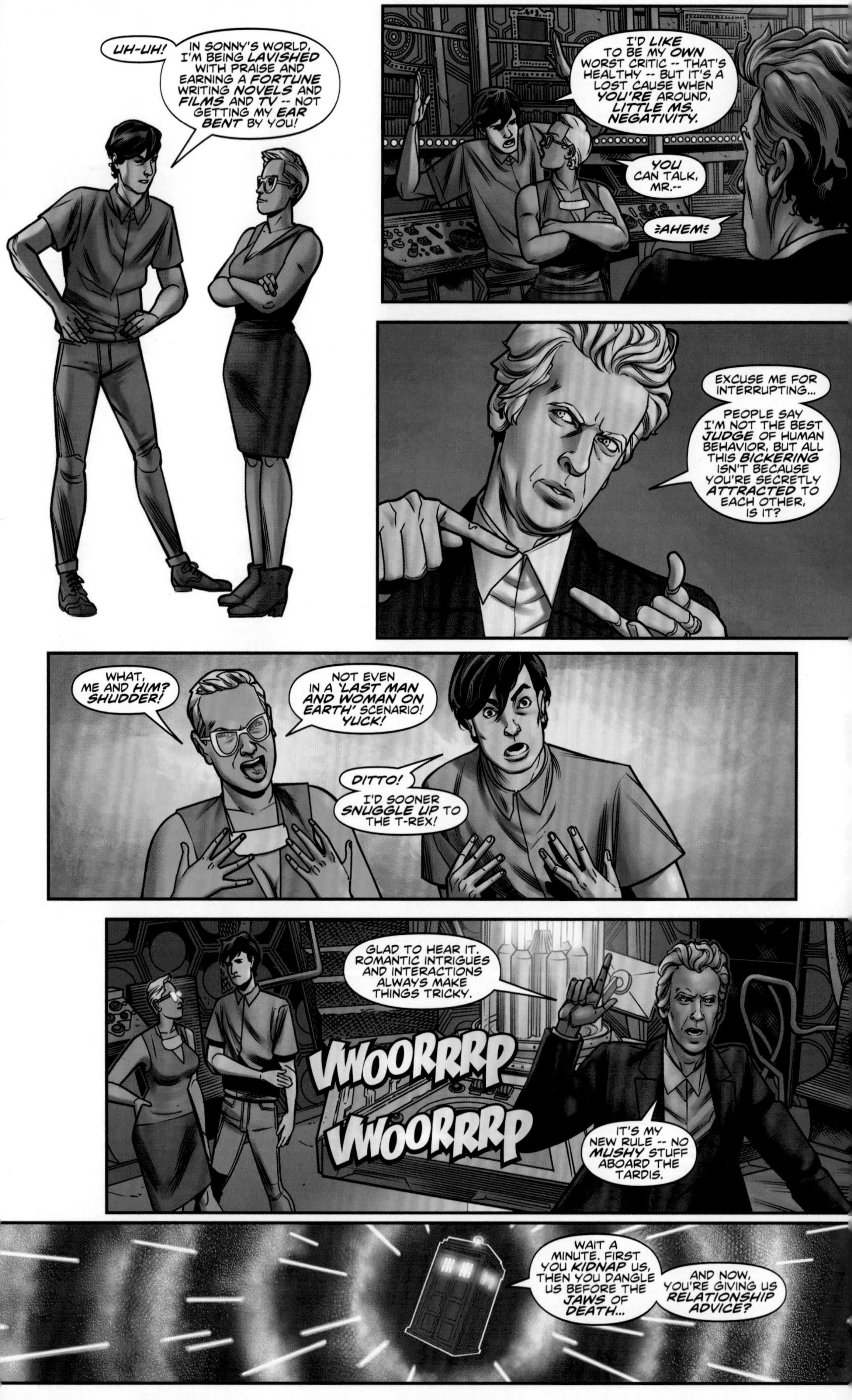

UH-UH!
IN SONNY'S WORLD, I'M BEING LAVISHED WITH PRAISE AND EARNING A FORTUNE WRITING NOVELS AND FILMS AND TV -- NOT GETTING MY EAR BENT BY YOU!
I'D LIKE TO BE MY OWN WORST CRITIC -- THAT'S HEALTHY -- BUT IT'S A LOST CAUSE WHEN YOU'RE AROUND, LITTLE MS. NEGATIVITY.
YOU CAN TALK, MR.--
AHEM
EXCUSE ME FOR INTERRUPTING...
PEOPLE SAY I'M NOT THE BEST JUDGE OF HUMAN BEHAVIOR, BUT ALL THIS BICKERING ISN'T BECAUSE YOU'RE SECRETLY ATTRACTED TO EACH OTHER, IS IT?
WHAT, ME AND HIM? SHUDDER!
NOT EVEN IN A 'LAST MAN AND WOMAN ON EARTH' SCENARIO! YUCK!
DITTO!
I'D SOONER SNUGGLE UP TO THE T-REX!
GLAD TO HEAR IT. ROMANTIC INTRIGUES AND INTERACTIONS ALWAYS MAKE THINGS TRICKY.
VWOORRRP
VWOORRRP
IT'S MY NEW RULE -- NO MUSHY STUFF ABOARD THE TARDIS.
WAIT A MINUTE. FIRST YOU KIDNAP US, THEN YOU DANGLE US BEFORE THE JAWS OF DEATH...
AND NOW, YOU'RE GIVING US RELATIONSHIP ADVICE?

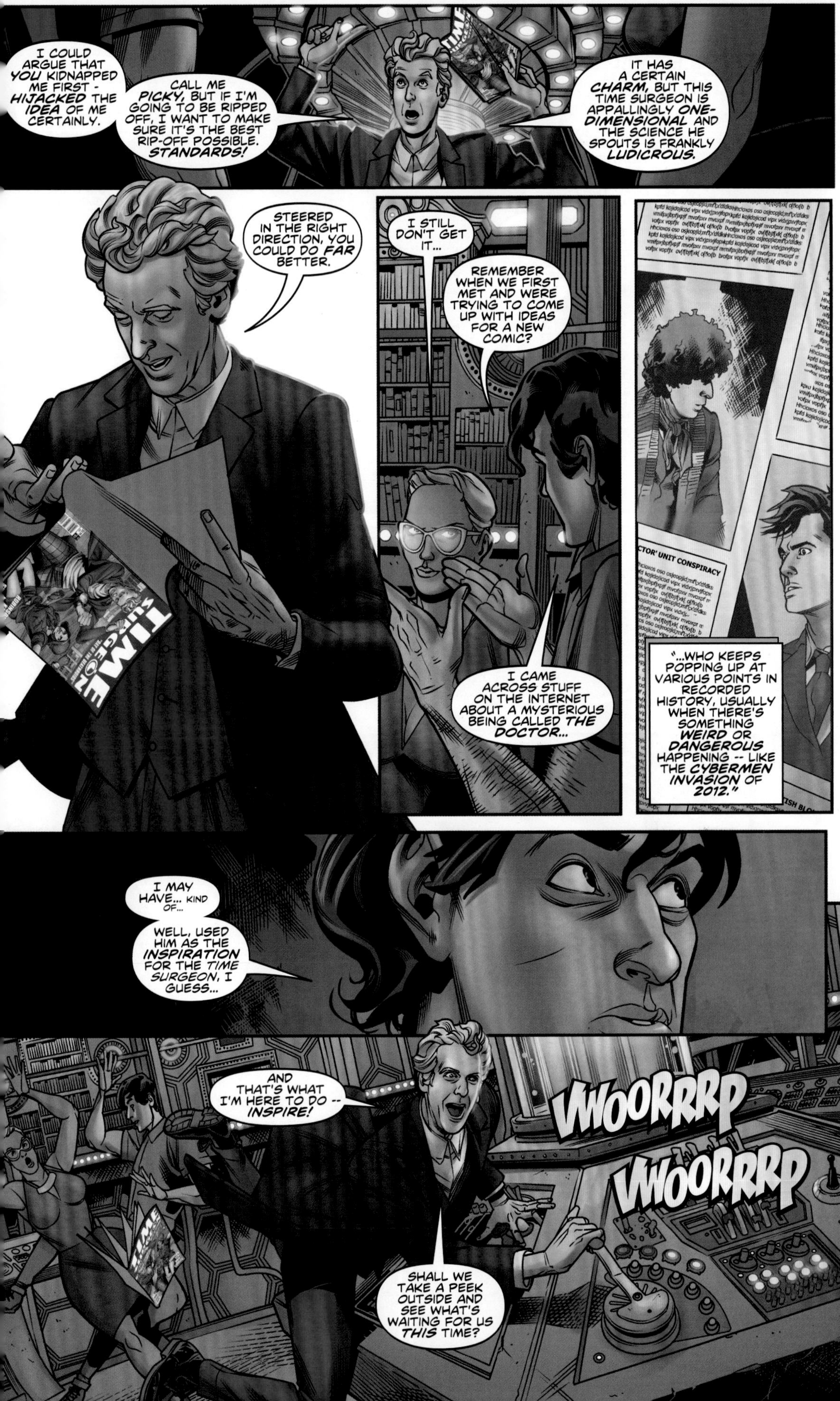
I COULD ARGUE THAT YOU KIDNAPPED ME FIRST - HIJACKED THE IDEA OF ME CERTAINLY.
CALL ME PICKY, BUT IF I'M GOING TO BE RIPPED OFF, I WANT TO MAKE SURE IT'S THE BEST RIP-OFF POSSIBLE. STANDARDS!
IT HAS A CERTAIN CHARM, BUT THIS TIME SURGEON IS APPALLINGLY ONE-DIMENSIONAL AND THE SCIENCE HE SPOUTS IS FRANKLY LUDICROUS.
STEERED IN THE RIGHT DIRECTION, YOU COULD DO FAR BETTER.
TIME SURGEON
I STILL DON'T GET IT...
REMEMBER WHEN WE FIRST MET AND WERE TRYING TO COME UP WITH IDEAS FOR A NEW COMIC?
I CAME ACROSS STUFF ON THE INTERNET ABOUT A MYSTERIOUS BEING CALLED THE DOCTOR...
CTOR' UNIT CONSPIRACY
"...WHO KEEPS POPPING UP AT VARIOUS POINTS IN RECORDED HISTORY, USUALLY WHEN THERE'S SOMETHING WEIRD OR DANGEROUS HAPPENING -- LIKE THE CYBERMEN INVASION OF 2012."
I MAY HAVE... KIND OF...
WELL, USED HIM AS THE INSPIRATION FOR THE TIME SURGEON, I GUESS...
AND THAT'S WHAT I'M HERE TO DO -- INSPIRE!
VWOORRRP
VWOORRRP
SHALL WE TAKE A PEEK OUTSIDE AND SEE WHAT'S WAITING FOR US THIS TIME?

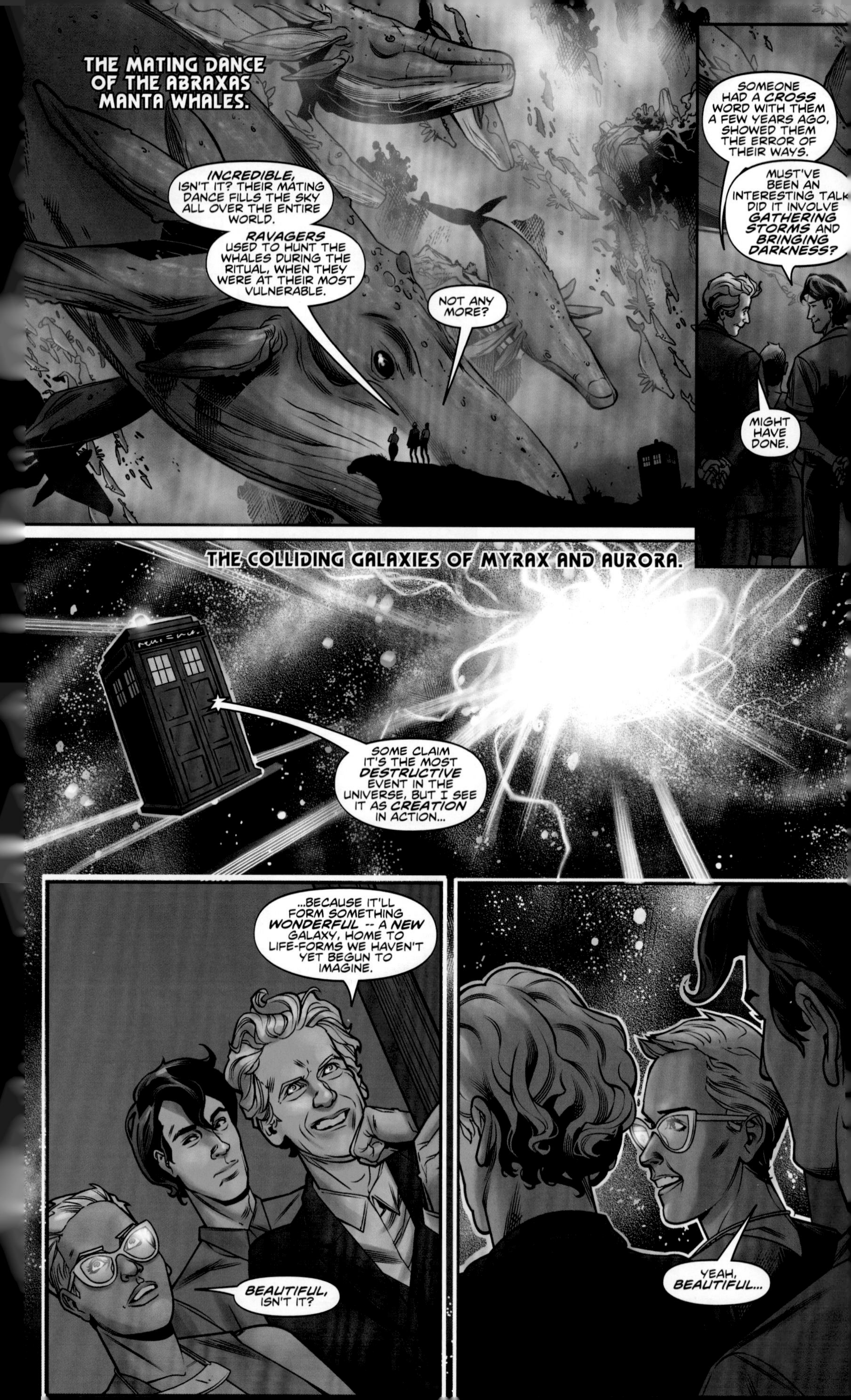
THE MATING DANCE OF THE ABRAXAS MANTA WHALES.
INCREDIBLE, ISN'T IT? THEIR MATING DANCE FILLS THE SKY ALL OVER THE ENTIRE WORLD.
RAVAGERS USED TO HUNT THE WHALES DURING THE RITUAL, WHEN THEY WERE AT THEIR MOST VULNERABLE.
NOT ANY MORE?
SOMEONE HAD A CROSS WORD WITH THEM A FEW YEARS AGO, SHOWED THEM THE ERROR OF THEIR WAYS.
MUST'VE BEEN AN INTERESTING TALK. DID IT INVOLVE GATHERING STORMS AND BRINGING DARKNESS?
MIGHT HAVE DONE.
THE COLLIDING GALAXIES OF MYRAX AND AURORA.
SOME CLAIM IT'S THE MOST DESTRUCTIVE EVENT IN THE UNIVERSE, BUT I SEE IT AS CREATION IN ACTION...
...BECAUSE IT'LL FORM SOMETHING WONDERFUL -- A NEW GALAXY, HOME TO LIFE-FORMS WE HAVEN'T YET BEGUN TO IMAGINE.
BEAUTIFUL, ISN'T IT?
YEAH, BEAUTIFUL...

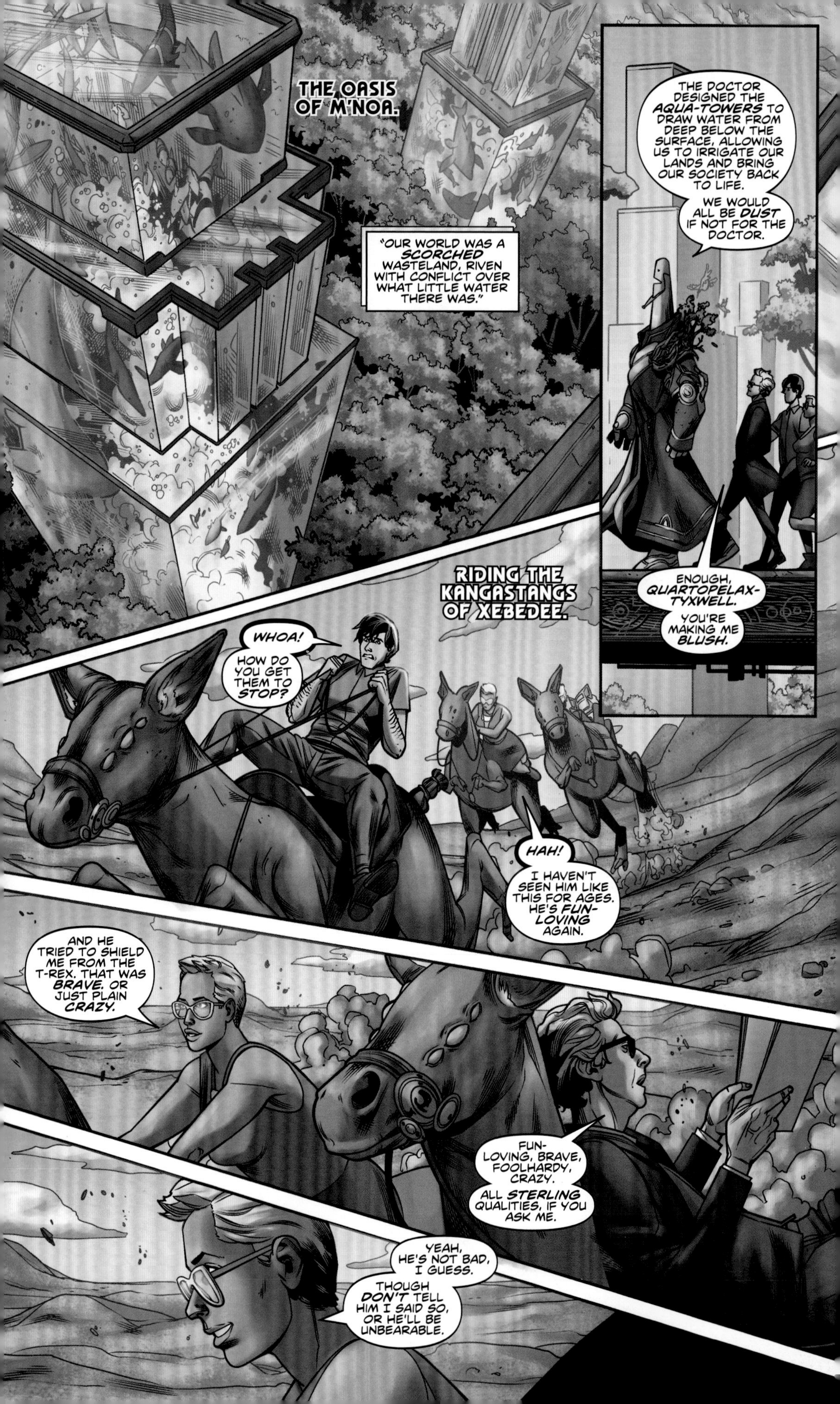

THE OASIS OF M'NOA.
"OUR WORLD WAS A SCORCHED WASTELAND, RIVEN WITH CONFLICT OVER WHAT LITTLE WATER THERE WAS."
THE DOCTOR DESIGNED THE AQUA-TOWERS TO DRAW WATER FROM DEEP BELOW THE SURFACE, ALLOWING US TO IRRIGATE OUR LANDS AND BRING OUR SOCIETY BACK TO LIFE.
WE WOULD ALL BE DUST IF NOT FOR THE DOCTOR.
ENOUGH, QUARTOPELAX-TYXWELL.
YOU'RE MAKING ME BLUSH.
RIDING THE KANGASTANGS OF XEBEDEE.
WHOA!
HOW DO YOU GET THEM TO STOP?
HAH!
I HAVEN'T SEEN HIM LIKE THIS FOR AGES. HE'S FUN-LOVING AGAIN.
AND HE TRIED TO SHIELD ME FROM THE T-REX. THAT WAS BRAVE. OR JUST PLAIN CRAZY.
FUN-LOVING, BRAVE, FOOLHARDY, CRAZY.
ALL STERLING QUALITIES, IF YOU ASK ME.
YEAH, HE'S NOT BAD, I GUESS.
THOUGH DON'T TELL HIM I SAID SO, OR HE'LL BE UNBEARABLE.

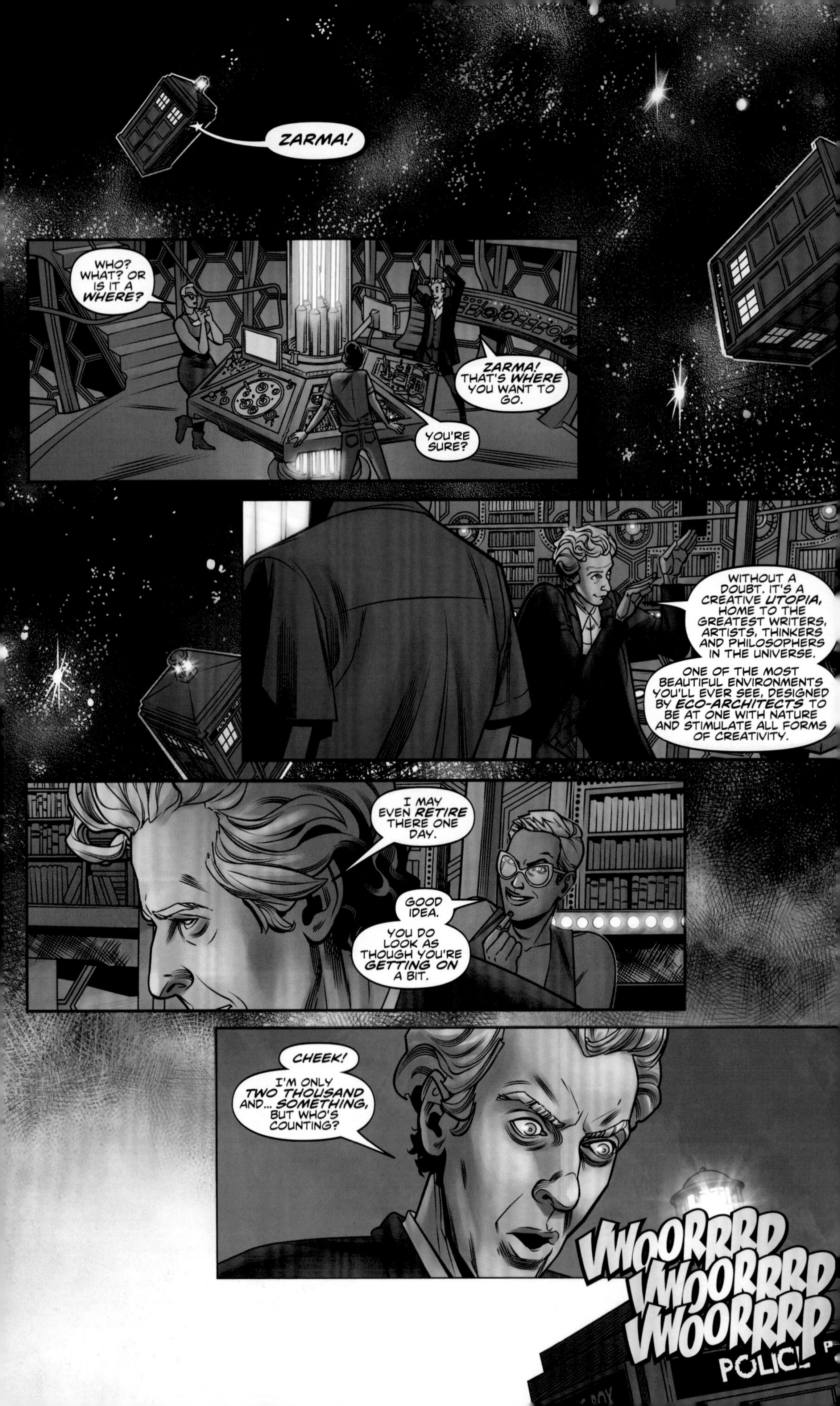
ZARMA!
WHO? WHAT? OR IS IT A WHERE?
ZARMA! THAT'S WHERE YOU WANT TO GO.
YOU'RE SURE?
WITHOUT A DOUBT. IT'S A CREATIVE UTOPIA, HOME TO THE GREATEST WRITERS, ARTISTS, THINKERS AND PHILOSOPHERS IN THE UNIVERSE.
ONE OF THE MOST BEAUTIFUL ENVIRONMENTS YOU'LL EVER SEE, DESIGNED BY ECO-ARCHITECTS TO BE AT ONE WITH NATURE AND STIMULATE ALL FORMS OF CREATIVITY.
I MAY EVEN RETIRE THERE ONE DAY.
GOOD IDEA.
YOU DO LOOK AS THOUGH YOU'RE GETTING ON A BIT.
CHEEK!
I'M ONLY TWO THOUSAND AND... SOMETHING, BUT WHO'S COUNTING?
VWOORRRD VWOORRRD VWOORRRP
POLICE

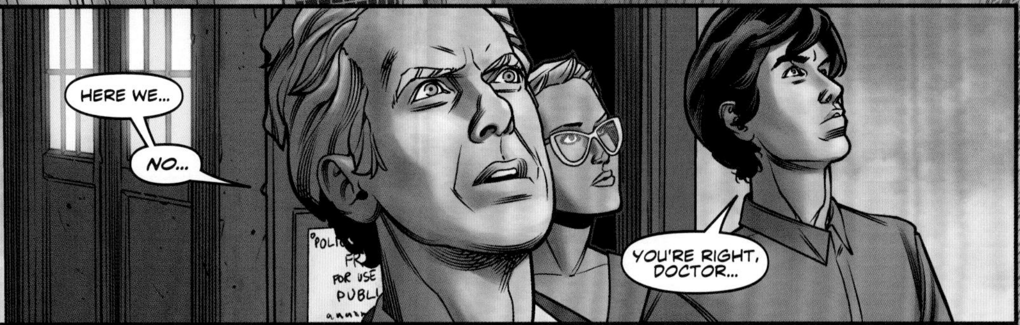
HERE WE...
NO...
YOU'RE RIGHT, DOCTOR...

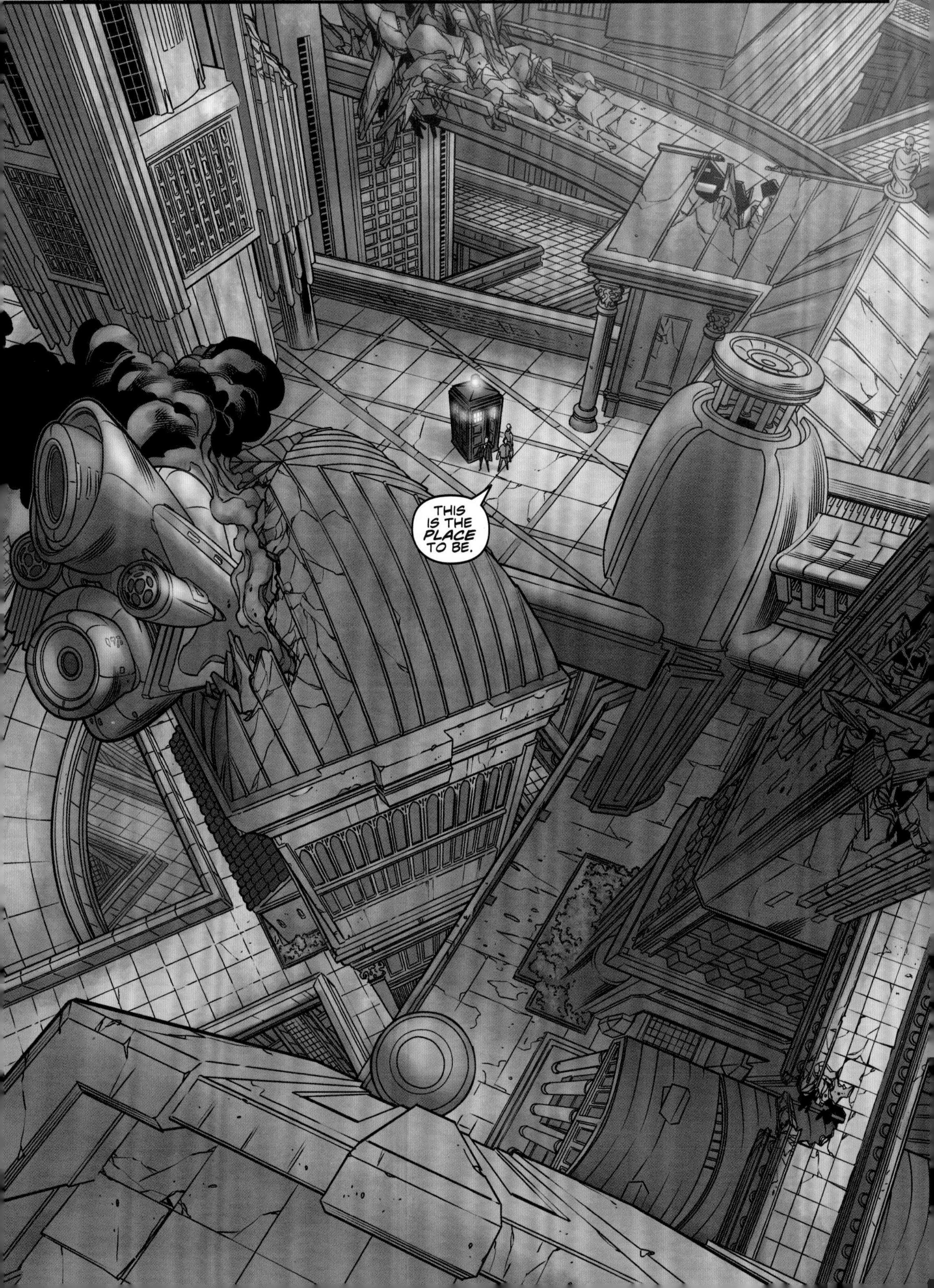
THIS IS THE PLACE TO BE.

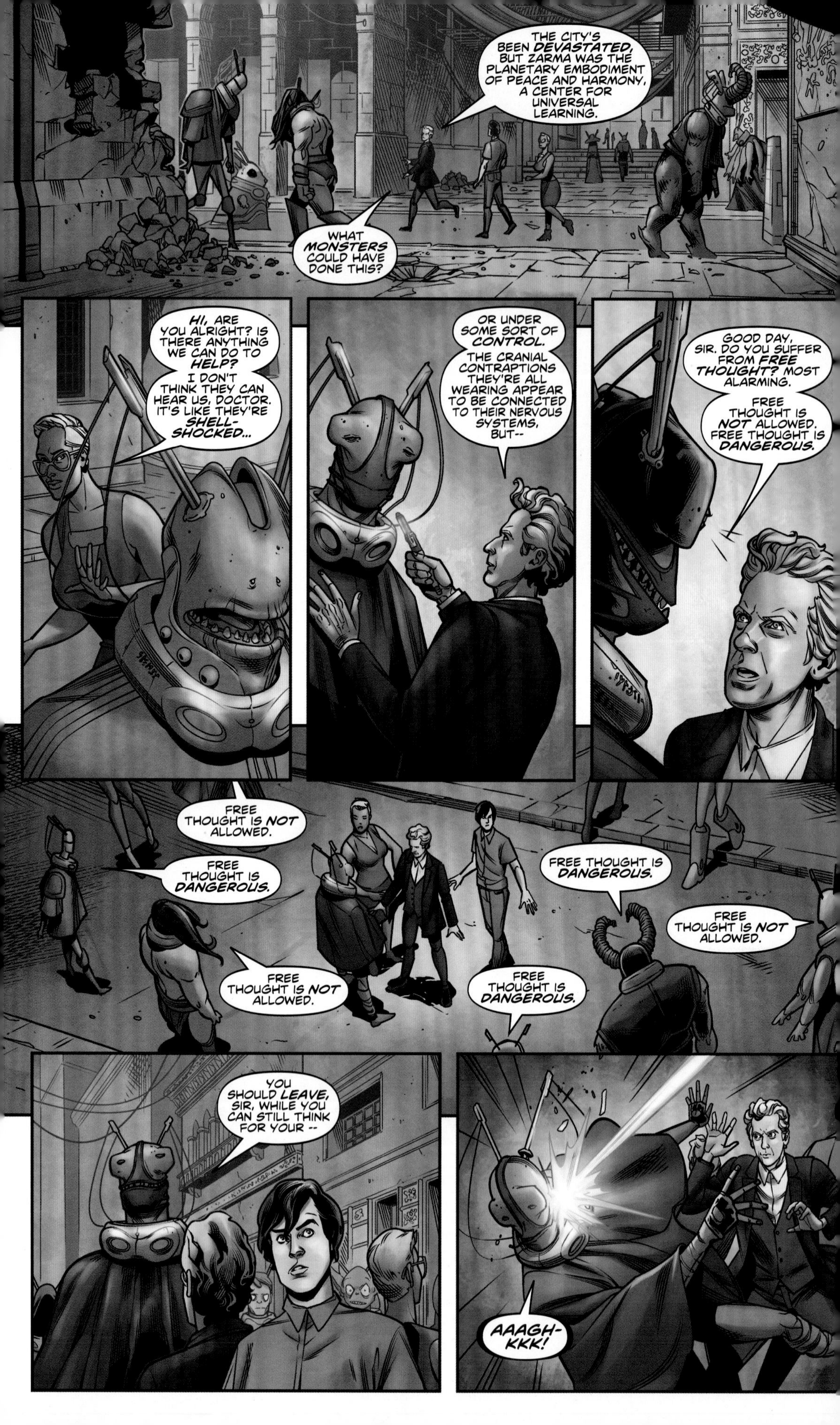
THE CITY'S BEEN DEVASTATED, BUT ZARMA WAS THE PLANETARY EMBODIMENT OF PEACE AND HARMONY, A CENTER FOR UNIVERSAL LEARNING.
WHAT MONSTERS COULD HAVE DONE THIS?
HI, ARE YOU ALRIGHT? IS THERE ANYTHING WE CAN DO TO HELP?
I DON'T THINK THEY CAN HEAR US, DOCTOR. IT'S LIKE THEY'RE SHELL-SHOCKED...
OR UNDER SOME SORT OF CONTROL.
THE CRANIAL CONTRAPTIONS THEY'RE ALL WEARING APPEAR TO BE CONNECTED TO THEIR NERVOUS SYSTEMS, BUT--
GOOD DAY, SIR. DO YOU SUFFER FROM FREE THOUGHT? MOST ALARMING.
FREE THOUGHT IS NOT ALLOWED. FREE THOUGHT IS DANGEROUS.
FREE THOUGHT IS NOT ALLOWED.
FREE THOUGHT IS DANGEROUS.
FREE THOUGHT IS DANGEROUS.
FREE THOUGHT IS NOT ALLOWED.
FREE THOUGHT IS NOT ALLOWED.
FREE THOUGHT IS DANGEROUS.
YOU SHOULD LEAVE, SIR, WHILE YOU CAN STILL THINK FOR YOUR --
AAAGH-KKK!

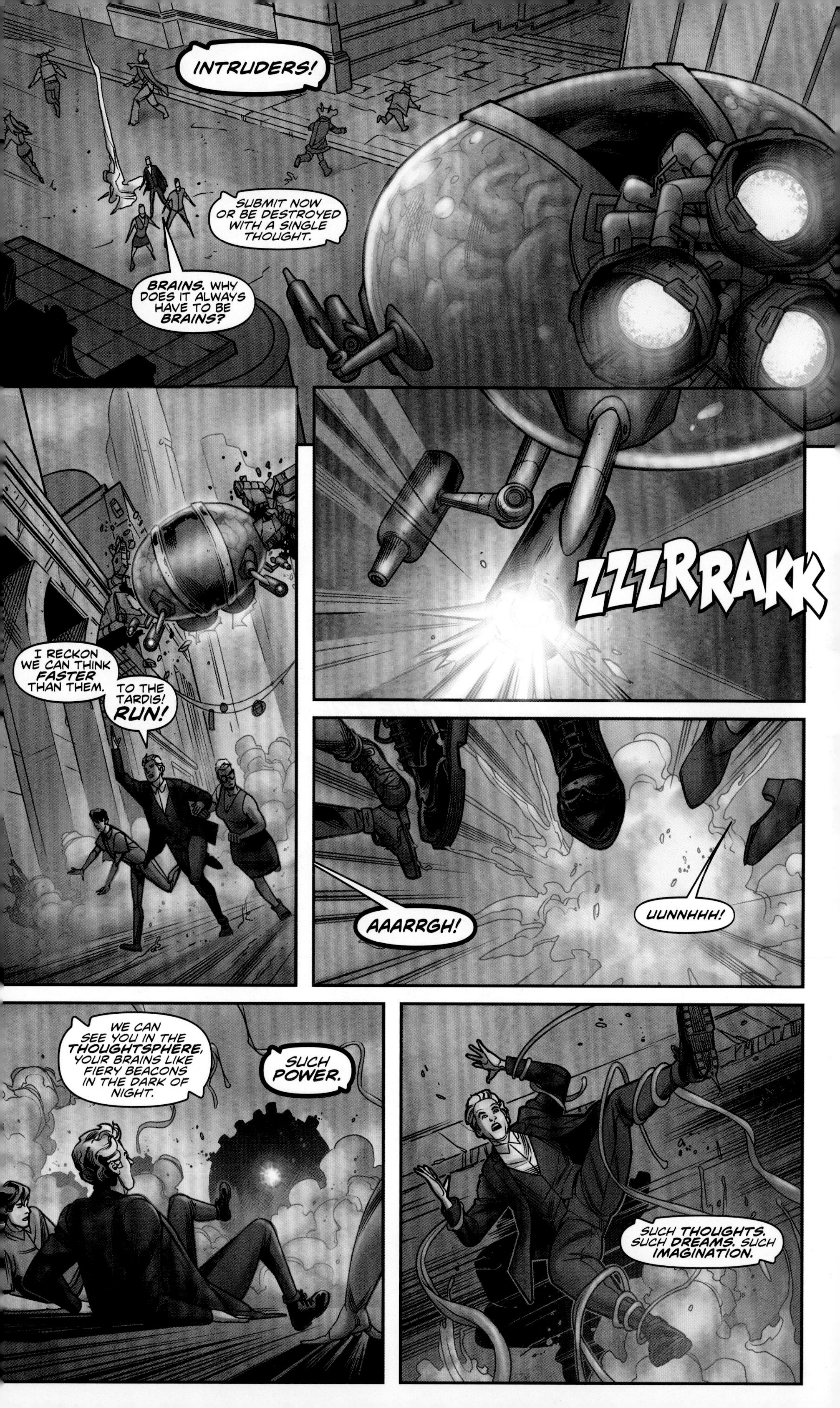

INTRUDERS!
SUBMIT NOW OR BE DESTROYED WITH A SINGLE THOUGHT.
BRAINS. WHY DOES IT ALWAYS HAVE TO BE BRAINS?
I RECKON WE CAN THINK FASTER THAN THEM.
TO THE TARDIS! RUN!
ZZZRRAKK
AAARRGH!
UUNNHHH!
WE CAN SEE YOU IN THE THOUGHTSPHERE, YOUR BRAINS LIKE FIERY BEACONS IN THE DARK OF NIGHT.
SUCH POWER.
SUCH THOUGHTS. SUCH DREAMS. SUCH IMAGINATION.

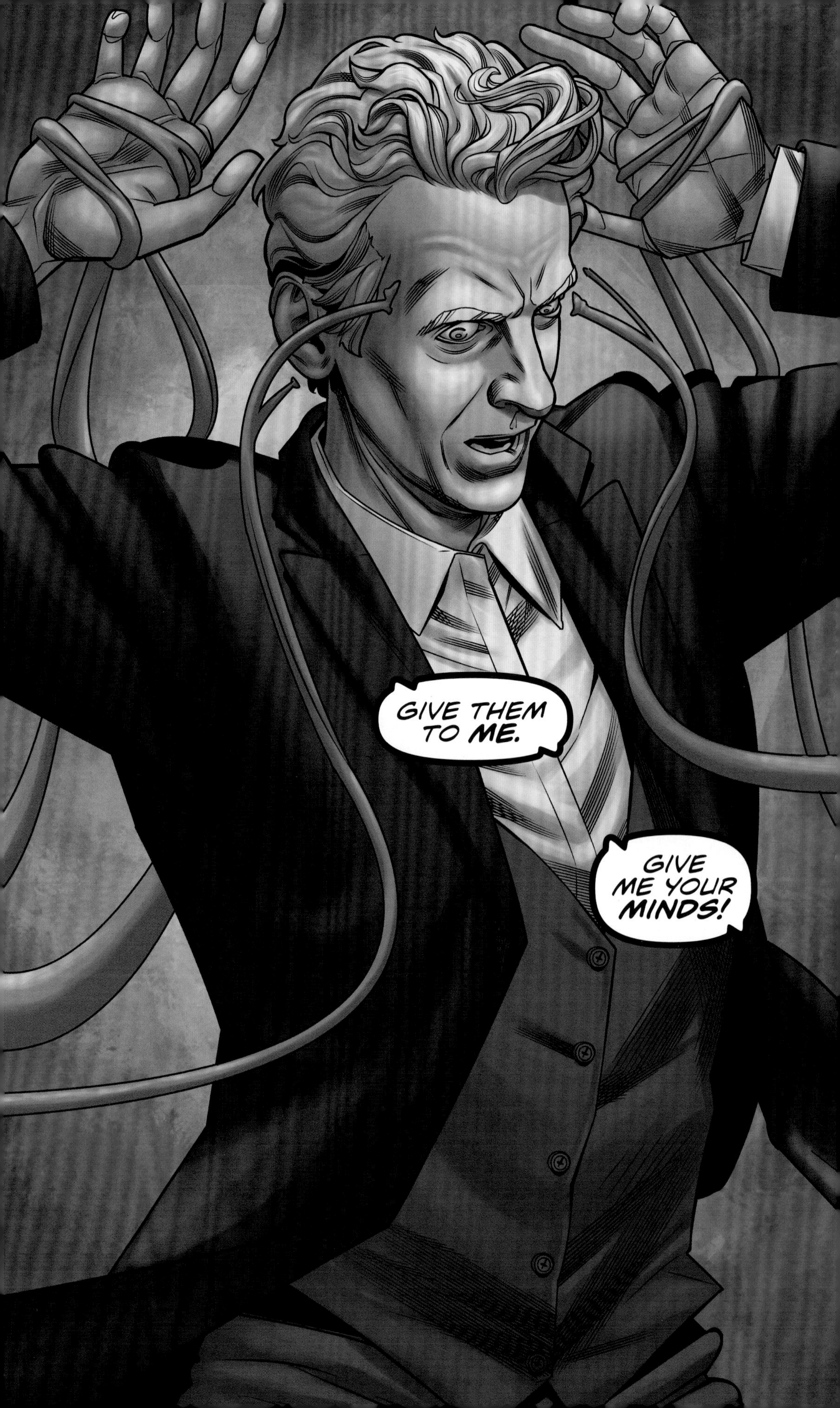
GIVE THEM TO ME.
GIVE ME YOUR MINDS!

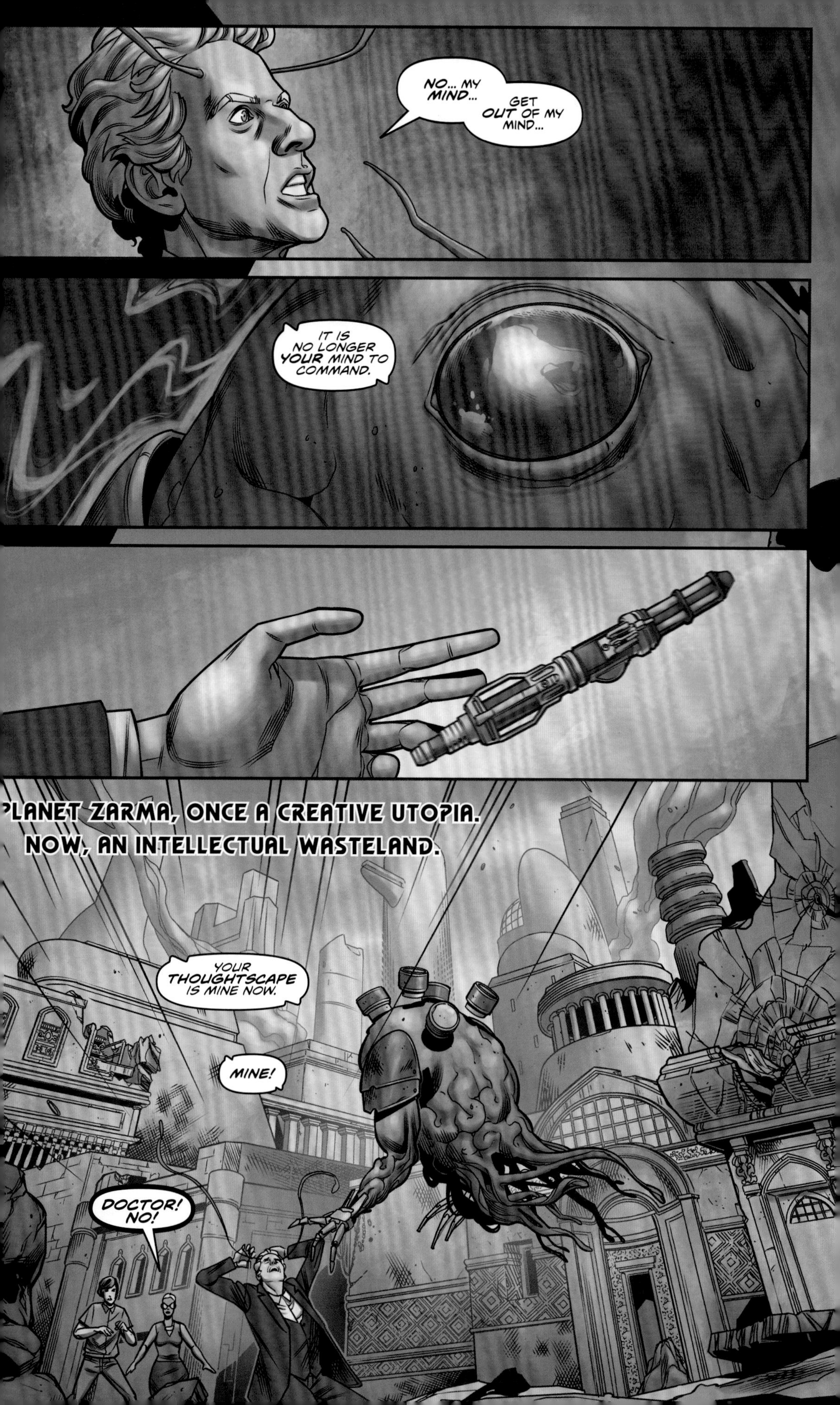
NO... MY MIND...
GET OUT OF MY MIND...
IT IS NO LONGER YOUR MIND TO COMMAND.
PLANET ZARMA, ONCE A CREATIVE UTOPIA.
NOW, AN INTELLECTUAL WASTELAND.
YOUR THOUGHTSCAPE IS MINE NOW.
MINE!
DOCTOR! NO!

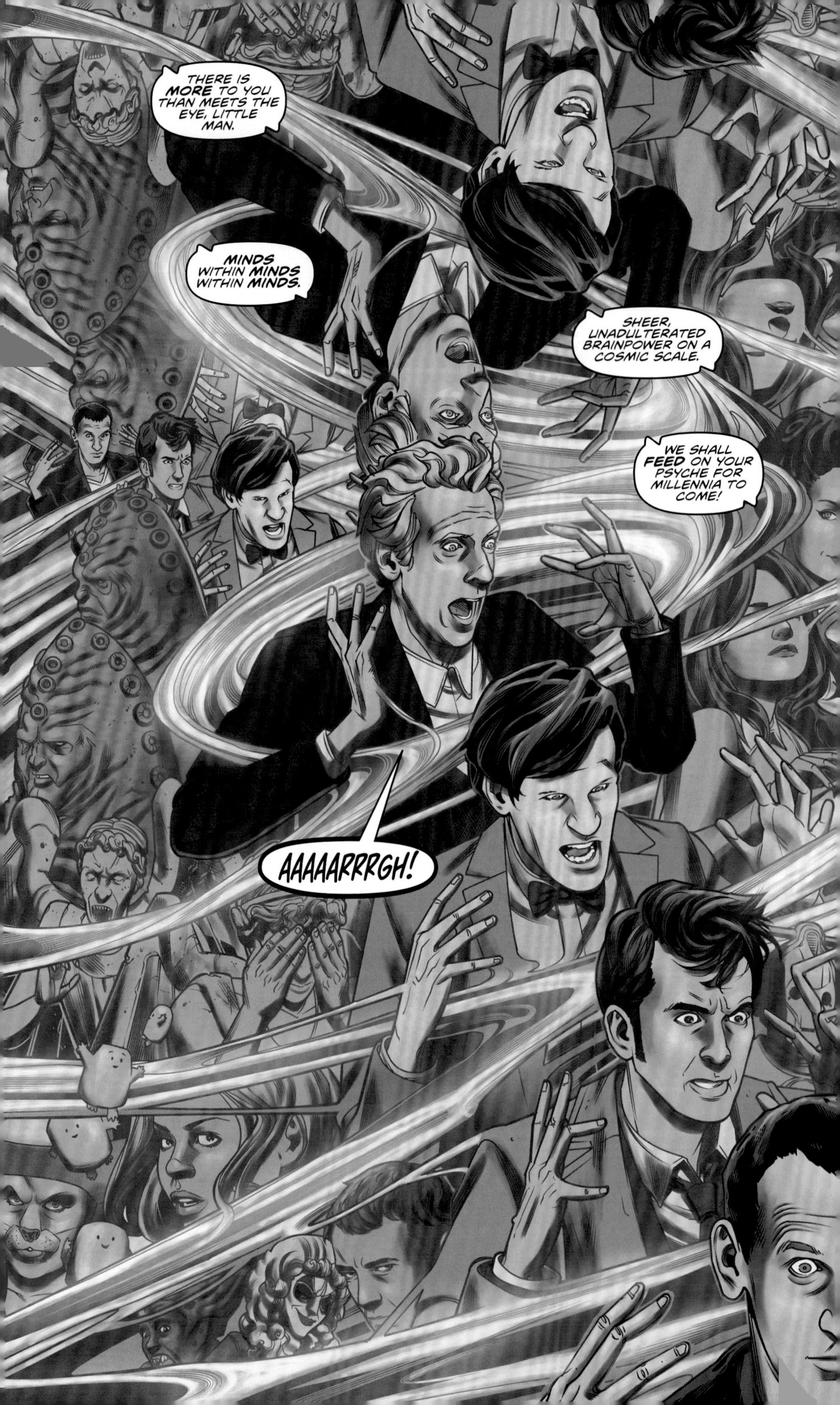
THERE IS MORE TO YOU THAN MEETS THE EYE, LITTLE MAN.
MINDS WITHIN MINDS WITHIN MINDS.
SHEER, UNADULTERATED BRAINPOWER ON A COSMIC SCALE.
WE SHALL FEED ON YOUR PSYCHE FOR MILLENNIA TO COME!
AAAAARRRGH!

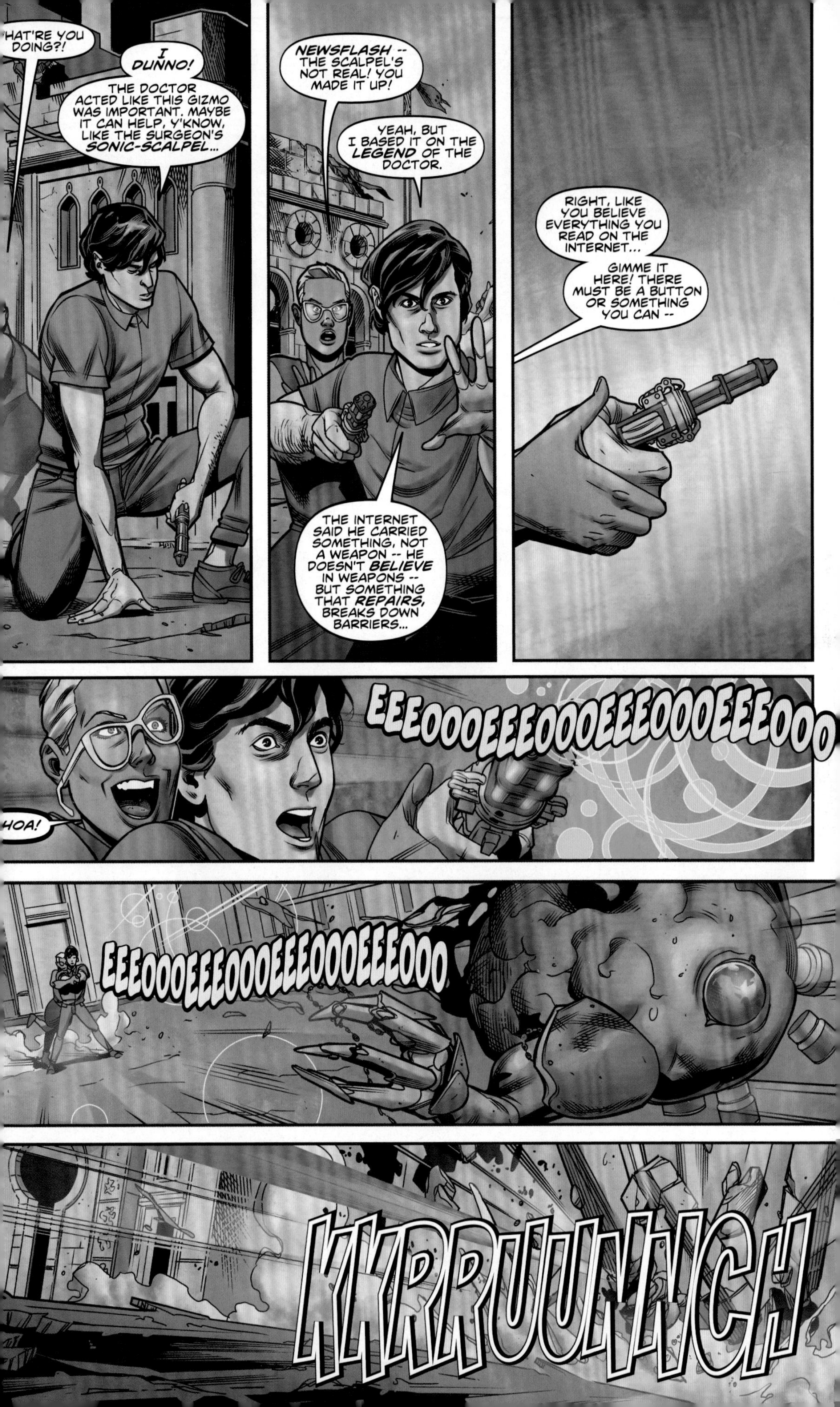

WHAT'RE YOU DOING?!
I DUNNO!
THE DOCTOR ACTED LIKE THIS GIZMO WAS IMPORTANT. MAYBE IT CAN HELP, Y'KNOW, LIKE THE SURGEON'S SONIC-SCALPEL...
NEWSFLASH -- THE SCALPEL'S NOT REAL! YOU MADE IT UP!
YEAH, BUT I BASED IT ON THE LEGEND OF THE DOCTOR.
THE INTERNET SAID HE CARRIED SOMETHING, NOT A WEAPON -- HE DOESN'T BELIEVE IN WEAPONS -- BUT SOMETHING THAT REPAIRS, BREAKS DOWN BARRIERS...
RIGHT, LIKE YOU BELIEVE EVERYTHING YOU READ ON THE INTERNET...
GIMME IT HERE! THERE MUST BE A BUTTON OR SOMETHING YOU CAN --
EEEOOOEEEOOOEEEOOOEEEOOO
WHOA!
EEEOOOEEEOOOEEEOOOEEEOOO
KKRRUUNNCH

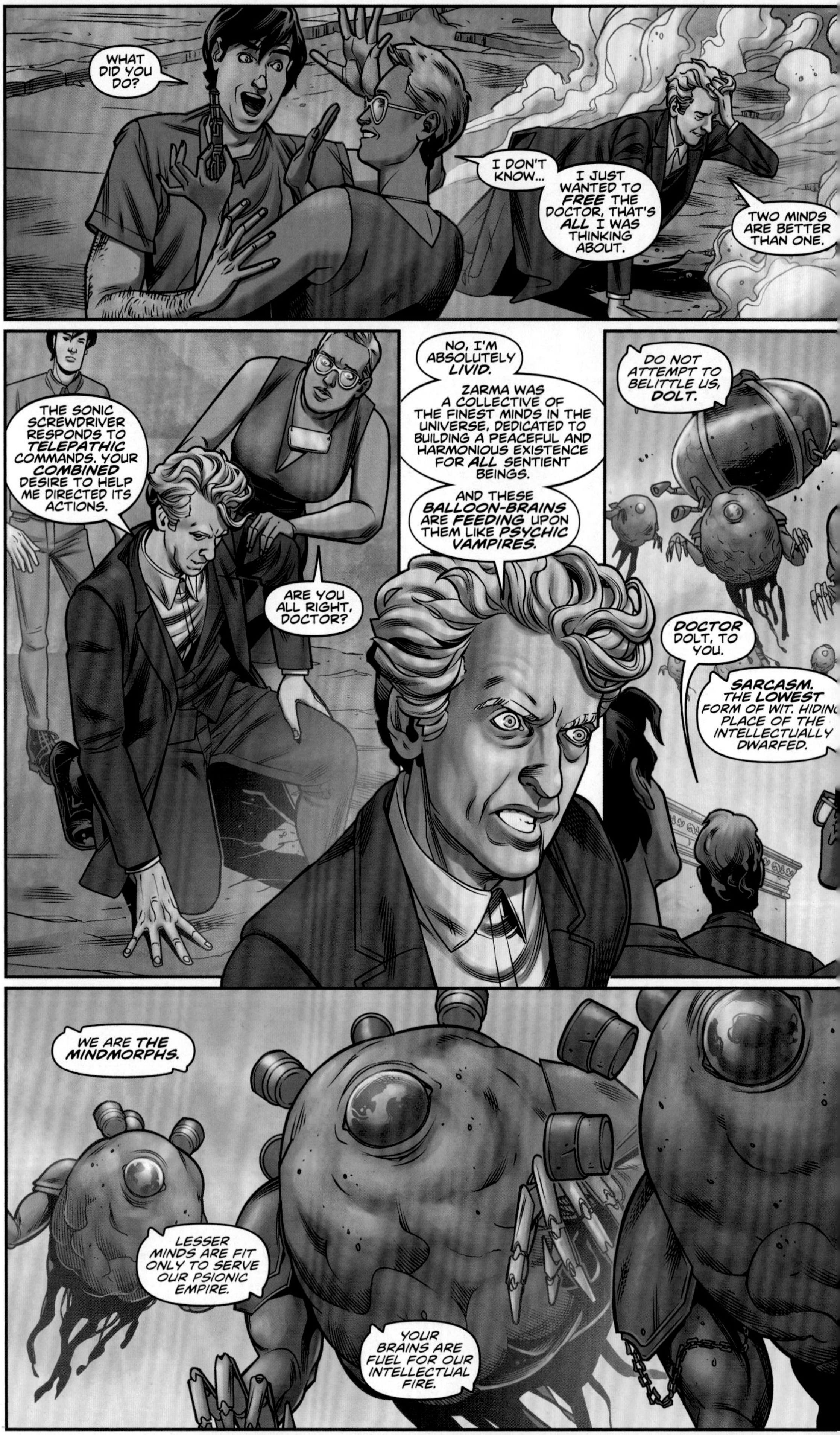
WHAT DID YOU DO?
I DON'T KNOW...
I JUST WANTED TO FREE THE DOCTOR, THAT'S ALL I WAS THINKING ABOUT.
TWO MINDS ARE BETTER THAN ONE.
THE SONIC SCREWDRIVER RESPONDS TO TELEPATHIC COMMANDS. YOUR COMBINED DESIRE TO HELP ME DIRECTED ITS ACTIONS.
ARE YOU ALL RIGHT, DOCTOR?
NO, I'M ABSOLUTELY LIVID.
ZARMA WAS A COLLECTIVE OF THE FINEST MINDS IN THE UNIVERSE, DEDICATED TO BUILDING A PEACEFUL AND HARMONIOUS EXISTENCE FOR ALL SENTIENT BEINGS.
AND THESE BALLOON-BRAINS ARE FEEDING UPON THEM LIKE PSYCHIC VAMPIRES.
DO NOT ATTEMPT TO BELITTLE US, DOLT.
DOCTOR DOLT, TO YOU.
SARCASM. THE LOWEST FORM OF WIT. HIDING PLACE OF THE INTELLECTUALLY DWARFED.
WE ARE THE MINDMORPHS.
LESSER MINDS ARE FIT ONLY TO SERVE OUR PSIONIC EMPIRE.
YOUR BRAINS ARE FUEL FOR OUR INTELLECTUAL FIRE.

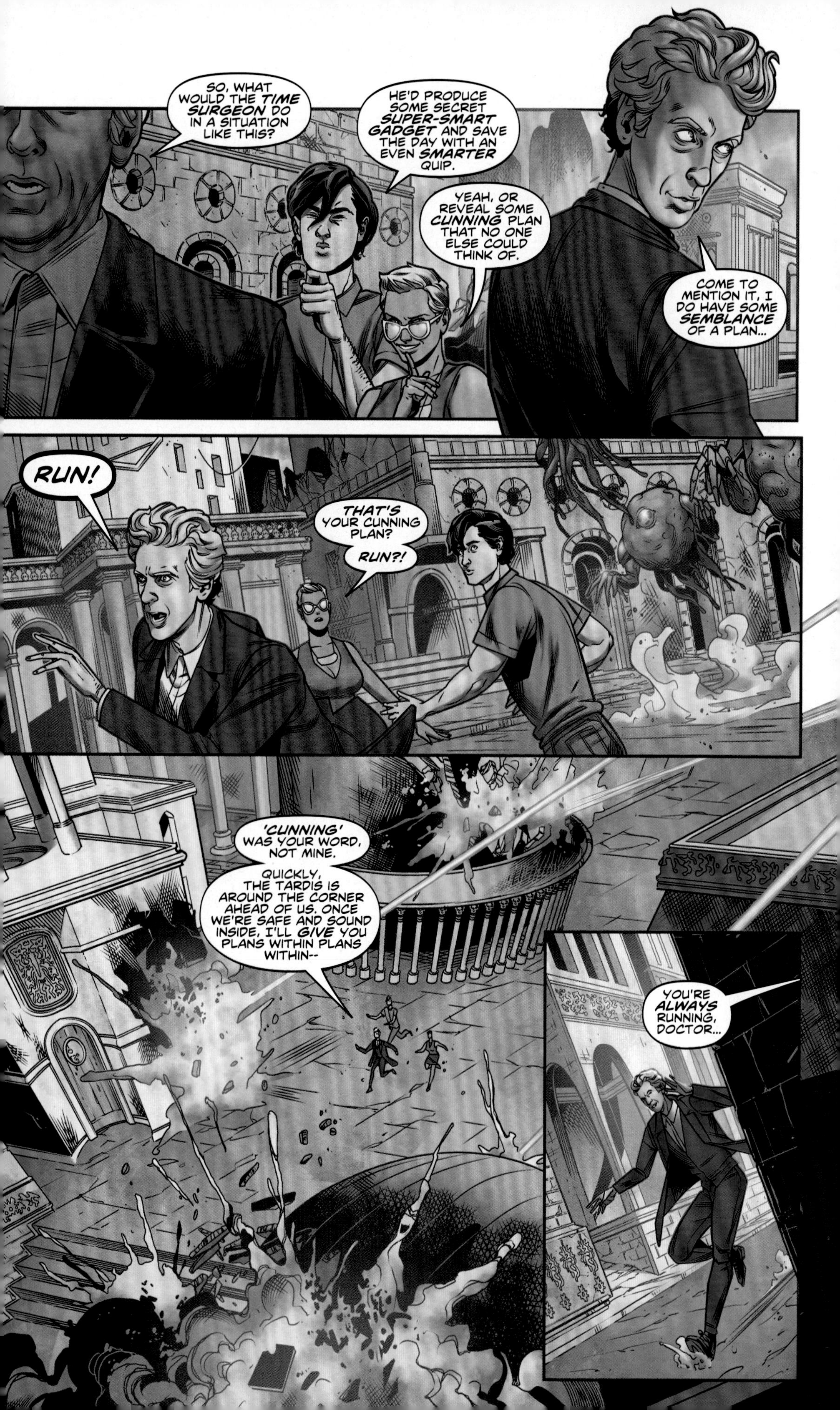
SO, WHAT WOULD THE TIME SURGEON DO IN A SITUATION LIKE THIS?
HE'D PRODUCE SOME SECRET SUPER-SMART GADGET AND SAVE THE DAY WITH AN EVEN SMARTER QUIP.
YEAH, OR REVEAL SOME CUNNING PLAN THAT NO ONE ELSE COULD THINK OF.
COME TO MENTION IT, I DO HAVE SOME SEMBLANCE OF A PLAN...
RUN!
THAT'S YOUR CUNNING PLAN?
RUN?!
'CUNNING' WAS YOUR WORD, NOT MINE.
QUICKLY, THE TARDIS IS AROUND THE CORNER AHEAD OF US. ONCE WE'RE SAFE AND SOUND INSIDE, I'LL GIVE YOU PLANS WITHIN PLANS WITHIN--
YOU'RE ALWAYS RUNNING, DOCTOR...

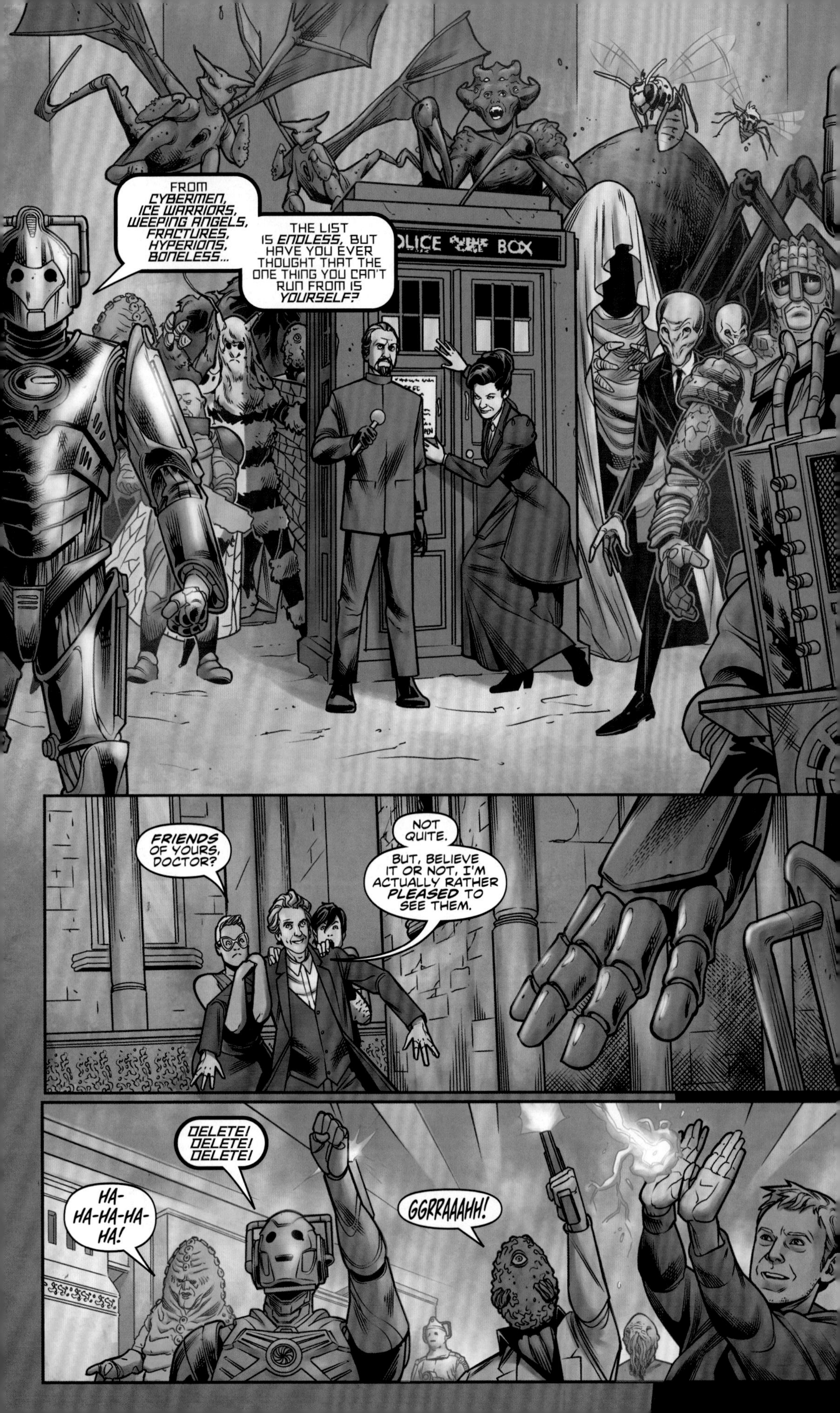
FROM CYBERMEN, ICE WARRIORS, WEEPING ANGELS, FRACTURES, HYPERIONS, BONELESS...
THE LIST IS ENDLESS, BUT HAVE YOU EVER THOUGHT THAT THE ONE THING YOU CAN'T RUN FROM IS YOURSELF?
FRIENDS OF YOURS, DOCTOR?
NOT QUITE.
BUT, BELIEVE IT OR NOT, I'M ACTUALLY RATHER PLEASED TO SEE THEM.
HA-HA-HA-HA-HA!
DELETE! DELETE! DELETE!
GGRRAAAHH!

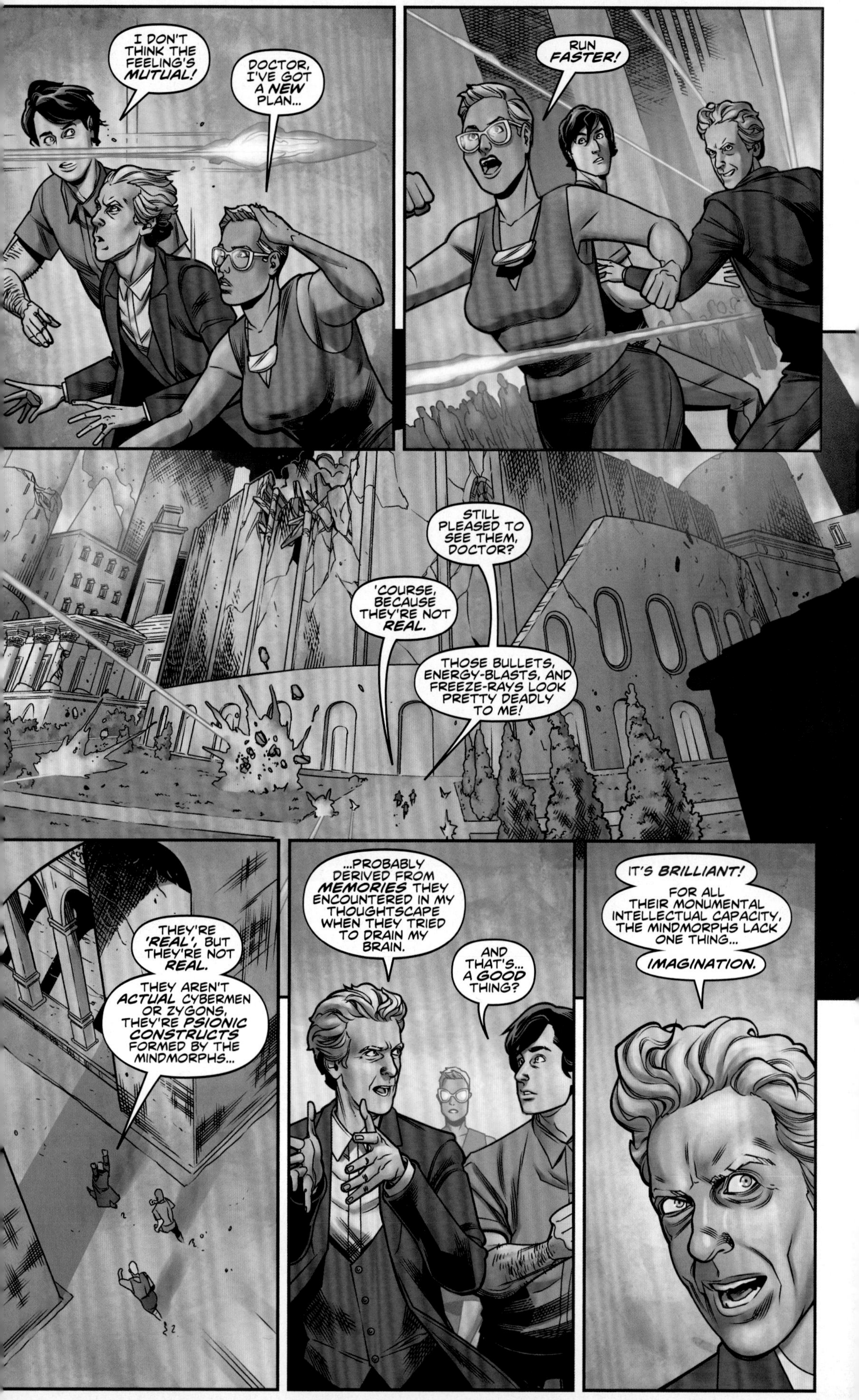
I DON'T THINK THE FEELING'S MUTUAL!
DOCTOR, I'VE GOT A NEW PLAN...
RUN FASTER!
STILL PLEASED TO SEE THEM, DOCTOR?
'COURSE, BECAUSE THEY'RE NOT REAL.
THOSE BULLETS, ENERGY-BLASTS, AND FREEZE-RAYS LOOK PRETTY DEADLY TO ME!
THEY'RE 'REAL', BUT THEY'RE NOT REAL.
THEY AREN'T ACTUAL CYBERMEN OR ZYGONS, THEY'RE PSIONIC CONSTRUCTS FORMED BY THE MINDMORPHS...
...PROBABLY DERIVED FROM MEMORIES THEY ENCOUNTERED IN MY THOUGHTSCAPE WHEN THEY TRIED TO DRAIN MY BRAIN.
AND THAT'S... A GOOD THING?
IT'S BRILLIANT!
FOR ALL THEIR MONUMENTAL INTELLECTUAL CAPACITY, THE MINDMORPHS LACK ONE THING...
IMAGINATION.

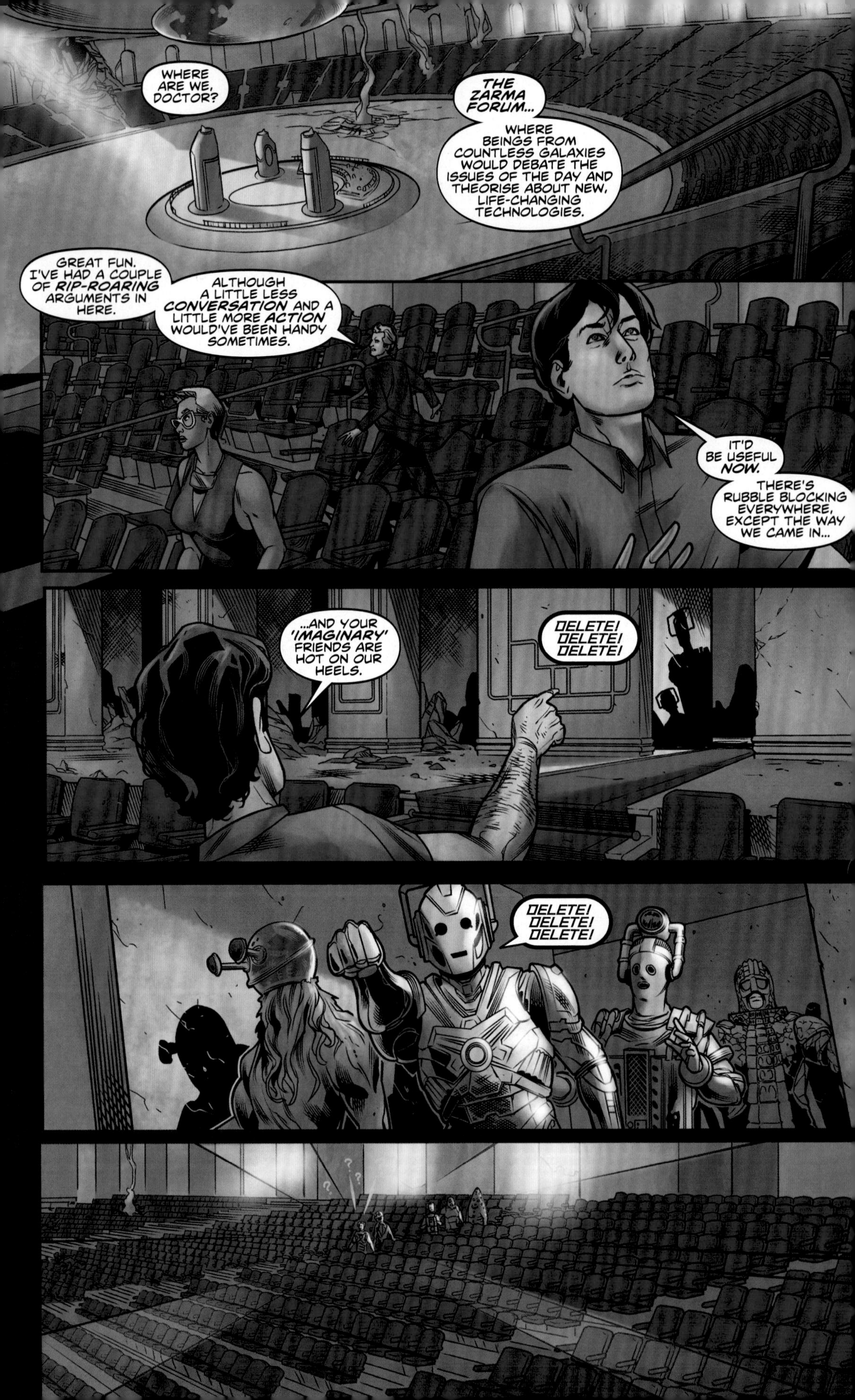
WHERE ARE WE, DOCTOR?
THE ZARMA FORUM...
WHERE BEINGS FROM COUNTLESS GALAXIES WOULD DEBATE THE ISSUES OF THE DAY AND THEORISE ABOUT NEW, LIFE-CHANGING TECHNOLOGIES.
GREAT FUN. I'VE HAD A COUPLE OF RIP-ROARING ARGUMENTS IN HERE.
ALTHOUGH A LITTLE LESS CONVERSATION AND A LITTLE MORE ACTION WOULD'VE BEEN HANDY SOMETIMES.
IT'D BE USEFUL NOW.
THERE'S RUBBLE BLOCKING EVERYWHERE, EXCEPT THE WAY WE CAME IN...
...AND YOUR 'IMAGINARY' FRIENDS ARE HOT ON OUR HEELS.
DELETE! DELETE! DELETE!
DELETE! DELETE! DELETE!
? ? ?

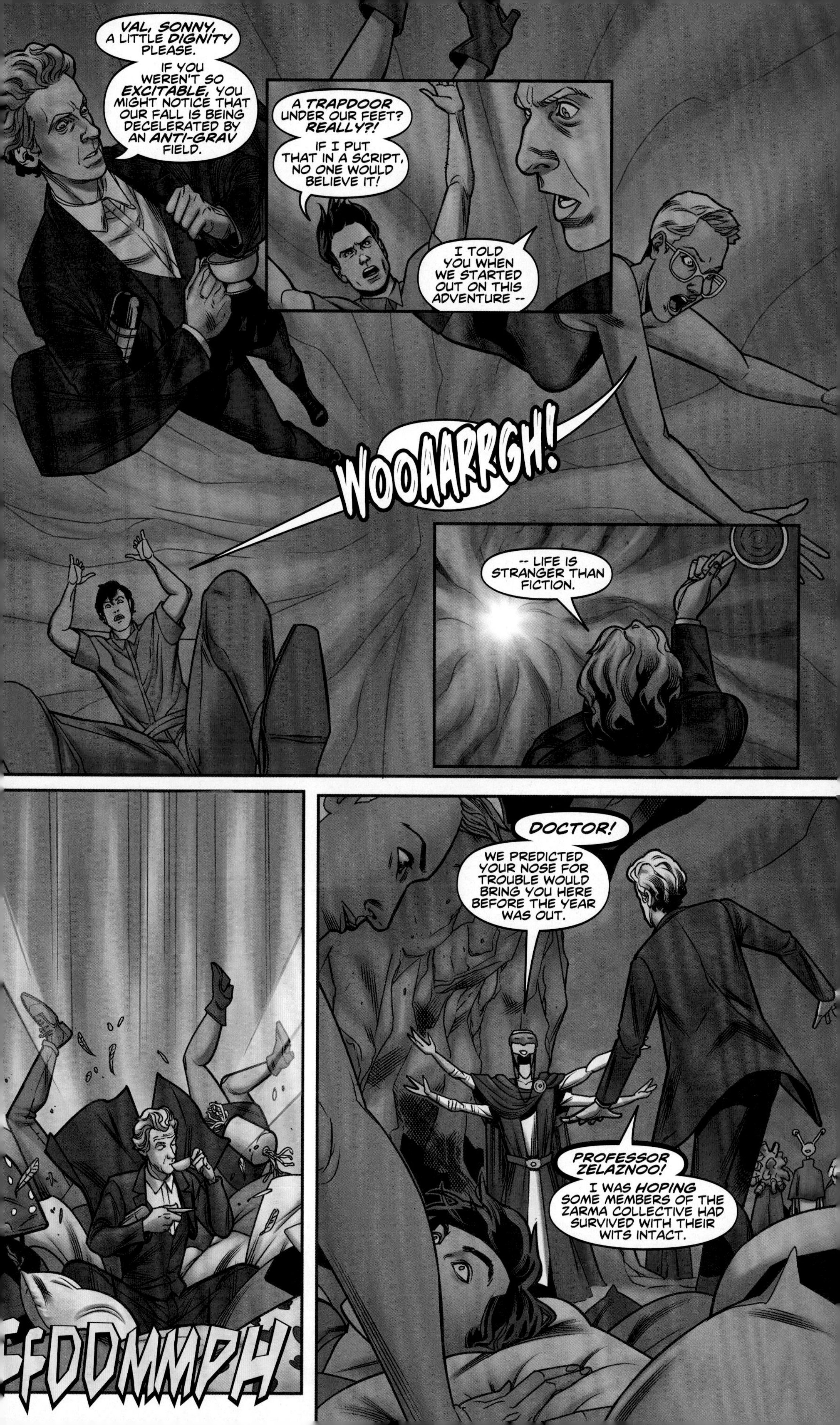
VAL, SONNY, A LITTLE DIGNITY PLEASE.
IF YOU WEREN'T SO EXCITABLE, YOU MIGHT NOTICE THAT OUR FALL IS BEING DECELERATED BY AN ANTI-GRAV FIELD.
A TRAPDOOR UNDER OUR FEET? REALLY?!
IF I PUT THAT IN A SCRIPT, NO ONE WOULD BELIEVE IT!
I TOLD YOU WHEN WE STARTED OUT ON THIS ADVENTURE --
WOOAARRGH!
-- LIFE IS STRANGER THAN FICTION.
FOOMMPH
DOCTOR!
WE PREDICTED YOUR NOSE FOR TROUBLE WOULD BRING YOU HERE BEFORE THE YEAR WAS OUT.
PROFESSOR ZELAZNOO!
I WAS HOPING SOME MEMBERS OF THE ZARMA COLLECTIVE HAD SURVIVED WITH THEIR WITS INTACT.

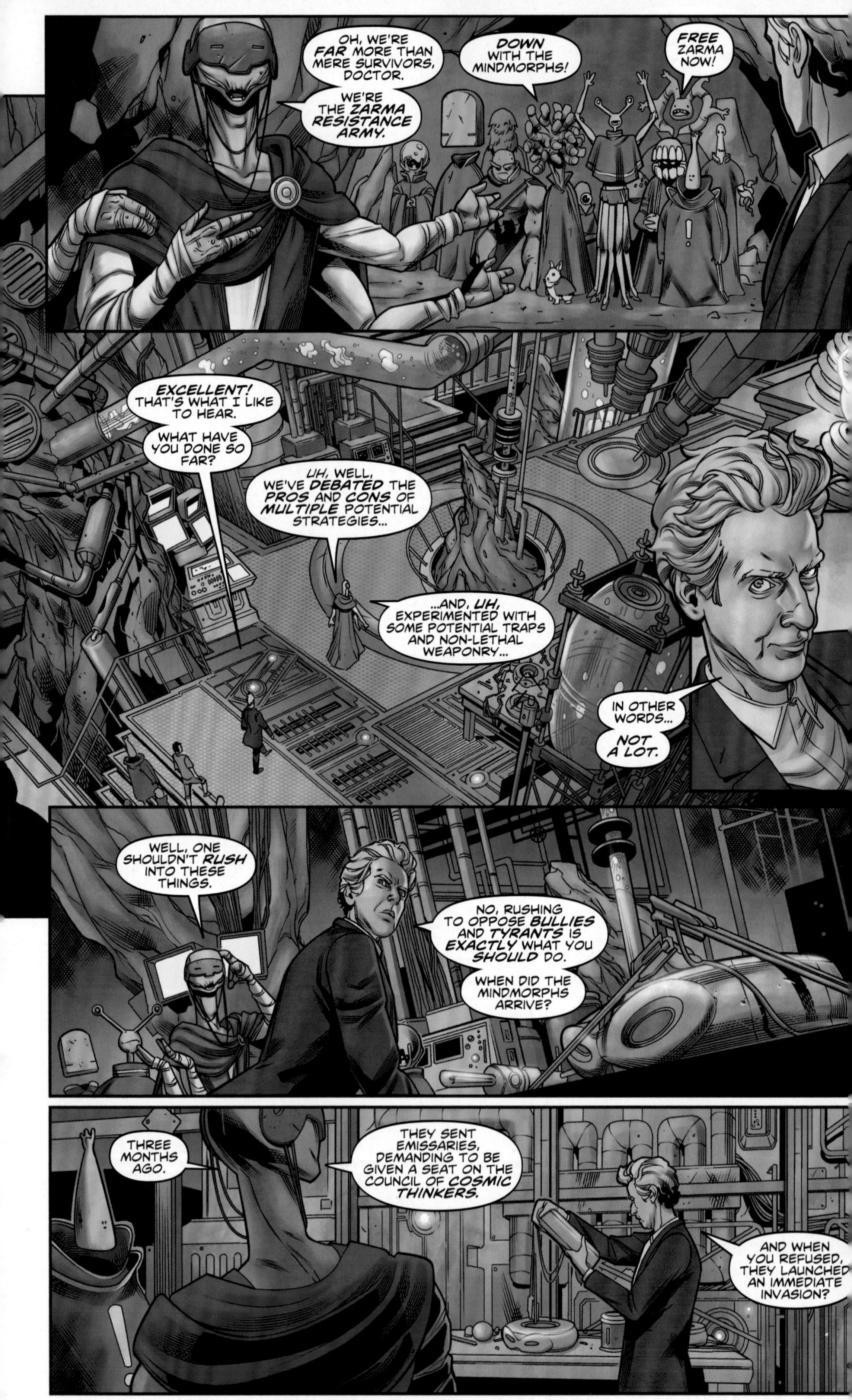
OH, WE'RE FAR MORE THAN MERE SURVIVORS, DOCTOR.
WE'RE THE ZARMA RESISTANCE ARMY.
DOWN WITH THE MINDMORPHS!
FREE ZARMA NOW!
EXCELLENT! THAT'S WHAT I LIKE TO HEAR.
WHAT HAVE YOU DONE SO FAR?
UH, WELL, WE'VE DEBATED THE PROS AND CONS OF MULTIPLE POTENTIAL STRATEGIES...
...AND, UH, EXPERIMENTED WITH SOME POTENTIAL TRAPS AND NON-LETHAL WEAPONRY...
IN OTHER WORDS...
NOT A LOT.
WELL, ONE SHOULDN'T RUSH INTO THESE THINGS.
NO, RUSHING TO OPPOSE BULLIES AND TYRANTS IS EXACTLY WHAT YOU SHOULD DO.
WHEN DID THE MINDMORPHS ARRIVE?
THREE MONTHS AGO.
THEY SENT EMISSARIES, DEMANDING TO BE GIVEN A SEAT ON THE COUNCIL OF COSMIC THINKERS.
AND WHEN YOU REFUSED, THEY LAUNCHED AN IMMEDIATE INVASION?

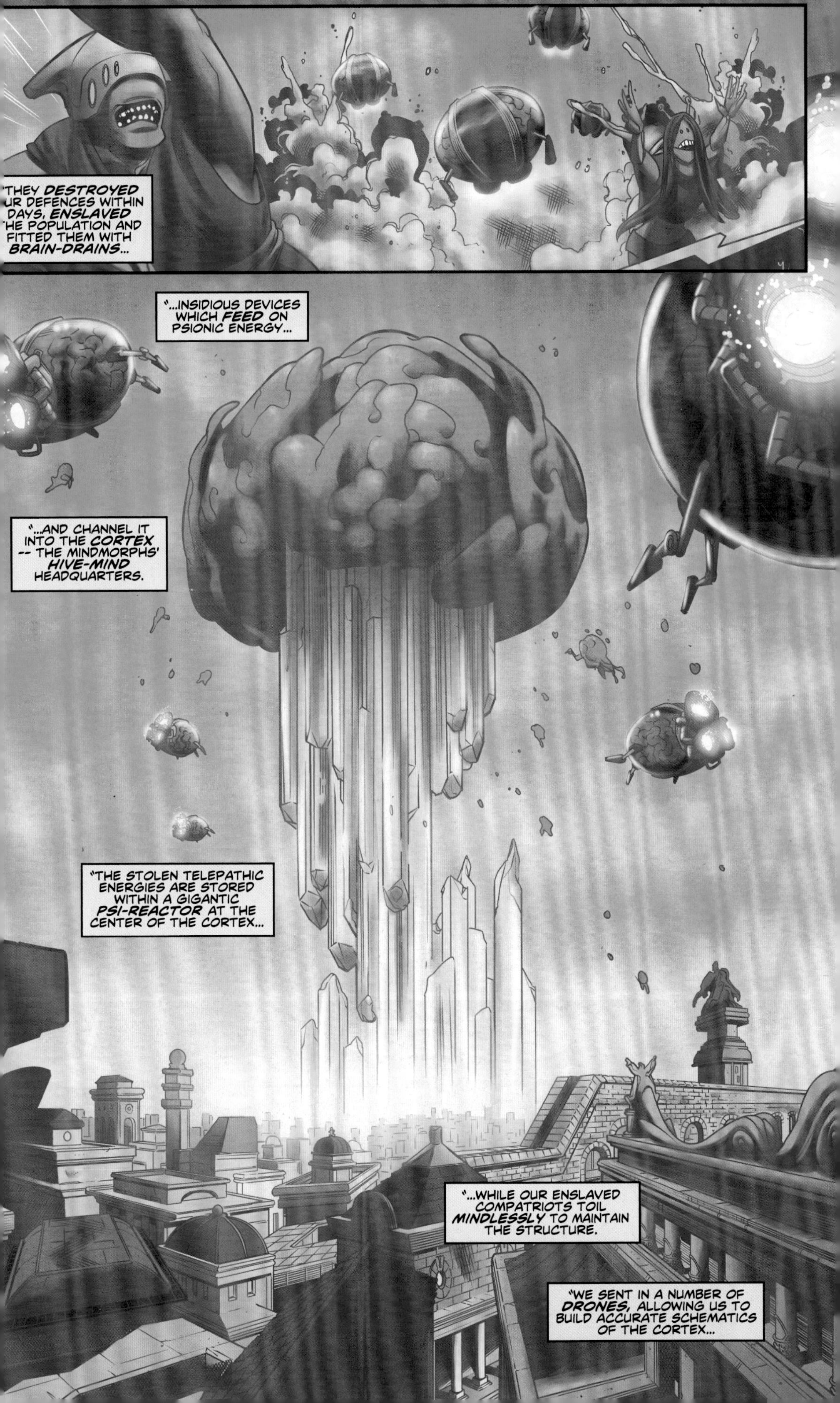
"THEY DESTROYED UR DEFENCES WITHIN DAYS, ENSLAVED THE POPULATION AND FITTED THEM WITH BRAIN-DRAINS...
"...INSIDIOUS DEVICES WHICH FEED ON PSIONIC ENERGY...
"...AND CHANNEL IT INTO THE CORTEX -- THE MINDMORPHS' HIVE-MIND HEADQUARTERS.
"THE STOLEN TELEPATHIC ENERGIES ARE STORED WITHIN A GIGANTIC PSI-REACTOR AT THE CENTER OF THE CORTEX...
"...WHILE OUR ENSLAVED COMPATRIOTS TOIL MINDLESSLY TO MAINTAIN THE STRUCTURE.
"WE SENT IN A NUMBER OF DRONES, ALLOWING US TO BUILD ACCURATE SCHEMATICS OF THE CORTEX...

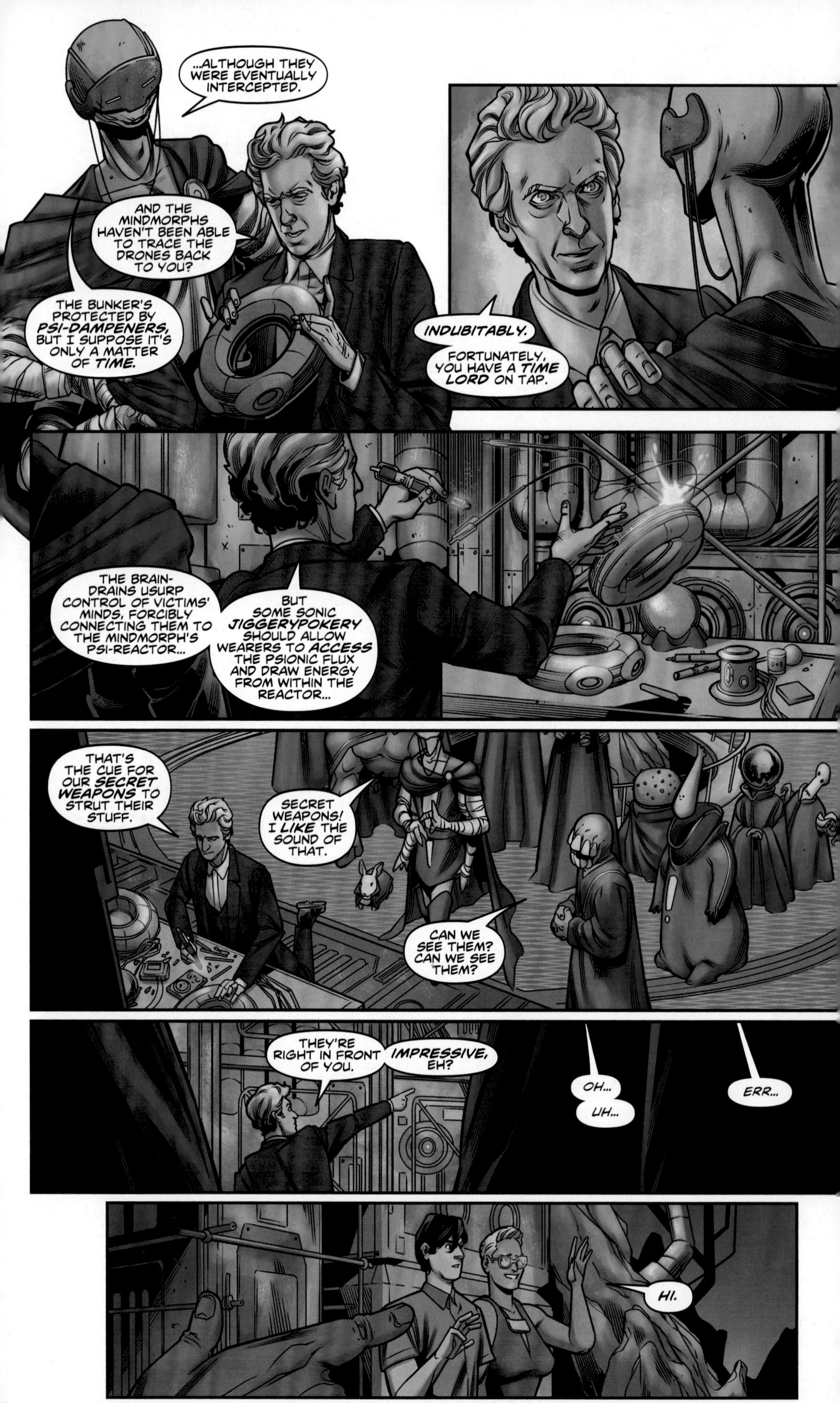
...ALTHOUGH THEY WERE EVENTUALLY INTERCEPTED.
AND THE MINDMORPHS HAVEN'T BEEN ABLE TO TRACE THE DRONES BACK TO YOU?
THE BUNKER'S PROTECTED BY PSI-DAMPENERS, BUT I SUPPOSE IT'S ONLY A MATTER OF TIME.
INDUBITABLY.
FORTUNATELY, YOU HAVE A TIME LORD ON TAP.
THE BRAIN-DRAINS USURP CONTROL OF VICTIMS' MINDS, FORCIBLY CONNECTING THEM TO THE MINDMORPH'S PSI-REACTOR...
BUT SOME SONIC JIGGERYPOKERY SHOULD ALLOW WEARERS TO ACCESS THE PSIONIC FLUX AND DRAW ENERGY FROM WITHIN THE REACTOR...
THAT'S THE CUE FOR OUR SECRET WEAPONS TO STRUT THEIR STUFF.
SECRET WEAPONS! I LIKE THE SOUND OF THAT.
CAN WE SEE THEM? CAN WE SEE THEM?
THEY'RE RIGHT IN FRONT OF YOU.
IMPRESSIVE, EH?
OH...
UH...
ERR...
HI.

THE CORTEX.

ALERT! CORTEX COMMAND TO ALL MINDMORPHS. UNEXPLAINED FLUCTUATIONS WITHIN THE REACTOR.

A HOSTILE PRESENCE IS ATTEMPTING TO INFILTRATE THE CORTEX.

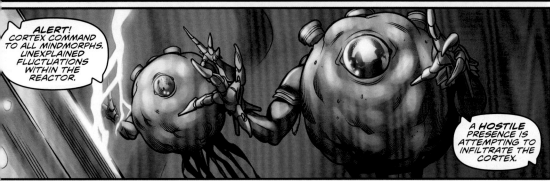

AN ENEMY ATTACK MAY BE IMMINENT.

SCAN ALL THRALLS.

DESTROY ANY WHO EXHIBIT SIGNS OF FREE WILL OR INDEPENDENT THOUGHT.

ARE YOU ABSOLUTELY *SURE* ABOUT THIS, DOCTOR? I MEAN, I *WRITE* COMICS!

AND I *DRAW* THEM! WE DON'T FEEL VERY, WELL... *SECRET* WEAPONRY.

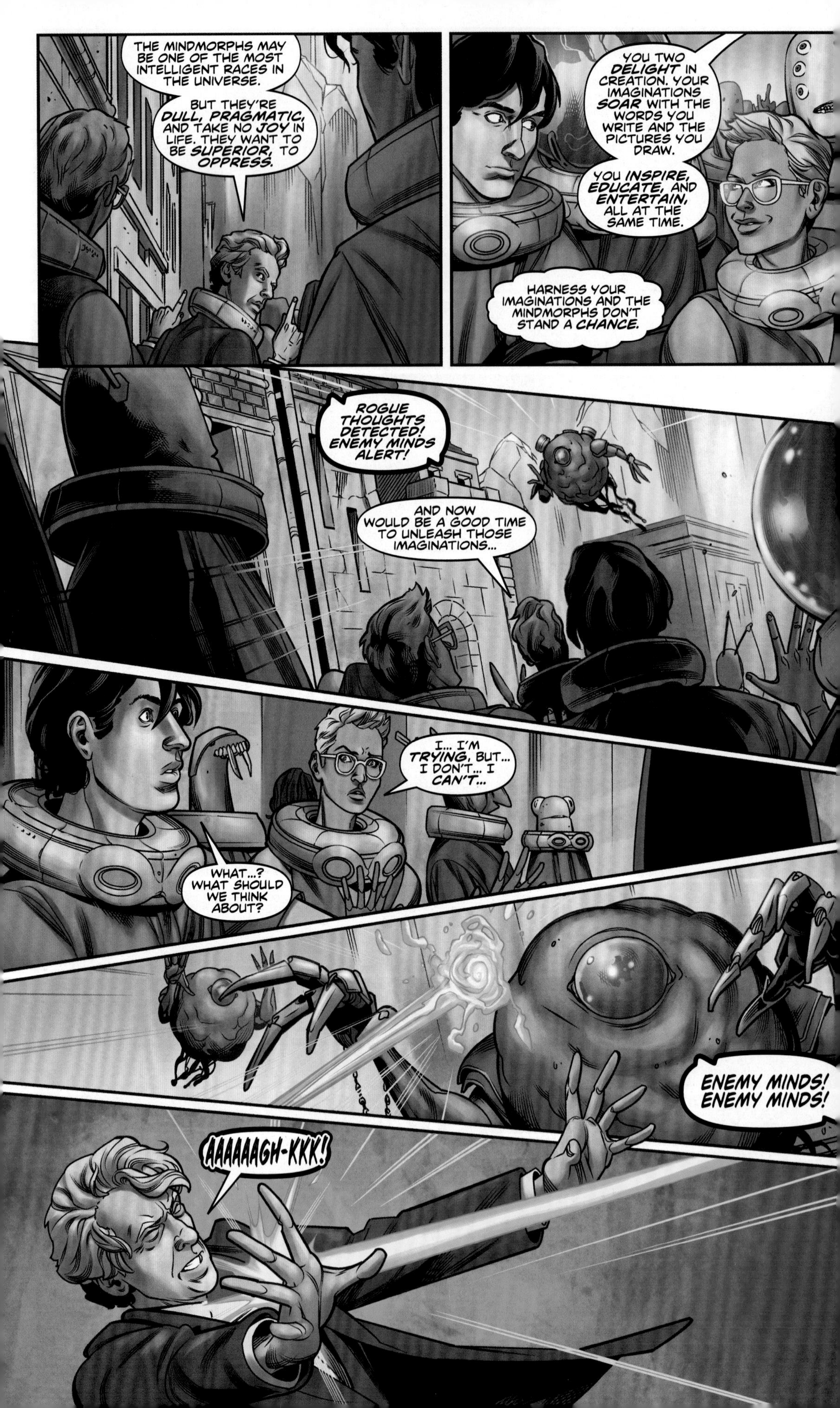
THE MINDMORPHS MAY BE ONE OF THE MOST INTELLIGENT RACES IN THE UNIVERSE.
BUT THEY'RE DULL, PRAGMATIC, AND TAKE NO JOY IN LIFE. THEY WANT TO BE SUPERIOR, TO OPPRESS.
YOU TWO DELIGHT IN CREATION. YOUR IMAGINATIONS SOAR WITH THE WORDS YOU WRITE AND THE PICTURES YOU DRAW.
YOU INSPIRE, EDUCATE, AND ENTERTAIN, ALL AT THE SAME TIME.
HARNESS YOUR IMAGINATIONS AND THE MINDMORPHS DON'T STAND A CHANCE.
ROGUE THOUGHTS DETECTED! ENEMY MINDS ALERT!
AND NOW WOULD BE A GOOD TIME TO UNLEASH THOSE IMAGINATIONS...
I... I'M TRYING, BUT... I DON'T... I CAN'T...
WHAT...? WHAT SHOULD WE THINK ABOUT?
ENEMY MINDS! ENEMY MINDS!
AAAAAAGH-KKK!

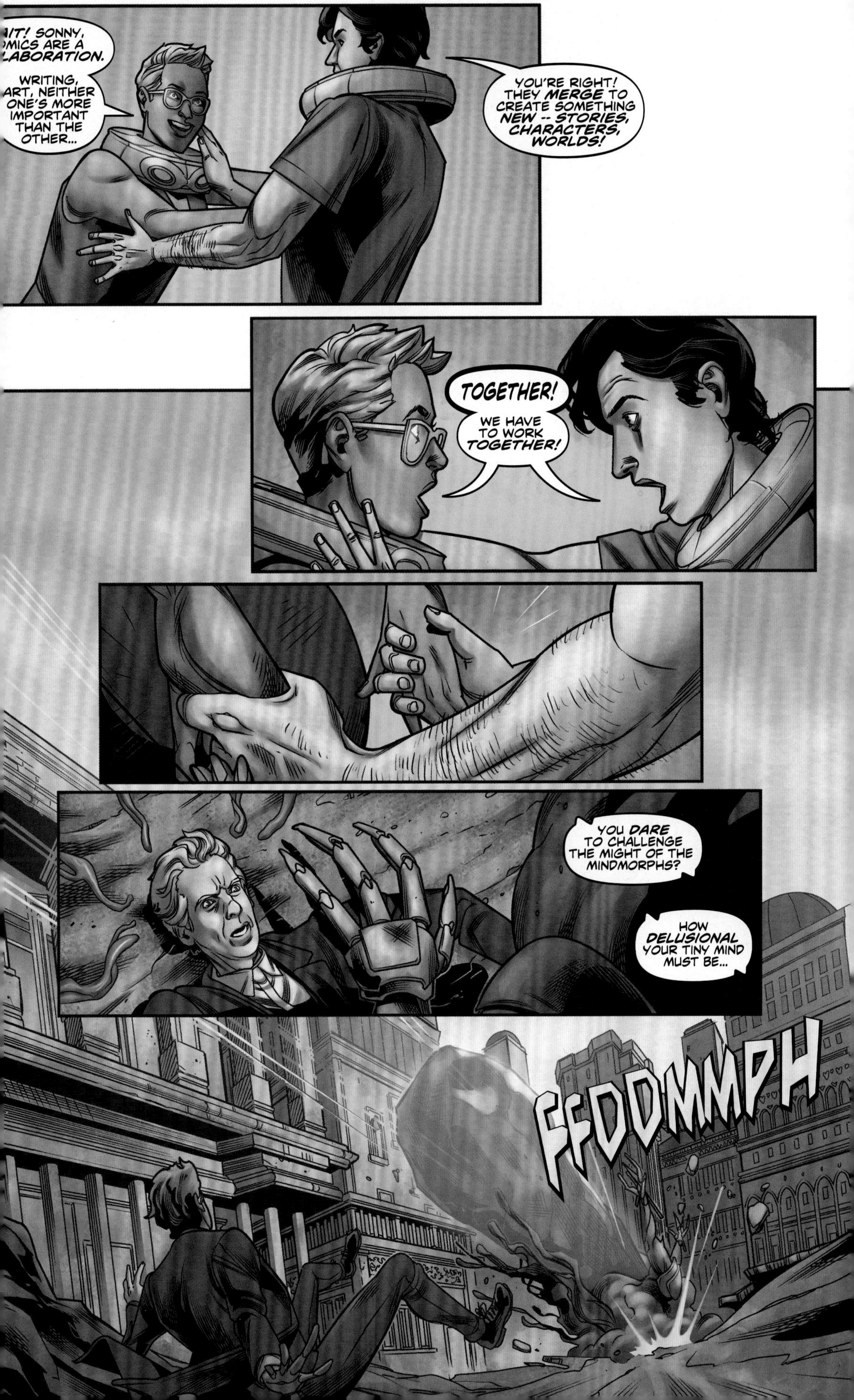

AIT! SONNY, OMICS ARE A LABORATION.
WRITING, ART, NEITHER ONE'S MORE IMPORTANT THAN THE OTHER...
YOU'RE RIGHT! THEY MERGE TO CREATE SOMETHING NEW -- STORIES, CHARACTERS, WORLDS!
TOGETHER!
WE HAVE TO WORK TOGETHER!
YOU DARE TO CHALLENGE THE MIGHT OF THE MINDMORPHS?
HOW DELUSIONAL YOUR TINY MIND MUST BE...
FFDOMMPH

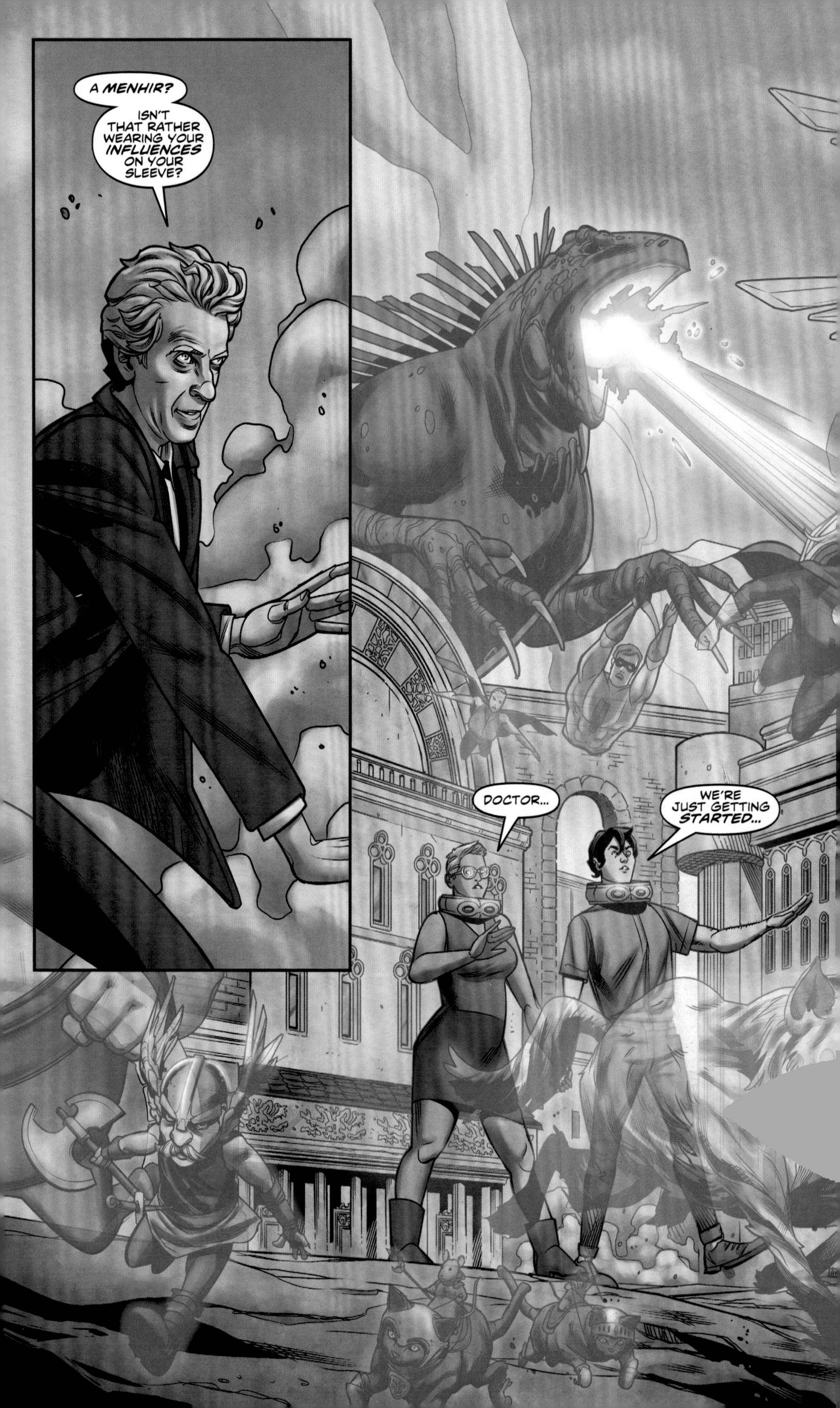

A MENHIR?
ISN'T THAT RATHER WEARING YOUR INFLUENCES ON YOUR SLEEVE?
DOCTOR...
WE'RE JUST GETTING STARTED...

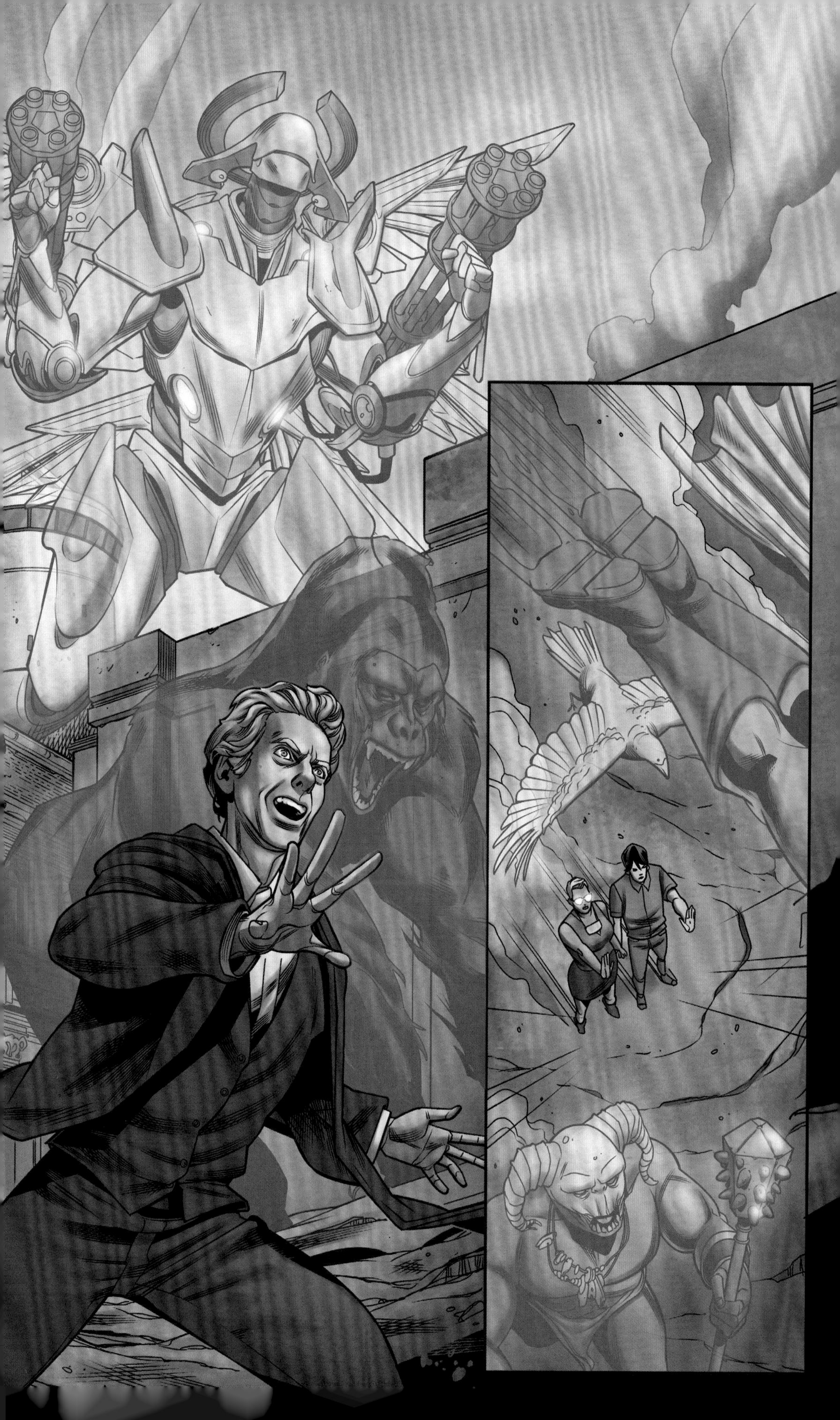

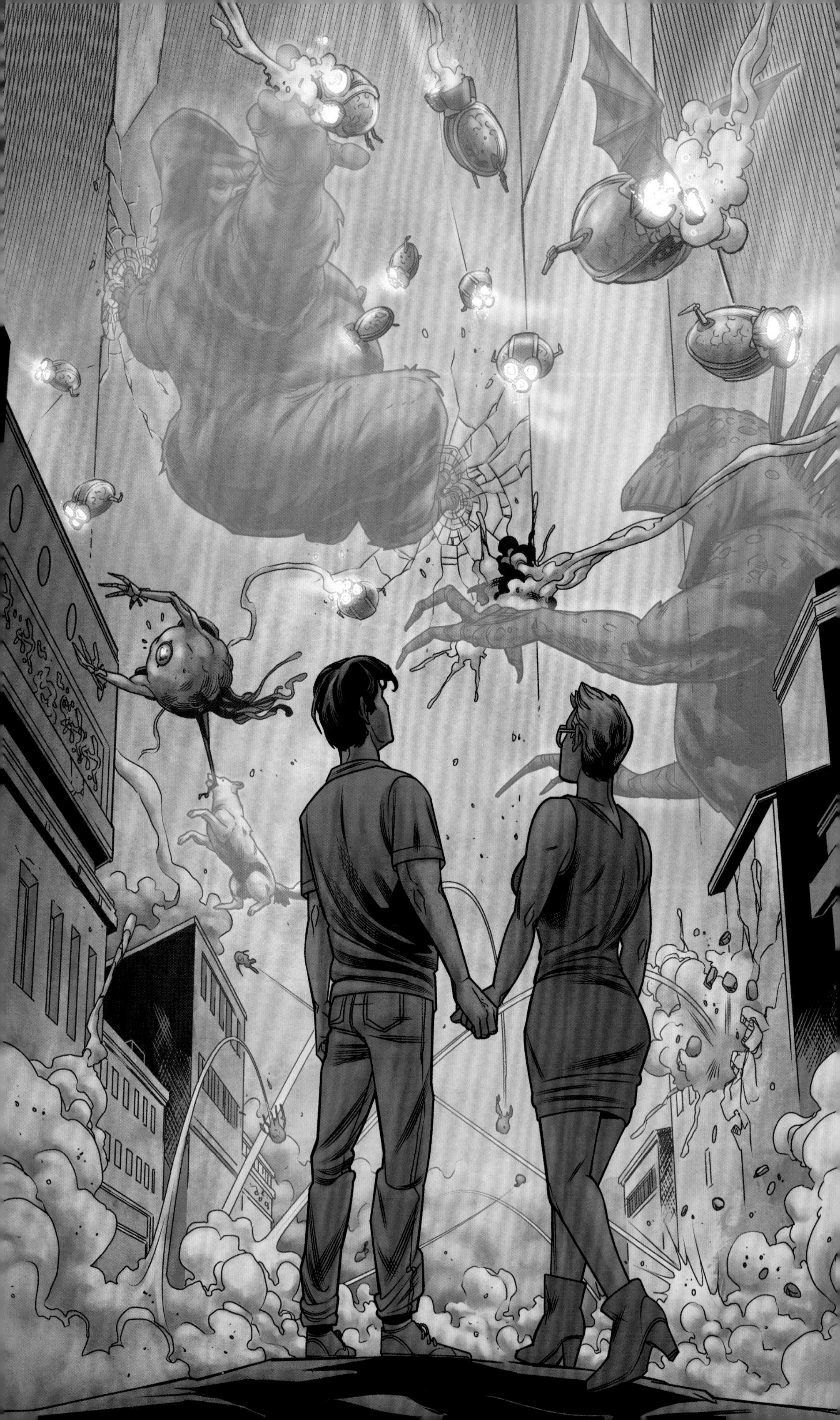

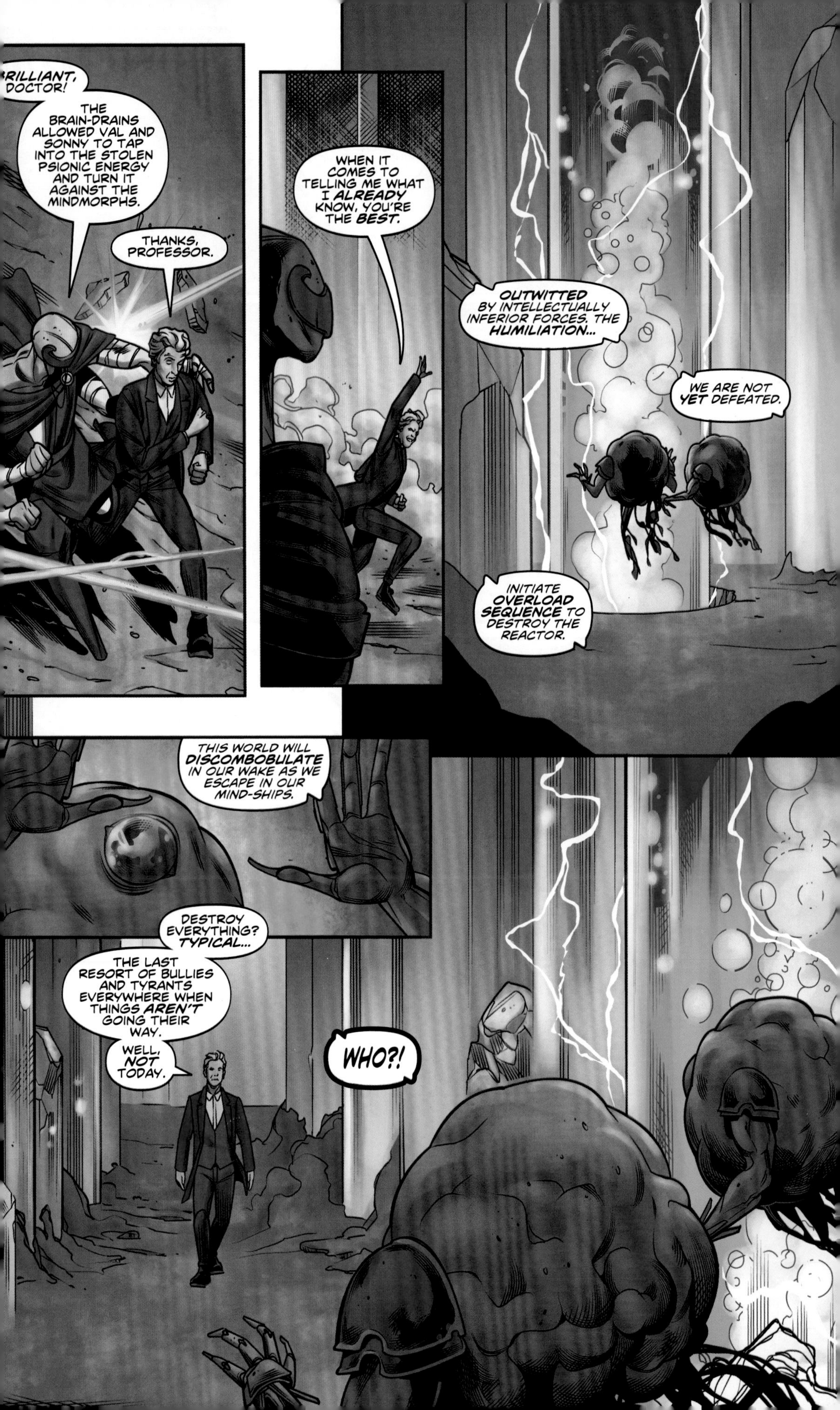
BRILLIANT, DOCTOR!
THE BRAIN-DRAINS ALLOWED VAL AND SONNY TO TAP INTO THE STOLEN PSIONIC ENERGY AND TURN IT AGAINST THE MINDMORPHS.
THANKS, PROFESSOR.
WHEN IT COMES TO TELLING ME WHAT I ALREADY KNOW, YOU'RE THE BEST.
OUTWITTED BY INTELLECTUALLY INFERIOR FORCES. THE HUMILIATION...
WE ARE NOT YET DEFEATED.
INITIATE OVERLOAD SEQUENCE TO DESTROY THE REACTOR.
THIS WORLD WILL DISCOMBOBULATE IN OUR WAKE AS WE ESCAPE IN OUR MIND-SHIPS.
DESTROY EVERYTHING? TYPICAL...
THE LAST RESORT OF BULLIES AND TYRANTS EVERYWHERE WHEN THINGS AREN'T GOING THEIR WAY.
WELL, NOT TODAY.
WHO?!

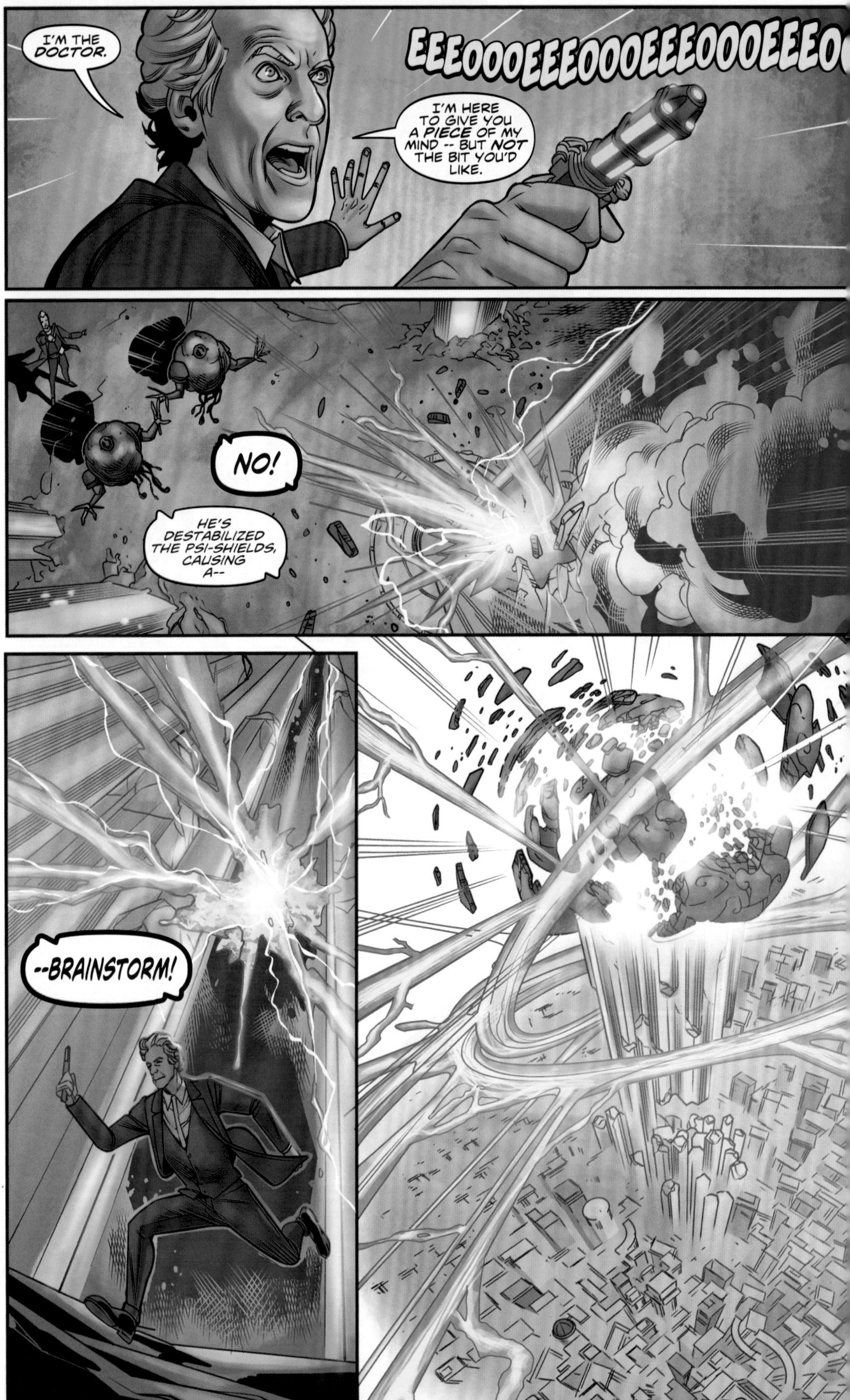
I'M THE DOCTOR.
EEEOOOEEEOOOEEEOOOEEEO
I'M HERE TO GIVE YOU A PIECE OF MY MIND -- BUT NOT THE BIT YOU'D LIKE.
NO!
HE'S DESTABILIZED THE PSI-SHIELDS, CAUSING A--
--BRAINSTORM!

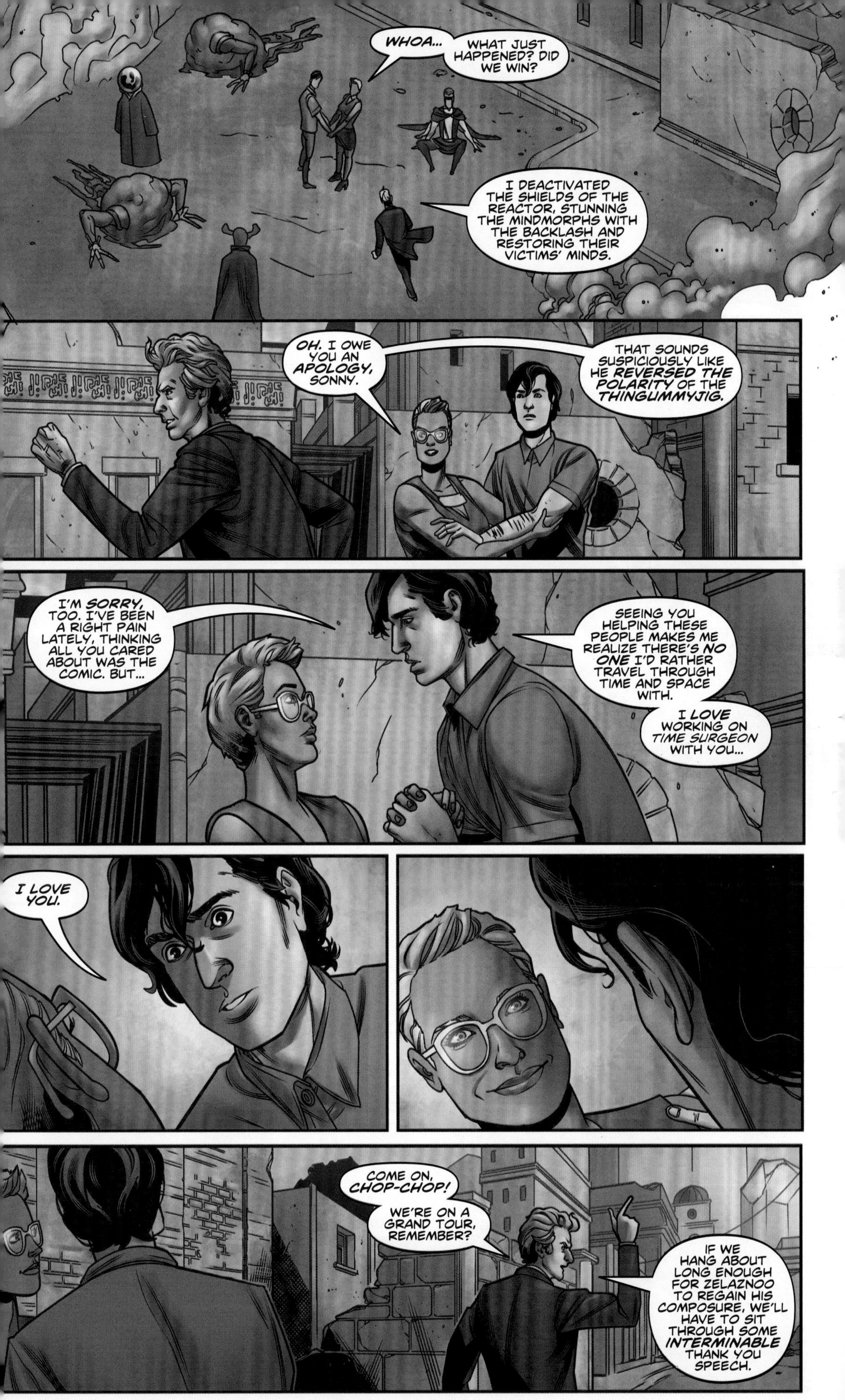
WHOA... WHAT JUST HAPPENED? DID WE WIN?
I DEACTIVATED THE SHIELDS OF THE REACTOR, STUNNING THE MINDMORPHS WITH THE BACKLASH AND RESTORING THEIR VICTIMS' MINDS.
OH. I OWE YOU AN APOLOGY, SONNY.
THAT SOUNDS SUSPICIOUSLY LIKE HE REVERSED THE POLARITY OF THE THINGUMMYJIG.
I'M SORRY, TOO. I'VE BEEN A RIGHT PAIN LATELY, THINKING ALL YOU CARED ABOUT WAS THE COMIC. BUT...
SEEING YOU HELPING THESE PEOPLE MAKES ME REALIZE THERE'S NO ONE I'D RATHER TRAVEL THROUGH TIME AND SPACE WITH.
I LOVE WORKING ON TIME SURGEON WITH YOU...
I LOVE YOU.
COME ON, CHOP-CHOP!
WE'RE ON A GRAND TOUR, REMEMBER?
IF WE HANG ABOUT LONG ENOUGH FOR ZELAZNOO TO REGAIN HIS COMPOSURE, WE'LL HAVE TO SIT THROUGH SOME INTERMINABLE THANK YOU SPEECH.

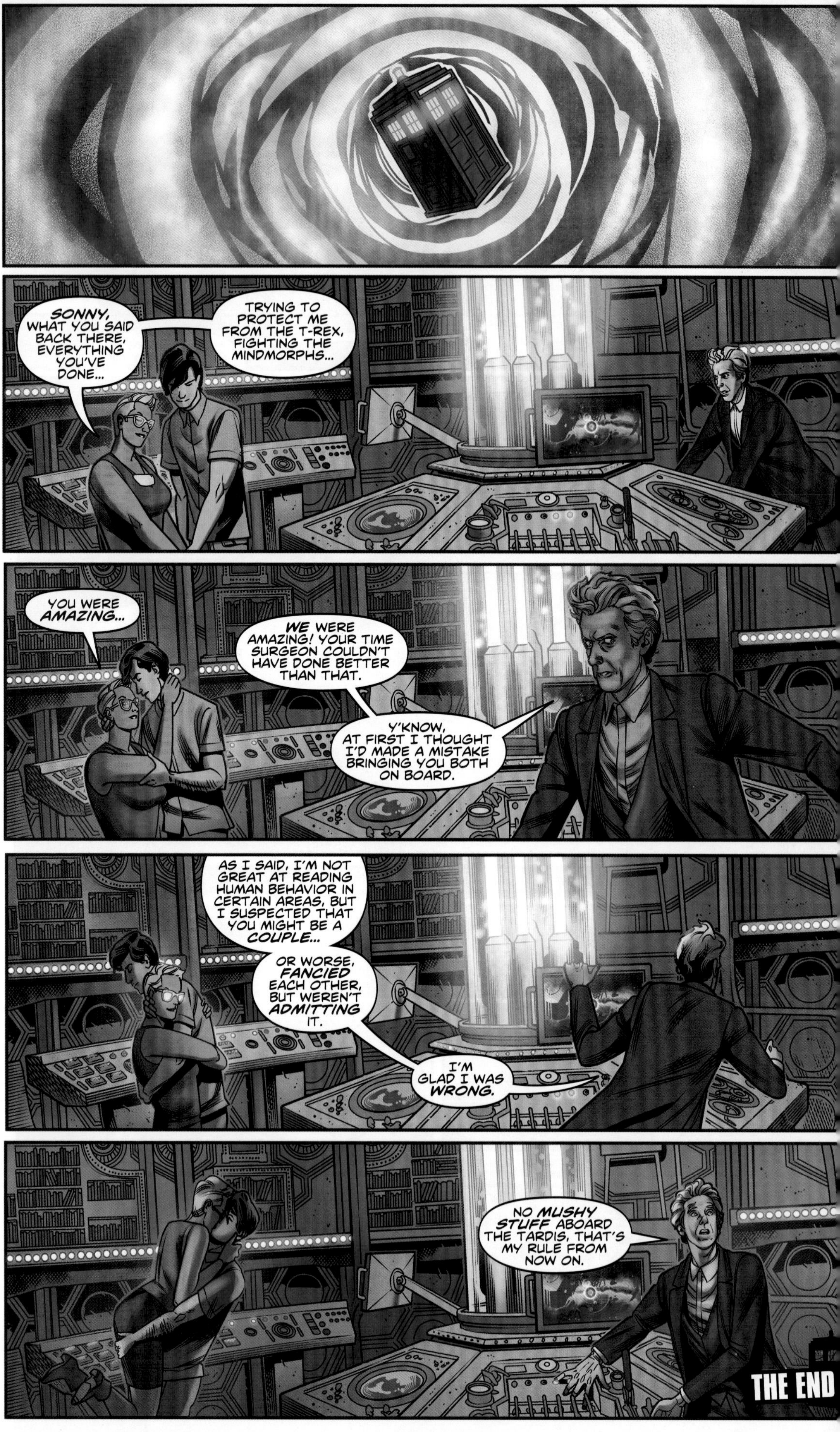
SONNY, WHAT YOU SAID BACK THERE, EVERYTHING YOU'VE DONE...
TRYING TO PROTECT ME FROM THE T-REX, FIGHTING THE MINDMORPHS...
YOU WERE AMAZING...
WE WERE AMAZING! YOUR TIME SURGEON COULDN'T HAVE DONE BETTER THAN THAT.
Y'KNOW, AT FIRST I THOUGHT I'D MADE A MISTAKE BRINGING YOU BOTH ON BOARD.
AS I SAID, I'M NOT GREAT AT READING HUMAN BEHAVIOR IN CERTAIN AREAS, BUT I SUSPECTED THAT YOU MIGHT BE A COUPLE...
OR WORSE, FANCIED EACH OTHER, BUT WEREN'T ADMITTING IT.
I'M GLAD I WAS WRONG.
NO MUSHY STUFF ABOARD THE TARDIS, THAT'S MY RULE FROM NOW ON.
THE END

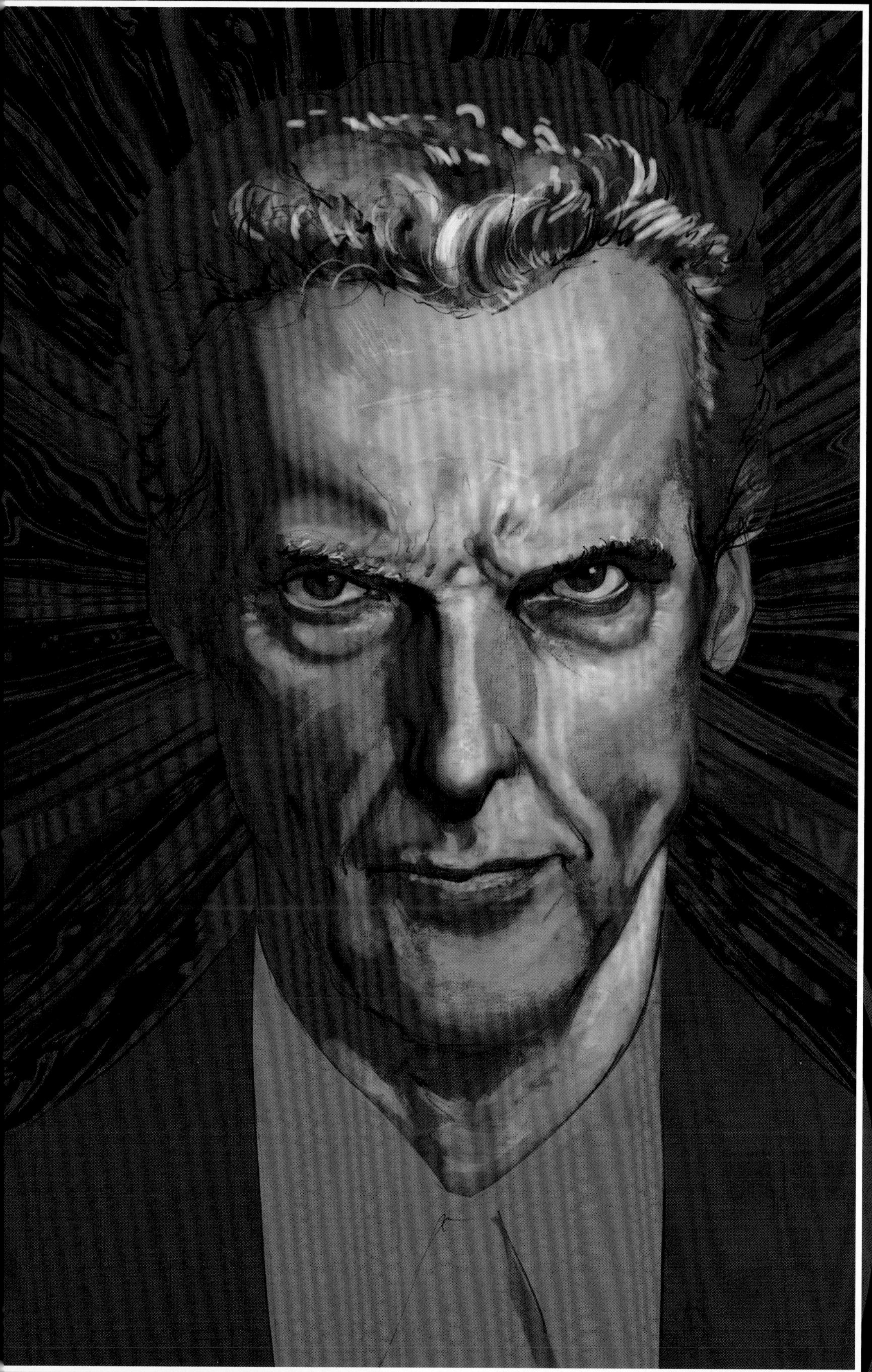

ISSUE #13

Cover: SIMON FRASER

JULIE D'AUBIGNY

A.K.A. LA MAUPIN

The real-life Julie d'Aubigny was a woman whose short life was filled with adventure, romance, and violence - just like her comic persona!

She was born in 1673, in France, to Gaston d'Aubigny - himself a secretary to Count d'Armagnac, the Master of the Horse for King Louis XIV. Gaston trained the King's court pages in the art of fencing, and felt that young Julie would benefit from learning the noble art. She trained alongside the boys, dressing as one, for most of her childhood.

She found favor early on with many high profile men in the French court, especially the Count d'Armagnac, who soon found her a husband, Monsieur de Maupin. However, de Maupin was sent away to an administrative post in the south of France shortly after the wedding, while Julie and d'Armagnac continued their affair.

Growing tired of d'Armagnac and her absent husband, Julie ran away to Marseille with a master swordsman named Sérannes, who was being hunted by the police at the time. Sérannes was accused of killing a man in a duel - and the police were very strict in enforcing anti-dueling laws and weapons regulations in Paris at the time.

Having no other way to earn money, she and Sérannes performed fencing and singing acts wherever they stayed to support themselves. While on the road, she auditioned at the music academy of Pierre Gaultier, a highly respected director, and impressed him so much with her natural singing talent that she was accepted into the academy, and began singing professionally in the town.

After declaring that she was bored with men, she started a relationship with a young blonde woman who initially mistook her for a man. Julie was infatuated, though the girl's parents opposed their relationship and promptly sent their daughter away to a convent to become a nun.

Daring and in love, La Maupin snuck into the convent and fled with the young girl, while setting the convent on fire to make the escape easier. Despite the elaborate ruse, the relationship did not last, and the girl returned to the convent.

Tried in absentia for arson and condemned to death by the Aix Parliament, Julie fled Marseilles for Paris to escape her punishment.

After months of singing in taverns while on the run, she was discovered by a man named Marechal, a talented musician. He offered to train her, and she began her journey as a theater performer.

She later met two maestros, Thévenard and Bouvard, who convinced the King to accept her into the Paris Opera company. Julie made her Opera debut in 1690 - it was said that she had the most beautiful voice in the world.

In 1695 she caused a commotion by kissing a young woman at a society ball, which prompted three noblemen to challenge her to a duel. Even though she prevailed, she once more had to flee Paris for violating the anti-dueling laws that were still in place.

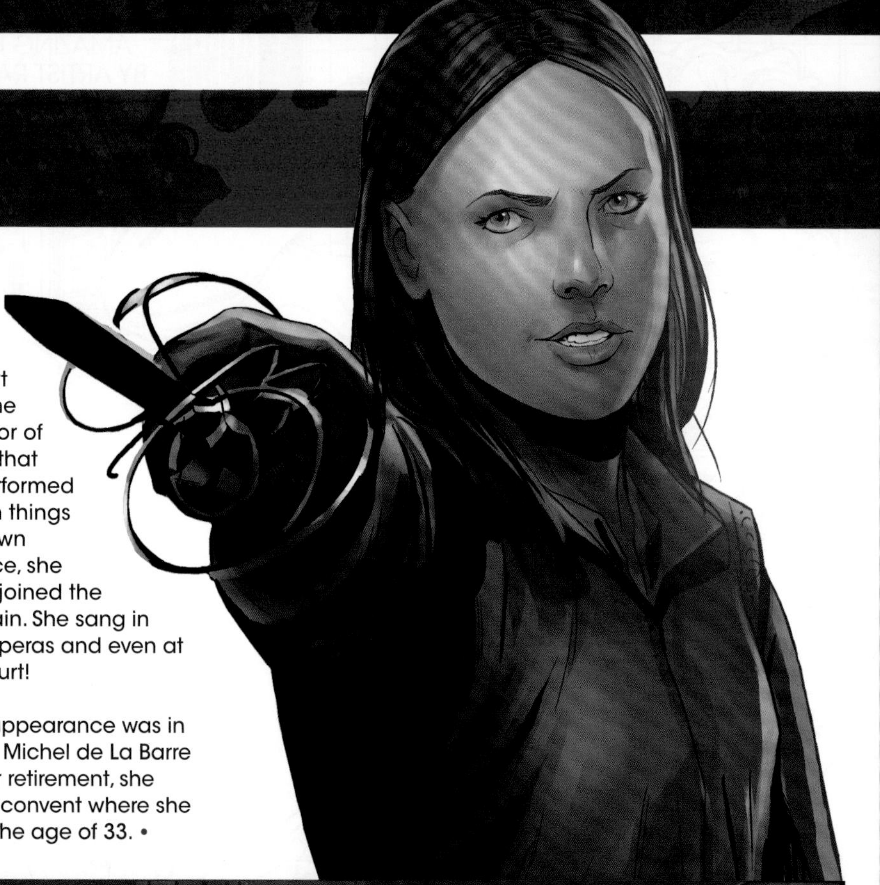

Brussels was her next destination, where for a short while she was the mistress of Elector of Bavaria. During that time she still performed in Operas. When things had calmed down enough in France, she went back and joined the Paris Opera again. She sang in several prolific operas and even at the Versailles court!

Her last Opera appearance was in *La Vénitienne* by Michel de La Barre in 1705. After her retirement, she took refuge in a convent where she died in 1707 at the age of 33. •

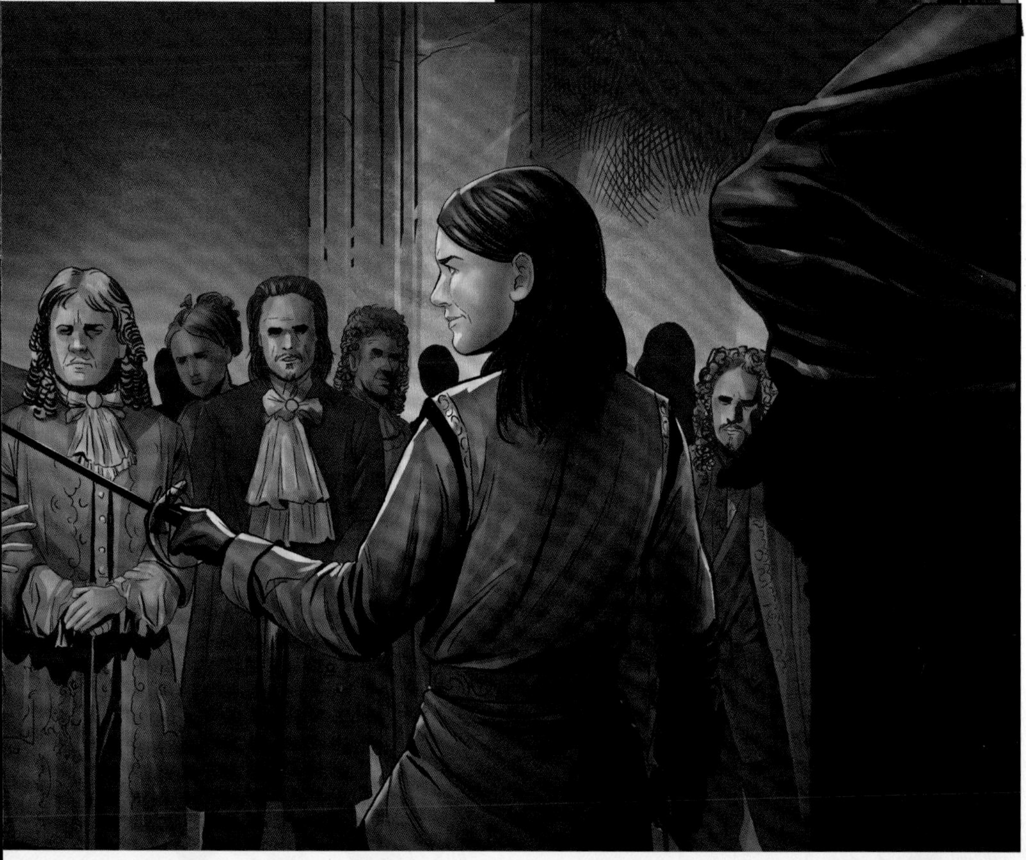

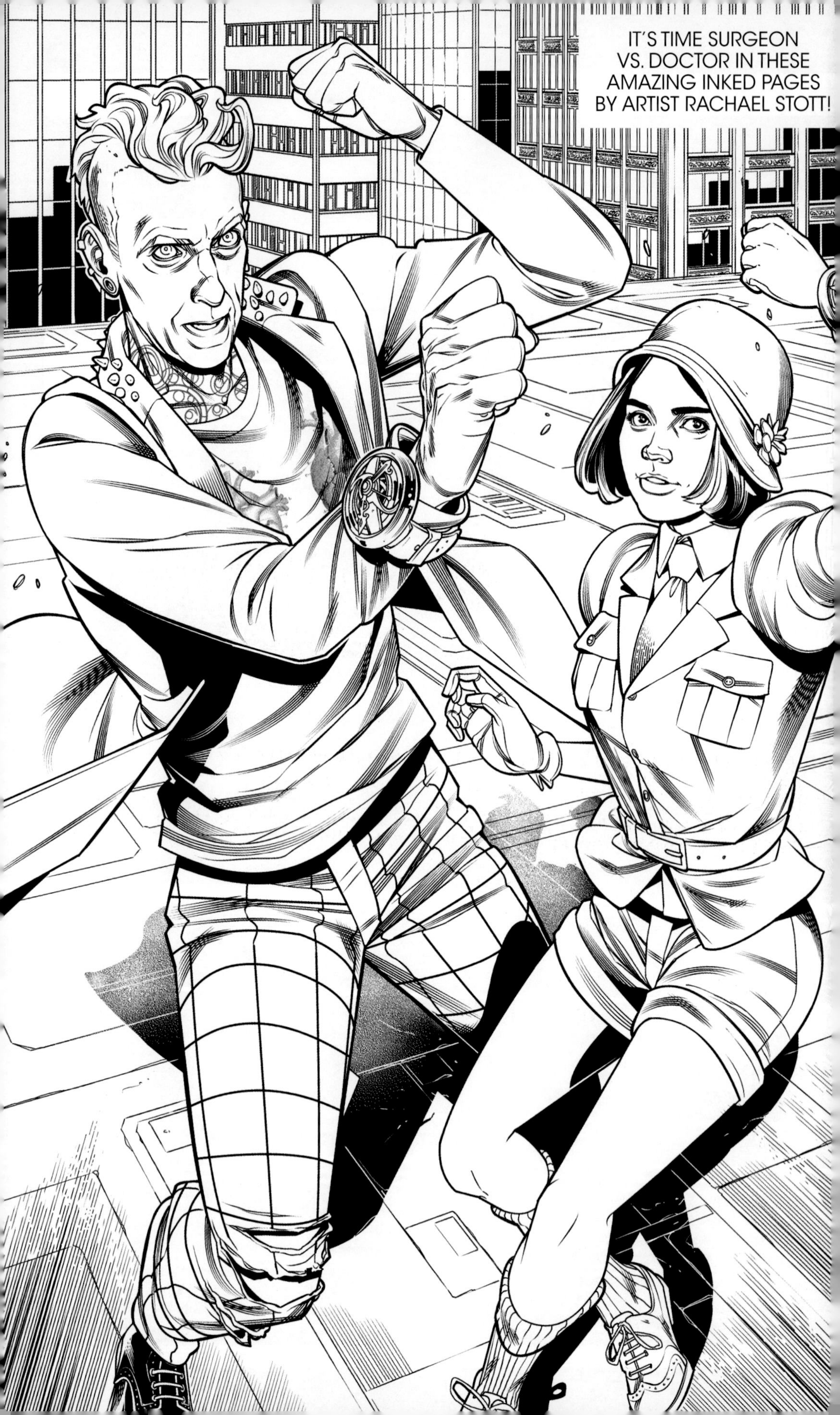
IT'S TIME SURGEON
VS. DOCTOR IN THESE
AMAZING INKED PAGES
BY ARTIST RACHAEL STOTT!

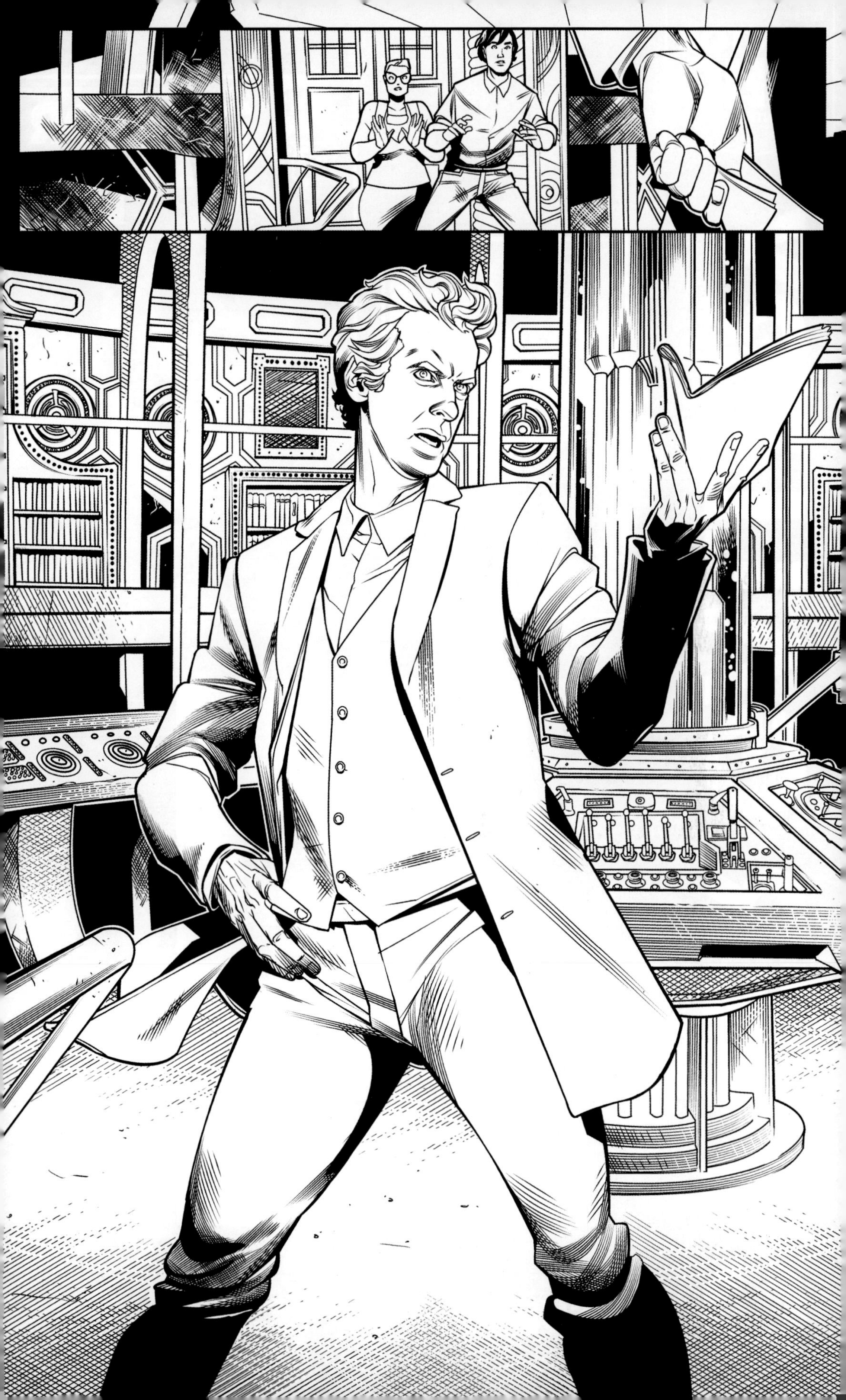

COVER GALLERY

A

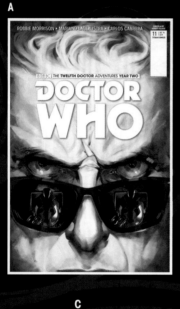

ROBBIE MORRISON • MARIANO LACLAUSTRA • CARLOS CABRERA
BBC THE TWELFTH DOCTOR ADVENTURES YEAR TWO
DOCTOR WHO

B

BBC THE TWELFTH DOCTOR ADVENTURES YEAR TWO
DOCTOR WHO
DOCTOR WHO
11 DEC '16 $3.99
COVER B WILL BROOKS
TITAN COMICS
ROBBIE MORRISON
MARIANO LACLAUSTRA
CARLOS CABRERA

C

BBC THE TWELFTH DOCTOR ADVENTURES YEAR TWO
DOCTOR WHO
DOCTOR WHO
ROBBIE MORRISON
MARIANO LACLAUSTRA
CARLOS CABRERA
COVER C SIMON MYERS
TITAN COMICS

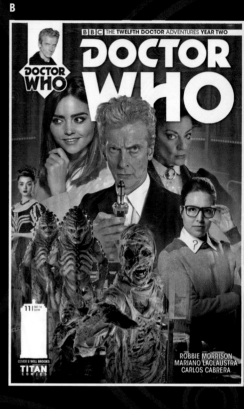

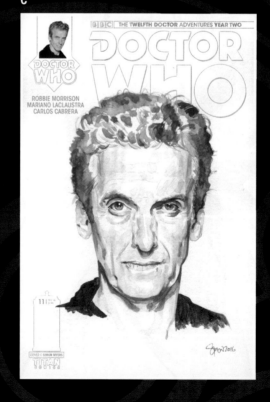

ISSUE #11

A. VERITY GLASS
B. PHOTO – WILL BROOKS
C. SIMON MYERS

A

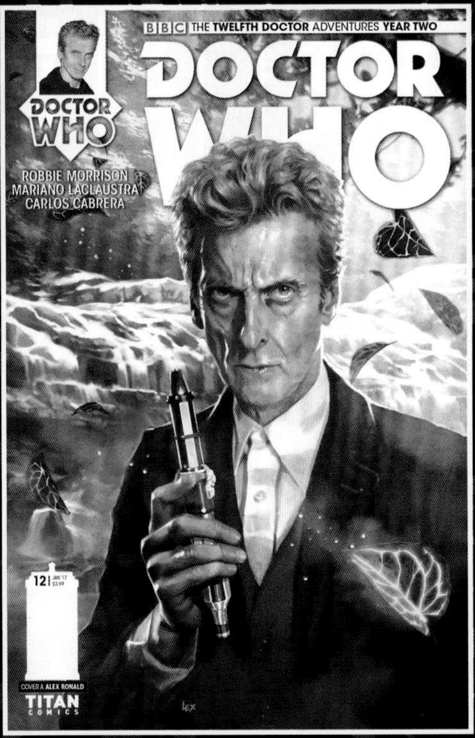
BBC THE TWELFTH DOCTOR ADVENTURES YEAR TWO
DOCTOR WHO
ROBBIE MORRISON
MARIANO LACLAUSTRA
CARLOS CABRERA
12
COVER A ALEX RONALD
TITAN COMICS

B

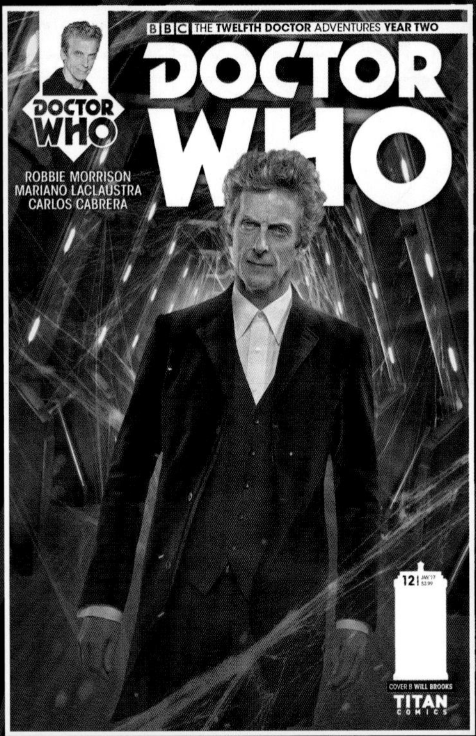
BBC THE TWELFTH DOCTOR ADVENTURES YEAR TWO
DOCTOR WHO
ROBBIE MORRISON
MARIANO LACLAUSTRA
CARLOS CABRERA
12
COVER B WILL BROOKS
TITAN COMICS

C

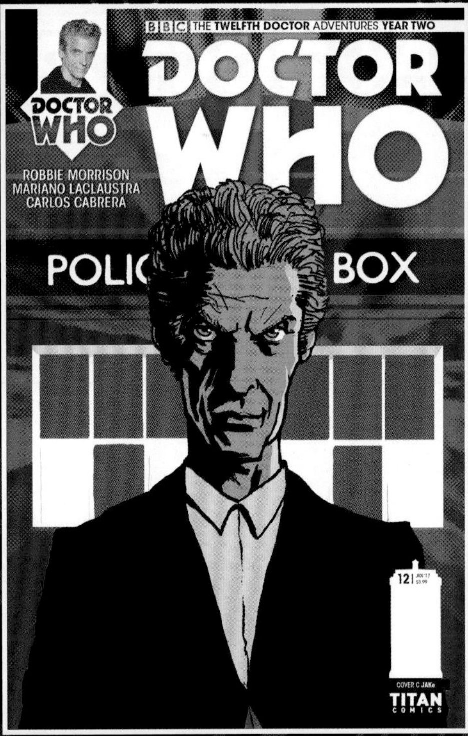
BBC THE TWELFTH DOCTOR ADVENTURES YEAR TWO
DOCTOR WHO
ROBBIE MORRISON
MARIANO LACLAUSTRA
CARLOS CABRERA
POLIC
BOX
12
COVER C JAKe
TITAN COMICS

ISSUE #12

A. ALEX RONALD
B. PHOTO – WILL BROOKS
C. JAKe

A

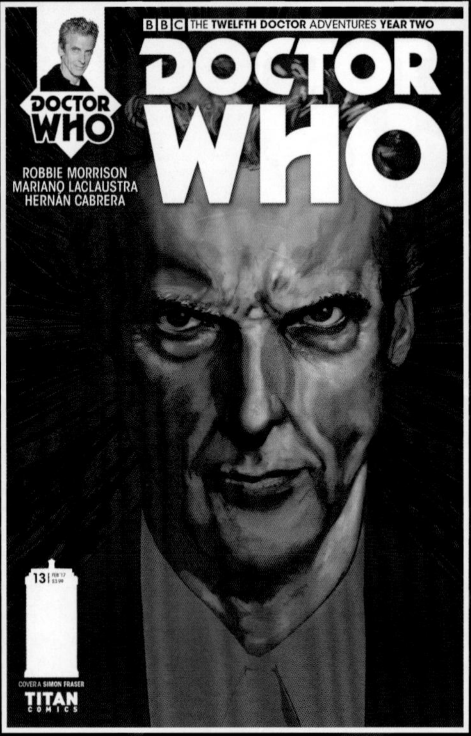
BBC THE TWELFTH DOCTOR ADVENTURES YEAR TWO
DOCTOR WHO
DOCTOR WHO
ROBBIE MORRISON
MARIANO LACLAUSTRA
HERNÁN CABRERA
13
COVER A SIMON FRASER
TITAN COMICS

B

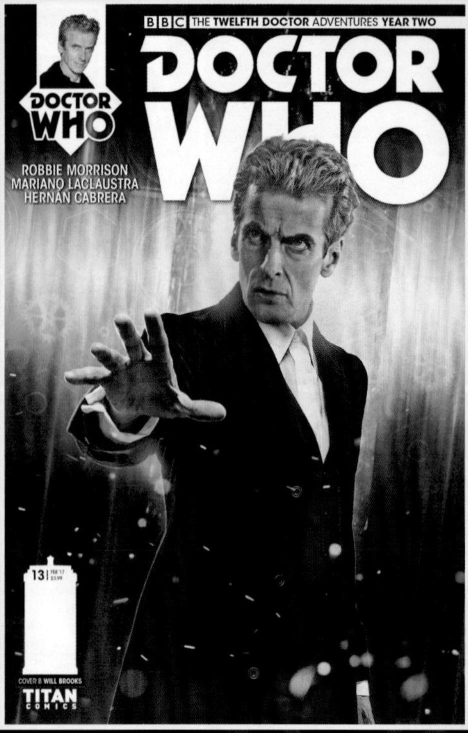
BBC THE TWELFTH DOCTOR ADVENTURES YEAR TWO
DOCTOR WHO
DOCTOR WHO
ROBBIE MORRISON
MARIANO LACLAUSTRA
HERNÁN CABRERA
13
COVER B WILL BROOKS
TITAN COMICS

C

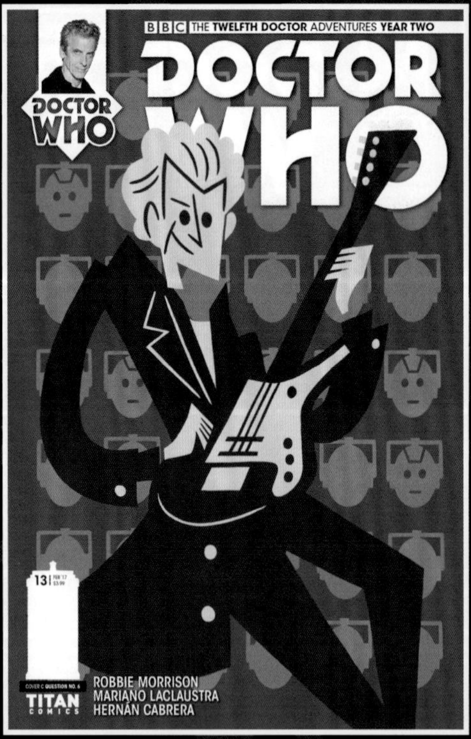
BBC THE TWELFTH DOCTOR ADVENTURES YEAR TWO
DOCTOR WHO
DOCTOR WHO
13
COVER C QUESTION NO. 6
TITAN COMICS
ROBBIE MORRISON
MARIANO LACLAUSTRA
HERNÁN CABRERA

D

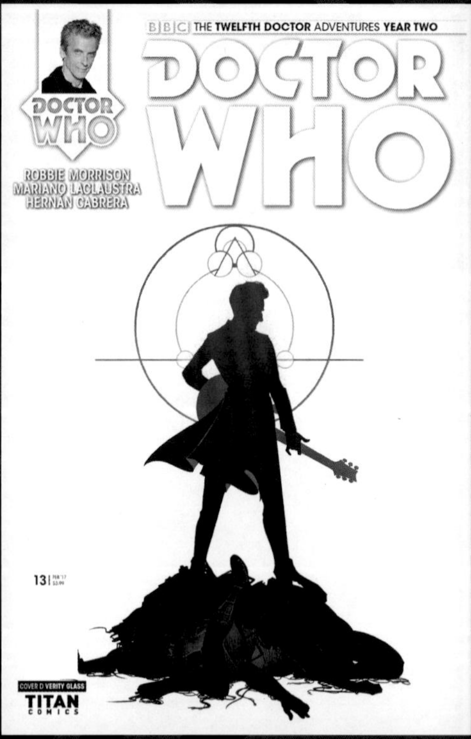
BBC THE TWELFTH DOCTOR ADVENTURES YEAR TWO
DOCTOR WHO
DOCTOR WHO
ROBBIE MORRISON
MARIANO LACLAUSTRA
HERNÁN CABRERA
13
COVER D VERITY GLASS
TITAN COMICS

ISSUE #13

A. SIMON FRASER
B. PHOTO – WILL BROOKS
C. QUESTION NO.6
D. VERITY GLASS

A

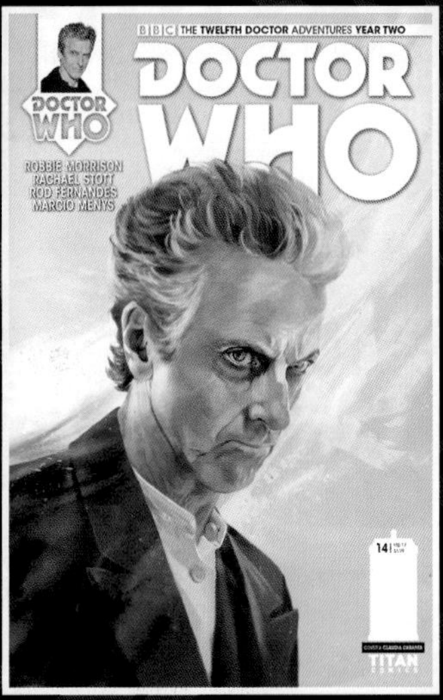
BBC THE TWELFTH DOCTOR ADVENTURES YEAR TWO
DOCTOR WHO
DOCTOR WHO
ROBBIE MORRISON
RACHAEL STOTT
ROD FERNANDES
MARCIO MENYS
14
TITAN

B

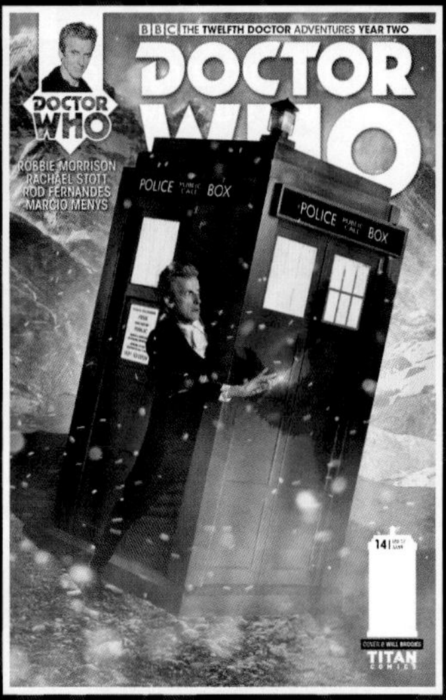
BBC THE TWELFTH DOCTOR ADVENTURES YEAR TWO
DOCTOR WHO
DOCTOR WHO
ROBBIE MORRISON
RACHAEL STOTT
ROD FERNANDES
MARCIO MENYS
POLICE BOX
POLICE BOX
14
TITAN

C

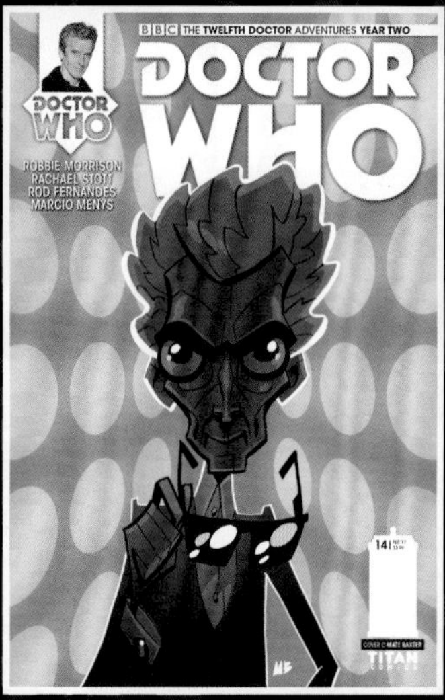
BBC THE TWELFTH DOCTOR ADVENTURES YEAR TWO
DOCTOR WHO
DOCTOR WHO
ROBBIE MORRISON
RACHAEL STOTT
ROD FERNANDES
MARCIO MENYS
14
TITAN

ISSUE #14

A. CLAUDIA CARANFA
B. PHOTO – WILL BROOKS
C. MATT BAXTER

A

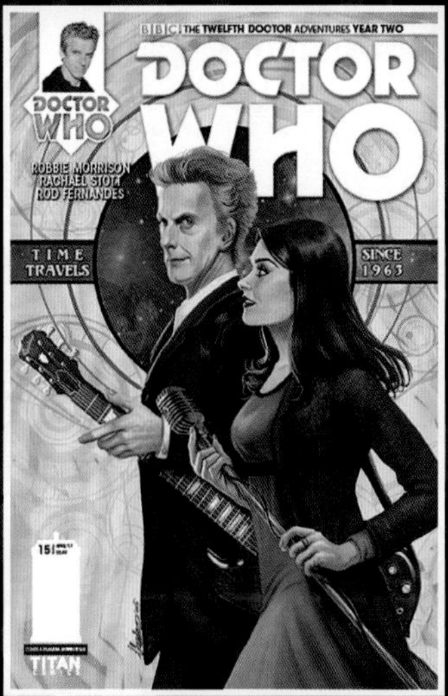
BBC THE TWELFTH DOCTOR ADVENTURES YEAR TWO
DOCTOR WHO
DOCTOR WHO
ROBBIE MORRISON
RACHAEL STOTT
ROD FERNANDES
TIME TRAVELS
SINCE 1963
15
TITAN

B

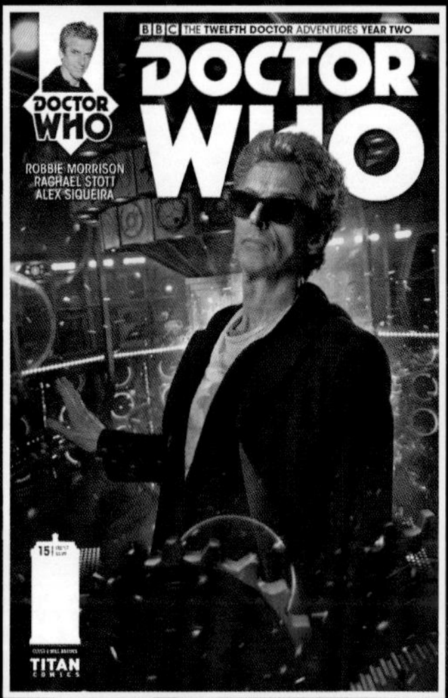
BBC THE TWELFTH DOCTOR ADVENTURES YEAR TWO
DOCTOR WHO
DOCTOR WHO
ROBBIE MORRISON
RACHAEL STOTT
ALEX SIQUEIRA
15
TITAN

C

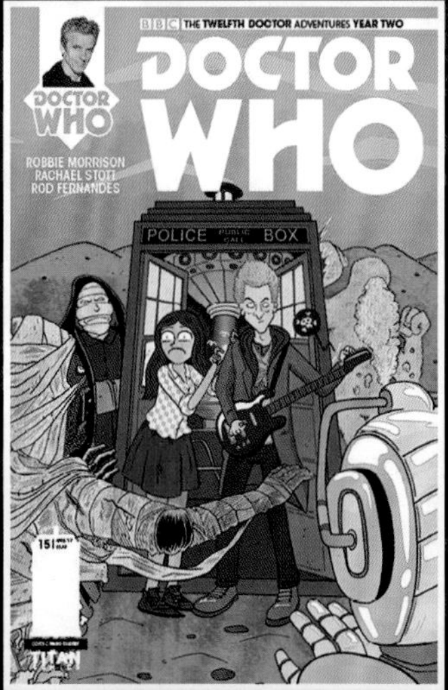
BBC THE TWELFTH DOCTOR ADVENTURES YEAR TWO
DOCTOR WHO
DOCTOR WHO
ROBBIE MORRISON
RACHAEL STOTT
ROD FERNANDES
POLICE BOX
15
TITAN

D

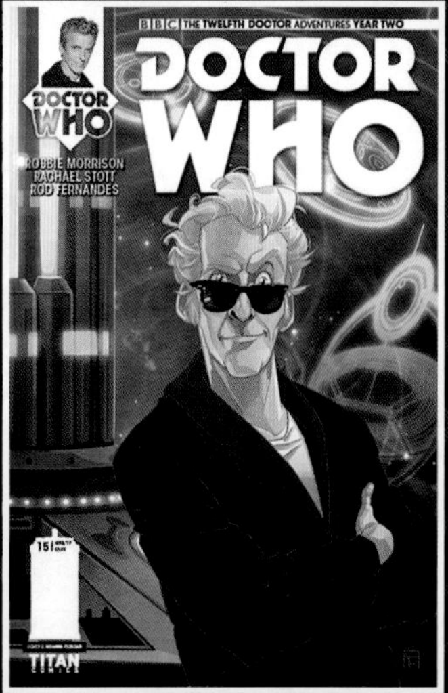
BBC THE TWELFTH DOCTOR ADVENTURES YEAR TWO
DOCTOR WHO
DOCTOR WHO
ROBBIE MORRISON
RACHAEL STOTT
ROD FERNANDES
15
TITAN

ISSUE #15

A. CLAUDIA IANNICIELLO
B. PHOTO – WILL BROOKS
C. MARC ELLERBY
D. ARIANNA FLOREAN

BBC

DOCTOR WHO READER'S GUID

With so many amazing *Doctor Who* comics collections, it can be diffi
know where to start! That's where this handy guide comes in.

THE TWELFTH DOCTOR – ONGOING

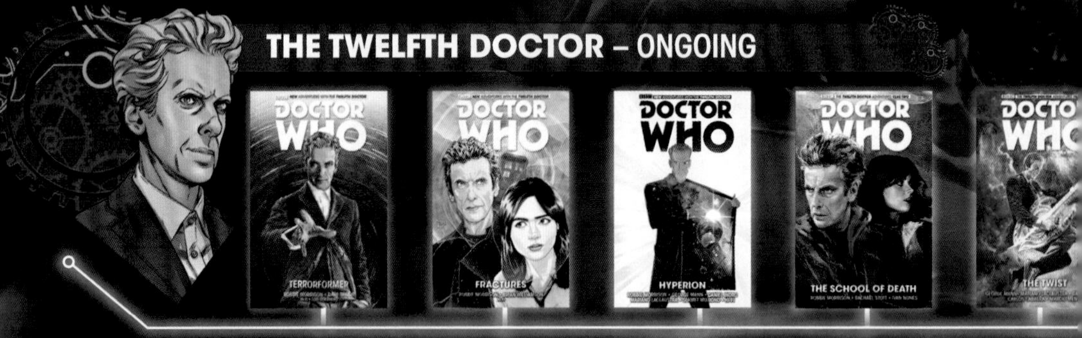

VOL. 1: TERRORFORMER

VOL. 2: FRACTURES

VOL. 3: HYPERION

YEAR TWO BEGINS! VOL. 4: SCHOOL OF DEATH

VOL. 5: THE TWIST

THE ELEVENTH DOCTOR – ONGOING

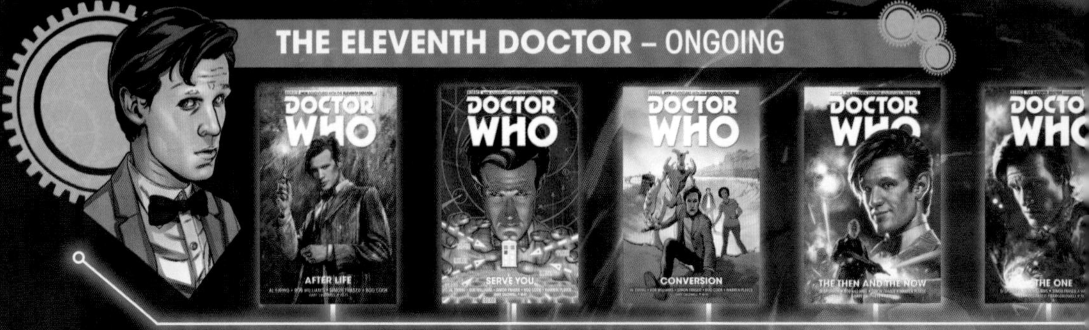

VOL. 1: AFTER LIFE

VOL. 2: SERVE YOU

VOL. 3: CONVERSION

YEAR TWO BEGINS! VOL. 4: THE THEN AND THE NOW

VOL. 5: THE ONE

THE TENTH DOCTOR – ONGOING

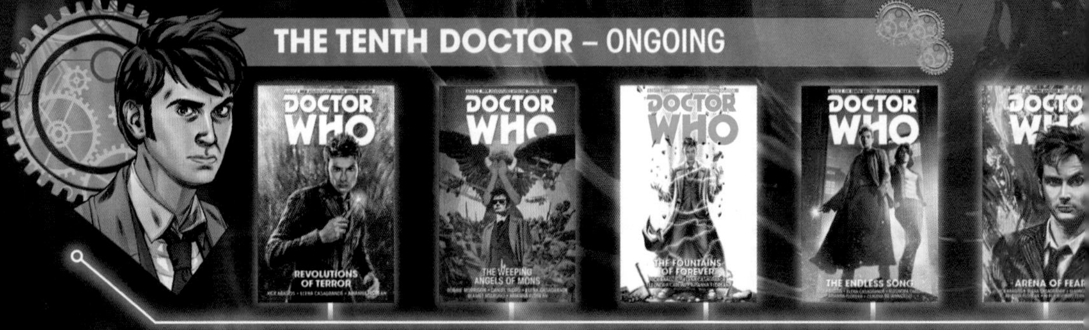

VOL. 1: REVOLUTIONS OF TERROR

VOL. 2: THE WEEPING ANGELS OF MONS

VOL. 3: THE FOUNTAINS OF FOREVER

YEAR TWO BEGINS! VOL. 4: THE ENDLESS SONG

VOL. 5: ARENA OF FE

THE NINTH DOCTOR – ONGOING

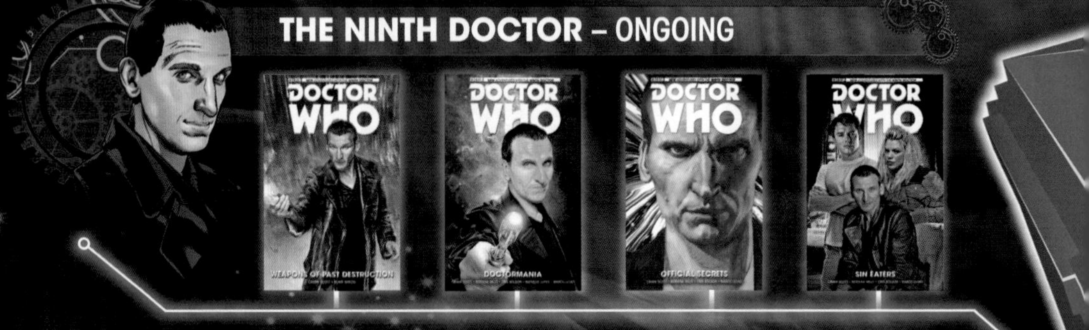

VOL. 1: WEAPONS OF PAST DESTRUCTION

VOL. 2: DOCTORMANIA

VOL. 3: OFFICIAL SECRETS

VOL. 4: SIN EATERS

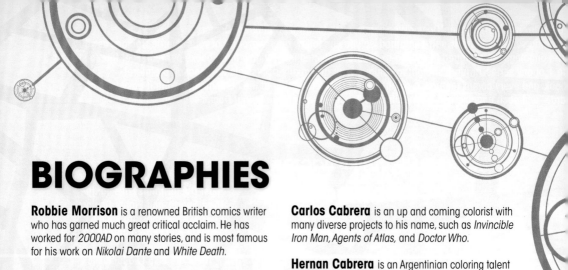

BIOGRAPHIES

Robbie Morrison is a renowned British comics writer who has garned much great critical acclaim. He has worked for *2000AD* on many stories, and is most famous for his work on *Nikolai Dante* and *White Death*.

Mariano Laclaustra is a creator with a background in the Fine Arts. A freelance artist based in Argentina, he has worked with publishers across Europe and the United States, including for *Dark Horse Presents*. In between drawing and coloring comics, he teaches oil painting.

Rachael Stott is a talented illustrator and winner of the Best Newcomer Artist at the British Comic Awards 2015. She has worked on *Planet of the Apes*, *Star Trek*, *Doctor Who*, and *Ghostbusters International*.

Carlos Cabrera is an up and coming colorist with many diverse projects to his name, such as *Invincible Iron Man*, *Agents of Atlas*, and *Doctor Who*.

Hernan Cabrera is an Argentinian coloring talent who has worked on *Legion*, *Priest*, and *God is Dead*, among many others.

Rodrigo Fernandes is a colorist whose beautiful work can be seen on titles such as *Vikings*, *Independence Day*, and *Doctor Who*.

8-7-17
8-3-19
3
2